BRITAIN FOR AND AGAINST EUROPE

Britain For and Against Europe

British Politics and the Question of European Integration

Edited by
DAVID BAKER
and
DAVID SEAWRIGHT

CLARENDON PRESS · OXFORD
1998

Oxford University Press, Great Clarendon Street, Oxford OX2 6DP

Oxford New York

*Athens Auckland Bangkok Bogota Bombay Buenos Aires
Calcutta Cape Town Dar es Salaam Delhi Florence Hong Kong Istanbul
Karachi Kuala Lumpur Madras Madrid Melbourne Mexico City
Nairobi Paris Singapore Taipei Tokyo Toronto Warsaw*

*and associated companies in
Berlin Ibadan*

Oxford is a registered trade mark of Oxford University Press

*Published in the United States
by Oxford University Press Inc., New York*

British Library Cataloguing in Publication Data
Data available

Library of Congress Cataloging in Publication Data
*Britain for and against Europe : British politics & the question of
European integration / edited by David Baker and David Seawright.
Includes bibliographical references and index.
1. European federation—Public opinion 2. Public opinion—Great
Britain. 3. Great Britain–Foreign relations–1945- 4. Great
Britain—Politics and government—1945- I. Baker, David, 1950-
II. Seawright, David.
JN15.B69   1998   337.4041—dc21   97–46961*

ISBN 0–19–828078–5

1 3 5 7 9 10 8 6 4 2

*Typeset by J&L Composition Ltd, Filey, North Yorkshire
Printed in Great Britain on acid-free paper by
Bookcraft (Bath) Limited, Midsomer Norton, Somerset*

To my parents, Bess and Cyril Baker

D.B.

For my mother, Anne

D.S.

ACKNOWLEDGEMENTS

The editors would like to thank all the contributors to this volume for producing such excellent chapters to the precise and exacting deadlines typical of such a complex project.

Special thanks are reserved for the other members of the Parliament Project at Nottingham Trent and Sheffield Universities—Andrew Gamble and Steve Ludlam. We would also like to thank our editors at Oxford University Press, Tim Barton who originally commissioned the project and Dominic Byatt and Sophie Ahmad who took over the project and greatly assisted our path through the acceptance and production minefields of an edited book. Thanks also to the anonymous reader for Oxford University Press whose comments enabled us to improve the book in important ways. Naturally, any errors are the responsibility of the editors and accepted as such by us.

CONTENTS

x   *Contents*

Conclusion
David Baker and David Seawright   222

LIST OF FIGURES AND TABLES

ABBREVIATIONS

AES	alternative economic strategy
AEU	Amalgamated Engineering Union
AMUE	Association of the Monetary Union of Europe
BBB	British Business Bureau
BCC	British Chambers of Commerce
BIFA	Banking, Insurance, and Finance Union
BLG	British Labour Group
BSE	bovine spongiform encephalopathy
CAP	Common Agricultural Policy
CBI	Confederation of British Industry
CEO	Chief Executive Office
CET	Common External Tariff
CFSP	Common Foreign and Security Policy
CJD	Creuzfeldt-Jacob disease
CND	Campaign for Nuclear Disarmament
CoR	Committee of Regions
DoE	Department of the Environment
DSS	Department of Social Security
DTI	Department of Trade and Industry
EBA	European Business Agenda
ECB	European Central Bank
ECSC	European Coal and Steel Community
EDC	European Defence Community
EDM	early day motion
EEC	European Economic Community
EFA	European Free Alliance
EFTA	European Free Trade Association
ELD	European Liberals and Democrats
ELDR	European Liberal Democratic and Reformist parties
EMU	economic and monetary union
EP	European Parliament
EPLP	European Parliamentary Labour Party
EPP	European People's Party
ERDF	European Regional Development Fund
ERM	Exchange Rate Mechanism
ERT	European Round Table of Industrialists

ESC	Economic and Social Council
ESRC	Economic and Social Research Council
ETUC	European Trade Union Confederation
EU	European Union
Euratom	European Atomic Energy Community
FCO	Foreign and Commonwealth Office
FPB	Forum of Private Business
FSB	Federation of Small Businesses
GMB	General Municipal and Boilermakers' Union
IGC	Intergovernmental Conference
IoD	Institute of Directors
ITN	Independent Television News
LBC	London Broadcasting Corporation
MAFF	Ministry of Agriculture, Fisheries, and Food
MEP	Member of European Parliament
MP	Member of Parliament
MSA	measure of sampling adequacy
MSF	Manufacturing Science and Finance Union
NAFTA	North American Free Trade Association
NATO	North Atlantic Treaty Organization
NEC	National Executive Committee
NLS	National Library of Scotland
OEEC	Organization for European Economic Cooperation
PASOK	Socialist Party of Greece
PC	Plaid Cymru
PES	Party of European Socialists
PLP	Parliamentary Labour Party
QMV	qualified majority voting
SDP	Social Democratic Party
SEA	Single European Act
SMEs	small and medium-sized enterprises
SNP	Scottish Nationalist Party
TGWU	Transport and General Workers' Union
TUC	Trades Union Congress
UKREP	United Kingdom Permanent Representation to the European Union
UNICE	Union of Industrial and Employers' Confederations of Europe
VAT	value added tax
VRPEP	Verbatim Report on the Proceedings of the European Parliament

LIST OF CONTRIBUTORS

DAVID BAKER is Reader in British Politics, Department of Politics and Economics, Nottingham Trent University

PETER BROWN PAPPAMIKAIL is Information Manager for the Party of European Socialists, Parliamentary Group, at the European Parliament, Brussels.

JIM BULLER is Lecturer in Politics, Department of Politics and International Relations, University of Birmingham.

SCOTT CLARKE is Lecturer in Politics, Department of Politics and Modern History, London Guildhall University.

JOHN CURTICE is Reader in Politics, Department of Government, Strathclyde University, Glasgow.

ANDREW GAMBLE is Professor of Politics, Department of Politics, and Pro-Vice Chancellor, University of Sheffield.

JUSTIN GREENWOOD is Jean Monnet Professor of European Public Policy, Robert Gordon University, Aberdeen.

STEVE LUDLAM is Lecturer in Politics, Department of Politics, University of Sheffield.

JAMES MITCHELL is Senior Lecturer in Politics, Department of Government, Strathclyde University, Glasgow.

BEN ROSAMOND is Lecturer in Politics, Department of Politics and International Studies, University of Warwick.

DAVID SEAWRIGHT is Lecturer in Politics, Department of Social Policy and Politics, Lincoln University Campus.

MARTIN J. SMITH is Senior Lecturer in Politics, Department of Politics, University of Sheffield.

LARA STANCICH is Research Assistant in European Public Policy, Robert Gordon University, Aberdeen.

GEORGE WILKES is a researcher in the School of Management, University of Cambridge.

DOMINIC WRING is Lecturer in Communication and Media Studies, Department of Media Studies, Loughborough University.

LIST OF CONTRIBUTORS

Introduction

David Baker and David Seawright

As Andrew Gamble observes in his chapter in this book, few would doubt that Britain's troubled relationship with the European Union has been one of the dominant and most divisive issues of modern British politics. Our title 'Britain for and against Europe' is a particularly apposite description of this relationship. The book primarily offers a research-based analysis of British elite attitudes towards Europe, including political parties, the civil service, trade unions, business, and the media. This analysis takes place at a time of what promises to be the most significant period in European history since the signing of the original Treaty of Rome. The book also includes a summary of Britain's troubled relationship with Europe over the last forty-five years and includes a final chapter that surveys Britain in Europe from a recent European perspective.

Britain has often been portrayed as the reluctant European partner in which the decisions to apply for membership were largely due to growing elite perceptions of Britain's relative economic weaknesses, the end of Empire, and the manifest failure of the special economic relationship with America to compensate for this. From the beginning, therefore, for many British politicians and officials, 'project Europe' was viewed more from national economic interests than any strong commitment to the wider political integrationist ideals of the founding fathers of Europe. Committed British Europeans like Edward Heath and Roy Jenkins, holding sincere beliefs in deeper European political cooperation to promote mutual prosperity and prevent another disastrous European war, have always existed, of course, but such sentiments have never really driven Britain's European agenda.

Since joining, the problem for the British is that the European Economic Community (EEC) has developed an overt political agenda becoming a European Union (EU), with large portions of parliamentary sovereignty inevitably ceded to European institutions. Successive British Prime Ministers who have faced difficulty in explaining and justifying developments in Britain's changing relationship with European institutions, even to their supporters, have resorted to clever party and media management to disguise the ongoing process of integration. The loss of sovereignty was depicted as a purely technical matter, necessary to modernize and strengthen British capital and labour, creating a modern economy and secure jobs; with little or no implications for ultimate parliamentary sovereignty. Both Wilson and Thatcher also made much domestic political capital out of their renegotiations of the terms of membership and financial contributions in Britain's favour. Wilson also employed a referendum on Europe in 1975 to decide the matter of membership largely for electoral and party management purposes.

But despite all these attempts by British governments of both parties to fudge the issues and evade responsibility for further integrationist developments, it has proved impossible to suppress a widespread series of high-level accusations that Europe has been to blame for Britain's declining world power and the underperformance of the economy. At the same time many have criticized the 'democratic deficit' that has arisen as European institutions have become more powerful without the necessary changes in the system of popular accountability (Hill 1996). At times such divisions have touched the agenda of party and electoral politics, as in the run-up to the 1975 referendum. Of these occasional eruptions the longest lasting and arguably the deepest was triggered by the signing of the Maastricht Treaty on 7 February 1992, since when British elite attitudes to Europe have tended to polarize as never before. A group of 'Eurosceptics', particularly although by no means exclusively in the Conservative Party, began a concerted and vociferous campaign, arguing that European Union is now revealed as a blueprint for a federalist political dystopia dominated by a Franco-German axis and based upon unaccountable rule by Brussels bureaucrats. As a result they have clashed repeatedly with so-called 'Europhiles', who are increasingly animated by a real fear of British withdrawal and a belief that the EU is vital to Britain's continued prosperity.

As Chapters 2 and 3 in this volume testify, this Europhile/Eurosceptic dichotomy is not at all simple, since both the Conservative and Labour parties contain individuals who are strongly for and against

Europe, drawn from within what are conventionally seen as the same ideological wings of the party. Equally, there is no single Eurosceptic or Europhile position, with some pro-Europeans rejecting a European Central Bank and some anti-Europeans accepting continued membership of a reduced EU. Indeed, this book offers substantial empirical evidence of the wide variety and complex nature of attitudes towards Europe amongst Britain's political, administrative, and economic elites and explodes a number of well-rehearsed myths about Britain's relations with Europe.

THE CHAPTERS

In Chapter 1 Andrew Gamble offers an important historical summary of Britain in Europe suggesting that, from its inception, the European issue arose within a context created by the long-term development of the British state. As a result, strategic choices and attitudes had already been shaped by events that occurred largely during the period of Britain's unrivalled power in the global political economy. This led to a strategy based upon dependence on open markets and foreign trade, coupled with the special relationship with America. Gamble argues that those rejecting any form of a Greater Europe have always sought to present an alternative political economy, whether based upon imperial preference and national protectionism as in the 1950s and 1960s, or free market nationalism, as in the 1980s and 1990s. Gamble further argues that it is against a background of perceived changing economic and security interests that the relationship of Britain to the process of European integration must be judged. This perspective helps to explain Britain's reluctance to become involved in the first place, and the continuing unease in some significant quarters over the way in which the Community has operated and developed since Britain joined.

As Gamble points out, major strategic choices such as those raised by the Maastricht Treaty of 1992 are rare in the life of any state and when they occur they encourage different perceptions and definitions of sovereignty and the national interest, to come into open conflict. This pushes to the surface vexed questions of interest, ideology, and identity, causing political realignments in parties, interest groups, and even governments (Baker et al. 1993*b*). As Steve Ludlam demonstrates in his chapter, such disagreements have the power to deeply divide even the most cohesive political groupings as can be seen in recent divisions in the Conservative Party, in which even the normally cohesive Thatcherite right of the party splintered into pro- and anti-European factions.

Given Gamble's scenario it is no surprise to discover that the remaining contributions to this volume emphasize the extent to which division and equivocation over Europe are still found deeply embedded within British political elites and institutions; a quarter of a century after signing the Treaty of Accession. For British elites, in Gamble's words, 'Europe is the issue that never seems to go away'.

One of the key issues of the Britain in Europe debate is obviously the extent to which national sovereignty is circumscribed by belonging to wider European institutions. In this context Ludlam in Chapter 2 and ourselves in Chapter 3, clearly demonstrate that internal party disputes over national sovereignty and Europe are extremely important in reflecting alternative agendas within both the Conservative and Labour parties. And that there is now scope for a revision of traditional left–right style ideological typologies on the issue of Europe.

Ludlam shows that European Union-post Maastricht has caused further turmoil within British Conservatism with the party racked by highly public divisions over Europe. As Ludlam points out, the Maastricht Treaty with its underlying supranationalist model of European integration, coupled with the legacy of bitterness at Margaret Thatcher's enforced resignation in November 1990, transformed earlier divisions into ones that ranked amongst the most damaging ever experienced by the party. Indeed, by 1996 factors that had hitherto prevented a catastrophic split in the party seemed to be weakening, as pro-Europeanist Conservatives began taking the possibility of a Conservative Party-led withdrawal from Europe seriously. In the face of these deep divisions, Major's continued leadership rested in good part on his being the leader least likely to trigger a split over Europe. The empirical evidence presented by Ludlam reveals that the Maastricht rebellion reflected very widespread Euroscepticism on the Conservative backbenches, far wider in fact than the numbers of MPs prepared to publicly defy the Whips would suggest (see also Baker et al. 1998). The scale and intensity of the rebellion under Major is also revealed to have been unprecedented. The evidence also suggests that on a range of issues encompassing sovereignty, economic and monetary union (EMU), subsidiarity, qualified majority voting (QMV), and the powers of EU institutions, potentially dangerous minorities of both

Eurosceptics and (perhaps more significantly) Euro-enthusiasts might be mobilized. Finally Ludlam demonstrates that while Conservative MPs have fallen broadly into two camps on national sovereignty ('absolutists' and 'poolers'), that this distinction is by no means clear-cut, with supporters of power-sharing to achieve the single market deeply divided over monetary integration. In the process, Ludlam's chapter powerfully confirms that the issue of sovereignty has become the most important fault-line in modern Conservatism.

Our chapter on Labour highlights the fact that Europe has traditionally had the power to divide the party, with official policy on Europe zigzagging between continued membership and a desire to withdraw. However, such official positions have always hidden real and continuing dissent within the party. The findings of our 1996 survey of Labour MPs and MEPs reveal that Labour has indeed moved some considerable way along the road of European integration since 1983, the 'high water mark' of official Labour Euroscepticism. But further analysis reveals clear divisions within the parliamentary party, existing along two sovereignty dimensions and two state interventionist dimensions. We find that Labour also remains a party with strong collectivist and interventionist values judged on the answers to the questions dealing with the social dimension of Europe. The divisions also cover the potentially explosive electoral issues of EMU and the consequences of the 1996 Inter-Governmental Conference (IGC). As with Ludlam's findings on the Conservatives, the sovereignty dimension cross-cuts traditional right–left ideological positions in New Labour, with the left of the Labour Party as split on Europe as the right. We therefore conclude that New Labour still has considerable potential for party fissures on the issue of European integration on particular issues.

James Mitchell in Chapter 5 and Scott Clarke and John Curtice in Chapter 4 highlight the different ideological emphasis placed on the European issue by Nationalists and Liberals. Significantly, just as Europe cuts across the traditional left–right divide in both Labour and Conservative parties, divisions on Europe according to Mitchell have also cut across what he terms the key fundamentalist–pragmatist cleavage inside the Scottish Nationalist Party (SNP). Thus, part of the willingness of the Nationalists to cede sovereignty to European institutions has been in order to distinguish themselves from the British governmental parties. This is paralleled by the policy of 'equidistance' carried out by the Liberals on Europe as revealed by Clarke and

Curtice. They add that another key influence on the Liberal Party's position was its long absence from the corridors of domestic power and the fact that Europe offered a more enticing prospect of both influence and resources.

A persistent theme amongst pro-integration nationalists was that being part of a large European authority was less threatening to Scottish and Welsh national identity than being part of a smaller, but more centrally organized British state. In fact Mitchell points out how far the SNP outstripped the Liberals as an agent of 'European-ization' in Scotland and how far the Scottish Nationalists, paradoxic-ally, used the idea of this apparent loss of sovereignty in their fight for independence. In the eyes of the Nationalists the pooling of sover-eignty with Brussels was much preferred to the centralized regime of Westminster. We find echoes of this mindset in the 'developing nations' of Eastern Europe where the idea of joining the European Union actually underpins their sovereignty, demonstrating their in-dependence from the former Soviet yoke. Mitchell further suggests that because divisions on Europe did not correlate with the main fault-line in the SNP, it failed to result in internal polarization.

Clarke and Curtice map out the classical liberal opposition to Europe, this free trade ideology rejecting the notion of trading blocs, with Europe being seen as merely a glorified customs union. From the 1960s onwards the 'social conscience liberals' won the ideological debate within the party and criticism of protectionist Europe is now, paradoxically, left to the neo-liberals of the Conservative Party. Thus, the free market nationalist right of the Conservative Party now voice some of the disagreements that the Liberals once did with Europe, preferring an 'open seas' policy. For them, Britain should resemble Hong Kong, eventually becoming a *European tiger economy*. How-ever, as Clarke and Curtice point out: 'Liberals can find as much ideological justification to be critical of the European Union as any Eurosceptic Conservative.'

In Chapter 6, Ben Rosamond delineates the changes in British trade unions' attitudes towards Europe. He demonstrates that until the mid-1980s it was a widely held belief within union ranks that socialism could only be realized within the nation state. Consequently British unions developed elaborate defences for parliamentary sovereignty, the corollary of which was a defence of national economic manage-ment. Rosamond singles out two significant developments that trans-formed trade union thinking on European integration during the late

1980s: first, the strategic possibilities afforded by British membership of the Community; and secondly, as part of a general reorientation of thinking on the British left, away from the combination of socialism and national political economy that produced the alternative economic strategy (AES) and towards Europe-wide strategies for the advancement of social progress. He identifies three broad groupings within the TUC coalition: 'pro-Commission' unions, 'sectoral pragmatists', and 'left sceptics'. The catalyst for a working pro-European policy coalition was a mixture of domestic embitterment fuelled by the anti-union legal and ideological onslaught of Thatcherite Conservative governments, juxtaposed with a union-friendly Commission that appeared to espouse ideas such as workers' rights and social partnership. Consequently, the unions have become amongst the most enthusiastic supporters of European Union and of the concept of pooled sovereignty, and according to Rosamond this Europeanization of union activities and concerns looks to be more or less permanent. However, there is also 'a marked dissonance', in Rosamond's terms, between the formal TUC position and the supply side policy of the Commission and trade union opposition to economic and monetary union could occur if higher unemployment occurs as a result.

Greenwood and Stancich in Chapter 7 argue that by and large British business cannot afford not to be positive towards Europe, since the British economy is now so deeply intertwined with that of the rest of Europe. Equally, they point out that the UK has a relatively good record of implementing directives in sectoral affairs, and that in 'low politics' domains British involvement in Europe is relatively unproblematic. This is a somewhat surprising finding, given the image of Britain as so often the 'awkward partner' in Europe (George 1990). However, they conclude that business may become increasingly reliant on its resources at the European level, unless what is perceived as the increasing idiosyncrasies of domestic channels change. In the process British business is likely to become even more integrated into mainstream European values.

In Chapter 8 Buller and Smith highlight the institutionally bounded interests that civil servants have developed in relation to the EU and how these interests may have affected both their behaviour and the organization of individual departments of state. They find little if any evidence of a *single* civil service attitude towards Europe because attitudes of civil servants vary according to departments, history, policies, and time. Departments differ in their approach to Europe, depending on whether they adopt an 'external' or 'internal' approach to Europe. Some like the Treasury, have adopted a 'foreign policy agenda' towards Europe. While others, like the Ministry of Agriculture, Fisheries, and Food (MAFF) and the Department of Trade and Industry (DTI), are quite comfortable in dealing with the issue in a 'domestic' context.

However, civil servants interviewed by Buller and Smith were quick to disclaim any notion that they had internalized a political ethos anywhere near that found among their continental counterparts. Consequently, they suggest that the 'British position', devoid of continental style bureaucratic semantics, but well coordinated on a common line, often gives an exaggerated appearance of 'awkwardness'.

In Chapter 10, Peter Brown Pappamikail reiterates this point of perceived awkwardness when Britain is viewed from the European end of the political telescope. From such a perspective Britain's political culture often appears largely based upon what he terms 'a damaging adversarial bipolar culture', which he traces to fundamentally differing conceptions of sovereignty. Most continentals, it seems, accept sovereignty as being 'multi-layered', while the British often view it as something indivisible. Consequently, Brown Pappamikail suggests that Europe is often viewed more as an aspect of foreign policy than domestic politics in Britain and that this has alienated our European partners.

This idea that the European Union is alien to the domestic body politic is given further emphasis by Brown Pappamikail's use of a unique set of interviews with European-based politicians. Gijs de Vries, for instance, states that in contrast to her European partners Britain always takes the view that she is negotiating with Brussels rather than negotiating in Brussels. He blames the 'Conservative press' for spreading the sceptic 'virus' which even affects the Liberals. But his comments are somewhat tempered by the findings of the chapters which deal with British political parties, namely that no British party, not even the Liberals, has given unanimous support to the idea of European integration.

Wilkes and Wring in Chapter 9, underline the fact that scepticism over Europe has not always been the preferred attitudinal position of the British press, whatever their presumed political stance on the traditional left–right spectrum. Indeed, the British press have never been exempt from the fact that Europe cuts across the conventional right–left division of the political spectrum. Consequently, as Wilkes and Wring point out, both the union-owned and left-leaning *Daily Herald* of the 1960s and its free market nationalist reincarnation the *Sun*, of the 1980s, opposed aspects of the ongoing European agenda.

Inevitably, given that this is a book about elite values, one vital aspect of the 'for and against' equation is almost entirely absent from the discussion, the opinions of British citizens, whose views the political elites in particular must take into account. The Gallup Index (first published in 1960) has consistently shown just how fickle and inconsistent British public opinion has been on the issue of Britain and Europe. They reveal both a high degree of volatility oscillating between 'for and against' and the second order nature of the issue which can also be seen from the historically low turnout by the British for European elections (see Gallup Political and Economic Index 1960–97, *passim*). In this context see the preliminary findings of a team at Nuffield College, Oxford, at present researching into the nature and degree of Euroscepticism in the wider British electorate, as expressed in terms of the vote for the Referendum Party in the 1997 general election (Heath et al. 1997).

Significantly, as Clarke and Curtice point out in their chapter, despite forty years of campaigning for Europe, Liberal Democrat voters are barely more pro-European than their Conservative or Labour counterparts. This reveals one constant in the Britain 'for and against' story, namely the refusal of the electorate to elevate Europe into a 'first order' issue. This is echoed in the figures for the SNP's electoral support contained in Table 5.5; where SNP supporters register the highest percentage for withdrawal in Scotland, in spite of the SNP's claim to be the party of Europe in Scotland.

As this book goes to press we cannot ignore the recent changes in the British political landscape brought about by the 'landslide' electoral victory of Labour in the 1997 general election (and we will address this in the Conclusion). But one thing remains constant—while the election may have changed the government, it will not alter the basic problems for British institutions and elites raised by the vexed question of Europe.

1

The European Issue in British Politics

Andrew Gamble

Britain's relationship with the European Union has been one of the dominant issues of British politics in the last fifty years. It has also been one of the most divisive. The debate has moved through a number of phases. The British government initially refused to participate in the negotiations which led to the setting up of the European communities in the 1950s. It then applied to join in the 1960s and was twice rebuffed. Entry was finally negotiated in 1971 and Britain became a full member in 1973. Since 1973 however the relationship between the British government and other European governments has been marked by distrust and conflict, and Britain's membership of the European Union, despite the referendum of 1975 which delivered substantial popular endorsement, has remained contentious.

Europe is the issue that never seems to go away. Controversy has continued to rage not only over the type of Europe Britain should be seeking to promote, but also and increasingly over whether Britain should remain a member at all. Both parties have shifted their position on the European Union, and in recent years have changed places. The Conservatives used to be seen as the party of Europe, while the majority of the Labour Party was opposed to it. In the 1990s however it is Labour which is the more pro-European party while the pro-European wing of the Conservative Party has struggled to keep control of policy towards Europe against a background of a rising tide of anti-European feeling in the party. In the 1970s Labour was more divided on the issue than the Conservatives and it was one of the factors in the split in 1981 which led to the creation of the Social Democratic Party. By the 1990s however it was Conservative divisions on Europe which were attracting attention, amidst speculation that they too might lead eventually to a split.

STRATEGIC CHOICES

What is at stake in the European controversy in British politics is a major choice about Britain's role in the global political economy, which involves questions of interest, ideology, and identity. Such choices occur rather rarely but when they do they often trigger political realignments which can constitute major turning points in the life of parties and governments.

The nature of the British political system with its tradition of executive government and simple plurality constituency voting rules imposes heavy penalties on parties which split. Only eight splits have occurred in the last 150 years (Baker et al. 1993*b*). Some of the most important have involved a strategic choice over Britain's role in the global political economy—particularly those in 1846 and 1903. Each involved a fierce clash between rival visions of the best future for Britain. Parties which split suffered subsequent electoral defeat, ideological marginalization, and in most cases a lengthy exclusion from office.

Europe is this kind of issue. It divides parties because it fuses together issues of sovereignty and identity with political economy in a novel and powerful way. Previous major conflicts over strategic choices in political economy, the Repeal of the Corn Laws in 1846 and Tariff Reform before 1914, did not involve questions of sovereignty directly, but rather the balance of interests within the British state. Europe has managed to involve both.

The European issue arose within a context created by past strategic choices made in the historical development of the British state. Britain was shaped by its experience as the leading commercial, financial, imperial, and industrial power in the global political economy. There were always tensions for example between the demands of the informal commercial empire and the formal administered empire; and between the global orientation of the commercial and financial interests of the leading sectors of the UK economy against the national focus of many other sectors, particularly in agriculture and some branches of manufacturing. The repeal of the Corn Laws marked the final defeat of those who had argued for protection of agriculture to promote a balanced economic development. The advocates of self-sufficiency lost and Britain committed itself still more deeply to a policy of open markets and dependence on foreign trade. Until 1916 Britain pursued a more complete policy of free trade, embracing goods, capital, and labour, than anything which has existed since. The system was underpinned by the financial stability created by the gold standard and the acceptance of the pound sterling as the leading international currency.

Britain's policy of maintaining markets open to all the world was threatened by the growth of territorial empires at the end of the nineteenth century and by the rapid industrialization of Germany and the United States. The two developments were accompanied by protectionist measures, aimed to safeguard new industry against the superior productivity and therefore cheaper production costs of British industry. Faced by the competitive challenge from these new rivals which was simultaneously economic and military, Britain had to decide whether its interests were best served by seeking to maintain the institutions of the liberal world order under which it had prospered so much during the nineteenth century, or whether it should reorganize itself as an empire against other empires, a cohesive bloc within the world economy to defend British interests. The heart of the Tariff Reform debate centred on the means by which the British Empire could be sustained in the twentieth century (Semmel 1960; Friedberg 1988).

The decision to give priority to the liberal world order rather than to the consolidation of the British Empire set the scene in the twentieth century for the gradual decline of Britain as a great power with global responsibilities. This process was delayed by Britain emerging on the winning side in the wars between the great powers in the first half of the twentieth century, but both victories, particularly the second, were only obtained with American assistance. The price of British victory over Germany was subordination to the United States, and a recognition that the restoration of a liberal world economic order required American leadership. Britain could no longer supply it by itself.

Britain emerged in 1945 undefeated, but the strategic choice it made in 1940 meant that its main global role was to be America's chief ally rather than an independent great power in its own right. The first twenty years after the war saw the dismantling of the British Empire and the painful adjustment by Britain to its diminished powers. The reconstruction under American aegis of a limited form of liberal world order allowed the partial restoration of sterling as an international currency, and the revival of the global strategies of its most successful companies. But the poor performance of the British domestic economy relative to other industrial economies was a constant source of vulnerability, which found its clearest expression in a series of sterling crises.

During the fifty years that have elapsed since the end of the Second World War Britain has made the transition from a great power with wide-ranging global responsibilities to a medium-sized power, with an economy which by the standards of its main competitors was under performing. It still retains some of the trappings of its former status, such as its permanent seat on the UN Security Council, as well as state agencies such as the intelligence apparatus and key economic sectors such as the defence industries which maintain a global reach. But in most other respects Britain's role has shrunk.

THE FIRST APPLICATION

It is against this background of changing economic and security interests that the relationship of Britain to the process of European integration must be judged. In the immediate post-war period British governments acknowledged the importance of Europe and the moves being taken to set up new European institutions. But they continued to give greater priority to the Empire and Commonwealth relationships and to Atlantic relationships. Churchill's argument that Britain stood at the point where three circles crossed—Europe, America, and the Empire—also gave priority to the Empire and America over Europe. British governments encouraged moves to European unity but had no intention of playing a leading role in European institutions. They saw Britain as having a different role and status from other European countries.

Despite therefore the warm words of encouragement given by Churchill and other British leaders to the early moves to European union, support at this stage for any serious involvement by Britain was limited to a small band of European enthusiasts. Britain withdrew from the negotiations which led to the European Coal and Steel Community, which was established in April 1952 following the Paris Treaty in April 1951, and also from the negotiations which established the EEC in January 1958 following the signing of the Treaty of Rome in March 1957. Part of the reason was the strong attachment of British elites to Britain's continuing global responsibilities, and to their desire to maintain both leadership of Europe and leadership of the Commonwealth. In the 1950s the British tried to persuade other

European members of OEEC (the Organization for European Economic Cooperation, established in 1948) to embrace a programme of unilateral reduction of import controls, currency convertibility, and non-discriminatory trade. The other European states however wanted to move towards the establishment of a customs union, regulated trade, and to maintain the power to discriminate against imports from countries outside the common external tariff, notably the United States. To the British the kind of community which many of the advocates of European cooperation wished to create was protectionist and inward-looking. They continued to argue for open, multilateral trading relationships, and began to reduce the import controls which had underpinned post-war reconstruction in the mistaken belief that British industries were now strong enough to compete in global markets without any support (Milward and Brennan 1996).

The gulf between Britain's perception of its economic and security interests and those of the other states of Western Europe explains the determination of British governments to stay aloof from the early attempts to build European union. The Treaty of Rome was signed without Britain in 1957. Yet only four years later, in July 1961, the British government submitted its first application for full membership.

The change was brought about by a substantial reassessment by important sections of the political elite of Britain's economic and security interests. The Suez episode in 1956 was one catalyst, since it painfully brought home to the British government how limited were the possibilities of independent action in pursuit of British interests abroad when American support was lacking. Another factor was the evidence that trade was growing very rapidly between developed industrial economies, particularly those in Western Europe, but was growing much more slowly with Britain's traditional markets in the Empire and Commonwealth. The dynamism of the Common Market in comparison with the fitful progress of the stop-go British economy seemed marked, and growing awareness of this began to win many converts in British industry and the British media to the need for Britain to become a member of the EEC. After Britain had pulled out of the negotiations at Messina in 1956, Britain had organized the European Free Trade Association (EFTA), an association of smaller European countries designed to promote the removal of trade barriers between them. But this was quickly seen to be no substitute for a closer association with the powerhouse of the European economy based round France, Germany, and the Benelux countries.

The initial application in 1961 formed part of a more general reassessment of Britain's place in the world, and the need to modernize British institutions. After Macmillan took over as Conservative leader following the failure at Suez, he moved to repair the damaged Atlantic relationship and to speed up the withdrawal from Empire. Macmillan had been one of the early supporters for a more positive European policy, and with the full backing of the Americans he was able to persuade his party that membership of the EEC was the logical next step. It could not be a substitute for Empire, because it commanded little of the emotional and ideological pull which Empire had for Conservatives. But it was put forward as serving both the interests of British industry and Conservative electoral interests. Maintaining and improving the rise in living standards required attaching Britain to one of the fastest growing regional economies in the world.

A formidable coalition of business, media, and political opinion was assembled in support of the application. Conservative opponents stressed the loss of national sovereignty. The rebels sought to construct an alternative political economy around what remained of imperial preference and the need to bind the Commonwealth together. But given the trends in trade this rested on sentiment rather than interest. The other main source of opposition at this time came from the Labour Party under Hugh Gaitskell, who articulated the concerns that Britain would lose its national sovereignty and distinctive national traditions (1,000 years of history, he called it), and more particularly that the emphasis on the creation of a common market would entrench market criteria as the arbiter of public policy and threaten the preservation of hard-won gains by the British Labour movement (Nairn 1973).

The first British application failed because of the French veto. De Gaulle had decided that Britain was not yet sufficiently European in its policy and outlook, by which he meant that Britain did not yet share France's strategic view of Europe. It still gave priority to its American links in both defence and economics, and therefore was unlikely to accept the direction in which the rest of the member states and especially France wished the Community to develop. De Gaulle's insight was as usual acute, although what he was advocating in the 1960s was not a federal vision of Europe, but a Europe of nation states under French leadership. He saw Britain's different preoccupations and traditions as a threat to the assertion of French leadership.

THE REFERENDUM ON MEMBERSHIP

The assessment made by Macmillan at the end of the 1950s that Britain's national interest was now to join the Common Market proved accurate. Once in government Labour reversed its earlier opposition, and made a second application in 1967 which was also turned down. Membership was not finally secured until after De Gaulle's death and a political deal between his successor, President Pompidou, and the new Conservative government under Edward Heath. There is little doubt that Harold Wilson would have accepted the same terms that Heath negotiated had he been re-elected in 1970. Pressures within the Labour Party forced the leadership back into a position of public opposition to the EEC. The majority of the Labour movement was strongly against the terms of entry negotiated in 1971 and this was to deepen in the years ahead. Wilson attempted to defuse opposition by promising that a future Labour government would renegotiate the terms of entry and then put them to a referendum. Back in government in 1974 the Labour leadership soon rediscovered its support for continued membership. The Cabinet supported the 'renegotiated terms' 16 : 7, but a majority of the Parliamentary Party voted against, and a special Labour conference voted 2 to 1 against. The referendum campaign however ended with a 2 to 1 vote in support of the government.

The referendum was expected to settle the issue once and for all. Britain was now clearly in the Community, and membership had been explicitly endorsed by the electorate and by the leaderships of the three main political parties. The ideological fault-lines however were still visible and they were to intensify in the years ahead. In the 1970s they ran deepest in the Labour Party. The parliamentary vote to accept the terms of entry in 1971 had only been passed because sixty-nine Labour MPs voted with the government, and twenty others abstained. They outweighed the thirty-nine Conservatives who voted against and the two who abstained. The Labour supporters of entry included the deputy leader, Roy Jenkins. Jenkins went on to play a leading role in the referendum campaigning for a Yes vote, and subsequently became President of the European Commission.

The gulf however between the leadership and the bulk of the Labour movement was not bridged by the referendum. The deep political and economic crisis of the 1970s kept the Labour Party moving to the left and developing a new programme, the alternative economic strategy, which aimed at guaranteeing employment and welfare through protectionist and interventionist policies. Its implementation clearly required withdrawal from the European Community, and this eventually became a manifesto commitment in 1983.

The argument of the Labour left against the European Community was that the rules of the Community prevented a Labour government adopting the measures it would need to revive the British economy. Reclaiming full national sovereignty was seen as essential to implement a radical interventionist programme, targeting investment to create a technologically advanced and high-productivity industrial base. The alternative economic strategy did not necessarily involve large increases in public ownership, but it did imply a radical revision of Britain's economic and security policies. The programme questioned not just the European Community but also NATO. It therefore repudiated some of the main lines of policy established under both parties since 1945.

This political economy of national protectionism had no echoes on the right in the 1970s and 1980s. The older protectionist tradition which had once been so strong in the Conservative Party, in support of imperial preference and before that of agricultural duties, had almost disappeared. Instead opposition to the European Community was organized around a different axis, the free market nationalist right. The first and most brilliant exponent of this position was Enoch Powell, but although he gained a few supporters, the majority of the free market right remained in the mainstream in support of Heath and entry to the EC. Powell's other allies in the Conservative Party were mostly imperialists. The number of MPs opposing the terms in 1972 was sufficient to deny the government a majority from its own supporters alone. Powell subsequently resigned from the Conservative Party at the 1974 election advising his supporters to vote Labour because Labour was promising a referendum on EC membership, and took a prominent part in the referendum campaign. Most of his allies at this time were drawn from the traditional imperialist wing of the party. What Powell foreshadowed however was the great rift that was to develop in the Conservative Party in the 1980s, and which had a different basis from the earlier divisions in the party over Europe.

The scale of Labour's election defeat in 1983 created a new dynamic in the party which discredited the alternative economic strategy and led to the abandonment of the commitment to withdraw from the European Community. The party swung increasingly to a pro-European stand, already foreshadowed by the pragmatic stance of many trade unions towards European cooperation. Faced by the ideological onslaught of the Thatcher government against so many aspects of the post-war social democratic order, the continued attachment of even centre-right governments in Europe to its main elements made Labour come to recognize that many of its social and economic objectives needed the European Community for their achievement.

At the moment of Labour's discovery of the European Community as the natural framework for the pursuit of social democratic objectives, many Conservatives were beginning to make the opposite discovery. The basis of the new divisions in the Conservative Party after 1985 was a splintering of the Thatcherite right into pro- and anti-European factions. All the Thatcherites supported the vision of the European Community as a free trade area, but they increasingly differed as to how the single market was to be achieved and maintained.

THE SINGLE MARKET AND MAASTRICHT

One of the salient facts about Britain's membership of the European Community since 1973 has been that the successful negotiation of entry has not stilled the internal debate. In Stephen George's phrase Britain has proved 'an awkward partner' (George 1990). The awkwardness began with the Heath government, and continued through every succeeding administration.

As far as Labour was concerned this was not so surprising. Given the extent of Labour divisions over Europe no one expected the relationship between Britain and Europe under Labour to be smooth. Following the renegotiation of the terms of entry the Labour government particularly after James Callaghan became Prime Minister proved pragmatic in its dealings with Europe, although Callaghan never made any secret of the priority he accorded to Britain's relationship with the United States. The main points of friction with Europe came over direct elections to the European Parliament and the first steps towards economic and monetary union. The Labour government's failure to deliver proportional representation as the voting system for the elections to the European Parliament meant that each European election produced a contingent of British MEPs which was unrepresentative of the British electorate.

Labour's reluctance to participate in moves to greater economic and monetary union led to the decision not to put the pound into the new European Monetary System approved at the Brussels summit in December 1978. The pragmatic acceptance by the Labour leadership of the need for cooperation with EC institutions was constrained by the lack of positive enthusiasm for Europe in the Labour leadership (especially following Roy Jenkins's departure to Brussels), and by the political reality that a majority of the labour movement remained hostile to the European Community and deeply suspicious of any moves towards further European integration. With its precarious parliamentary situation the Labour government was unlikely to take any risks with its European policy.

The European Community expected however that the return of the Conservatives to government in 1979 might herald a more constructive policy towards the community. Margaret Thatcher had supported Britain's continued membership of the European Union at the 1975 referendum as vital for the British national interest (even though she had not played a prominent part in the campaign). Thatcher had also criticized the decision of the Labour government not to join the European Monetary System. Once in government, however, a different pattern asserted itself. The first cause of friction was the British contribution to the budget, a problem left over from the original negotiations. It had not been solved then, and the issue had not been resolved in the renegotiation either. The difficulty was a structural one reflecting the way in which the Community budget was financed. Britain was a major contributor through the Common External Tariff (CET) and through VAT payments, the two main sources of Community revenues. But the main programme which the budget supported was the Common Agricultural Policy (CAP, established 1962), from which Britain received relatively little. The subsidies to small-scale agricultural production through the CAP were a political priority for several of the leading members of the EC, but not for Britain with its relatively efficient and large-scale agriculture. The solution for a positive European British government would have been either to accept the higher budget contribution as the price of belonging to the club, and enjoying the benefits for British companies of unrestricted access to European markets; or to press for the enlargement of the budget and the development of programmes such as the regional development fund (ERDF) which could be expected to provide much greater benefits for Britain.

Thatcher rejected both 'communautaire' solutions and pressed instead for Britain's money back (Gilmour 1993). The stridency of her negotiating style eventually won a compromise solution at the Fontainebleau summit in 1984, but it damaged long-term relationships, casting Britain in a role that was to become increasingly familiar of seeking to promote its own interests with no regard as to how Community institutions might be strengthened.

The reputation of Britain for intransigence and negative blocking of any moves towards greater integration firmly took root in the Thatcher years, but needs to be qualified. The greatest move of all to greater integration, the Single European Act, was achieved with strong support from the British, and there were other signs that the British at last were becoming more adept at playing the internal EC political game (George 1990: 205). Thatcher agreed to back the introduction of qualified majority voting to implement the new rules which were necessary to make the single market a reality, because she was aware that some states like Greece would veto many of the proposals fearing the effects of greater competition on many sectors of the Greek economy.

The signing of the Single European Act however also accelerated consideration of further measures to promote European union which culminated in the negotiations for the Maastricht Treaty in 1991. The achievement of a genuine single market was seen to require corresponding development of supranational institutions, in particular economic and monetary union, to support and regulate it so that it might achieve its full potential. At the same time Jacques Delors, the President of the Commission, and others warned that a balance would need to be struck between economic efficiency and the social rights and economic security of the working population. This implied a larger community budget and more programmes and legislation at the European level. There was particular concern on the left about the 'democratic deficit' in Europe, the lack of accountability and openness in the way in which the key European institutions functioned. Supporters of European integration advocated the transfer of more decision-making power to the European Parliament to give greater legitimacy to the decisions of the European Commission, and to make it more independent of the Council of Ministers.

It was the implications of the creation of the single market in promoting new moves towards economic and political union which divided the Thatcherite wing of the Conservatives. Many of them like

Geoffrey Howe accepted the logic that a single market needed in due course the creation of a single currency and such other agencies as were necessary to police it. The Thatcherite programme in Britain had targeted the political obstacles to the working of the free market and had endeavoured to sweep many of them away. It followed that if there was to be a real single market at the European level there had to be supranational administrative and legal institutions to ensure that local political obstacles in the various nation states were exposed and overcome. The problem for many Thatcherites however, including Thatcher herself, was that although they agreed with the goal they were not prepared to will the means if this meant transferring what they regarded as core aspects of British national sovereignty.

The central point of opposition was the proposal for economic and monetary union and a single currency. Many Conservatives feared that the transfer of monetary responsibilities to a European Central Bank would be followed by the transfer of fiscal responsibilities to the European Commission, and the loss of control by British governments of their ability to control or influence economic conditions in Britain (Holmes 1996). Economic policy would be determined at the European level, and might well be more interventionist and social democratic than the Conservatives were prepared to accept. In this way socialism could be imposed through the back door on Britain without the British people having voted for it.

Thatcher's key move, expressed particularly clearly in a brief passage in her celebrated Bruges speech, was to give absolute priority to national sovereignty over any move to supranational institutions. This was presented not as an anti-European policy but as an alternative European policy. Europe should be no more than an association of nation states, agreeing to set up institutions and common programmes where these were in the interests of all states. The implication of this view was that qualified majority voting (QMV) agreed under the Single European Act should be abolished, and certainly not extended; that the powers of the European Court to interpret the terms of the treaties which had established the European Union should not be able to override the national courts; and that the European Commission should have no independent power to initiate legislation but should be subordinate to the Council of Ministers.

The nationalist free market right has always stressed that adoption of these measures does not require Britain to leave the European Union. It merely requires the rest of the Union to accept the British view of the way the Union should develop. So long as the other member states still accept a role for supranational institutions which are not entirely subordinate to national governments, then there will continue to be conflict. Opinion has recently hardened in the nationalist free market right that a time may come therefore when the insistence of the majority of the members of the European Union in moving down a supranationalist path means that Britain will have to contemplate leaving the European Union.

POLITICAL ECONOMY OF THE EUROPEAN UNION

The supporters of Britain's membership of the European Union regard the anti-European drift of opinion in the Conservative Party as based on a fantasy that there is an alternative political economy to which Britain at the end of the twentieth century could turn, revealing the European project pursued during the last fifty years to have been a false trail.

Thatcher's resistance to committing Britain to membership of the European Monetary System was eventually overcome by the insistence of her colleagues, but she succeeded in defining the new terrain of anti-EU sentiment within the Conservative Party and in the country. Her falling out with several of her most senior colleagues, among them Nigel Lawson and Geoffrey Howe, was in part attributable to differences over Europe, and precipitated her own ousting from the leadership in 1990. Her successor, John Major, the Chancellor who had finally taken Britain into the European Monetary System in September 1990, was at first expected to strike a new note and chart a fresh direction for Britain's relationship with the European Union. He clearly intended to do so, speaking of his wish to see Britain at the heart of Europe. But his awareness of the tide of opinion in his own party was already apparent in the way in which he conducted the negotiations for the Maastricht Treaty, insisting on crucial opt-outs for Britain on the social chapter and on economic and monetary union.

He presented the outcome of the negotiations at Maastricht as a considerable triumph for British diplomacy, but his efforts were undermined by the catastrophe of Black Wednesday, on 16 September 1992. The forced suspension of sterling's membership of the Exchange Rate Mechanism (ERM) knocked away one of the crucial supports for the government's economic policy. If sterling had stayed within the ERM then the ground would have been prepared for Britain's eventual acceptance of a single currency and economic and monetary union. The forced exit ignited the opposition to the Maastricht Treaty and gave the government nine months of parliamentary battles to secure passage of the bill. It also permanently damaged the reputation of the government for economic competence. It led directly to the eruption of a civil war within the party over its leadership and future direction. Given his increasingly precarious majority as a result of by-election losses and defections, Major was obliged to adopt a vacillating and inconsistent policy in order to hold the factions of his party together. He steadily grew increasingly negative in his attitude towards Europe because of the growing strength of anti-European opinion in the party and in the Conservative media (Baker et al. 1996). In 1996 the row over BSE and British beef and the House of Commons vote which saw seventy-four backbenchers support Bill Cash's motion for a referendum on any further moves towards European integration revealed just how far the party had shifted from its former pro-European stance.

By 1996 the other members of the European Community were increasingly despairing of the British Conservatives chances of developing a consistent and positive European policy, and rather as they had done in the 1970s, they transferred their hopes to the opposition, and the New Labour of Tony Blair. The Conservatives were quick to seize on this and attempted to portray the Labour leader as 'the poodle of Brussels' and Labour as a federalist party which would abandon British sovereignty.

This might be a false hope. Apart from Edward Heath there has so far not been a British Prime Minister who was unequivocally pro-European. Even under Heath there were some early difficulties in Britain's relationships with its European partners. Are there perhaps reasons regardless of which party is in government why friction is likely to persist between Britain and the rest of the Community? Or is the friction merely the result of a period of transition?

The answer depends on the assumptions that are made about the causes of European integration. From an economic perspective integration is often treated as deriving from fundamental shifts in the organization of the European and world economy. National economies have become more interdependent and as a consequence interests have been formed in support of further and deeper economic integration. The continued political separation of Europe into nation states is an obstacle to this process of economic integration, which it is argued will gradually be overcome through the development of supranational institutions. On this view it is the trends towards regionalization of the European economic space through trade and investment flows which is the central reality of the past fifty years. The setting up of the original communities reflected an early grasp of this new political economy by the founder states. Once other countries including Britain recognized the same logic they applied for membership.

European integration can therefore be understood as a long-term process which is hindered or delayed by political decision-making, but not halted or seriously diverted. Sooner or later the political opposition to the next stages of integration will be overcome because of the irresistible pressure which arises from the new structure of interests in the European economy. Progress towards further integration is regarded as cyclical. It is fastest in periods of economic prosperity and economic growth. In periods of economic recession and stagnation progress is halted or slowed. But each new period of advance starts from a higher base so that the development of integration appears cumulative, an inexorable process leading to deeper and wider political and economic union, and the transfer of key functions from national governments to supranational institutions.

Opponents of European integration often argue that the end-point of this process will be the creation of a United States of Europe—a strong centralized state which replaces the existing nation states as a focus of legitimacy, identity, and executive competence. An alternative view however is that what we are witnessing is the emergence of a new kind of political system, the first post modern state, in which there are overlapping economic and political spaces, jurisdictions, and institutions (Ruggie 1993). Government functions are distributed among several different levels—European, national, and local. The nation state transfers some functions to European institutions and others to regional and local institutions, but it still retains an important range of decision-making powers. National sovereignty is qualified and limited but not dispelled. Most of the key issues in the debate over Britain's relationship to the European Union are over the extent to which national sovereignty should be limited by the transfer of decision-making to supranational institutions.

If the trend towards European economic integration is so powerful, what explains Britain's troubled relationship with the European Community, the reluctance to get involved in the first place, the constant fretting about the terms of entry, the friction over particular issues, and the unwillingness to accept the way in which the Community operates? From an economic perspective these are all transitional problems which reflect the particular legacies of Britain's past, and which can all in time be overcome. They are symptoms of a post-imperial trauma from which Britain will eventually emerge. The intensity of the European issue in British politics and the conflicts around it are seen as part of the process of adjustment.

A very different view emerges from political explanations of integration. The process of European integration is not seen either as irresistible or irreversible, but as the result of decisions made by national governments in line with their perceived national interests and in response to changing political and economic conditions in the world economy. The existence of long-term economic and social trends, and of various kinds of interdependence and interconnectedness in the global economy are not disputed, but governments and other political actors are recognized as having important degrees of autonomy in managing and adjusting to these pressures. Governments are not ciphers but agents, whose decisions sustain and modify the structures within which they operate.

One of the implications of political explanations of the European Union is that there is no presumption that the trend towards economic integration and political union is inevitable or irreversible. The calculations by government of their national interest or of their domestic political pressures may change, as a result of external as well as internal factors. The European Community can be interpreted primarily as a political project launched and sustained as the result of a political understanding between France and Germany, shaped in a particular political and economic context of the Cold War and the long post-war boom. The debates in the 1990s on the future of the European Union have been taking place in a very different context: the collapse of communism in Europe, the disintegration of the Soviet Union, the reunification of Germany, and the relative stagnation of the European economy relative to other parts of the world economy. On this view the loss of momentum in the European project evident in the 1990s may therefore not be due to political processes lagging behind economic, but may reflect a fundamental shift in the information available to political agents about the nature of their environment and the choices open to them.

A further question is whether Britain's relationship with the EU is best explained as the outcome of calculations made by British governments as to Britain's external national interest or as a result of national domestic policy choices. Are the interests which governments pursue primarily defined by national elites in isolation from domestic pressures, or are they more directly influenced by the concerns of the electorate? Much of the controversy over Europe and its persistence as an issue in British politics is due to different perceptions and definitions of the national interest, and whether the interests of the elites and of the people are the same or diverge.

At the centre of this debate is whether there really is no other choice for Britain than deepening economic and political integration with Europe, as many of the enthusiasts for integration contend. Sceptics note that the regionalization of the European economy which occurred in the forty years between 1950 and 1990 was closely related to the division of the world economy between the United States and the Soviet Union. The disintegration of the Soviet Union and its command economy opened the way for a new era of a unified global economy. The future patterns of regionalization in this global economy may be different and may fragment rather than further unify the West European economy. The disappearance of the former superpower confrontation brings into focus the economic division between East Asia, North America, and Western Europe, but the fears that a new world of regional blocs and inter-bloc rivalry are about to emerge are exaggerated (Gamble and Payne 1996). The end of the Cold War in Europe has undoubtedly weakened the European Union as a coherent economic and political project.

Political explanations of European integration deny that economic regionalization will necessarily deliver political union and suggest that the reason why European union has advanced as far as it has is because the various national elites calculated either that it promoted the interests of the state or their electoral interests or both. The political, administrative, business, and media elites in Britain have always supported membership of the European Community. No Cabinet of either party has come out against membership. Several key government departments, particularly the Foreign Office, have become very committed to Britain's place in Europe. Business opinion has remained broadly in favour of membership and of further steps to integration. The media is more divided, with the Conservative press since the 1980s becoming steadily anti-European, but the overall picture suggests that there remains a strong bias as far as the policy-making elites are concerned for Britain to remain a member of the Union. Membership confers significant benefits on Britain which could not be realized in any other way.

Despite the growing strength of the anti-European wing of the Conservative Party, therefore, there remains substantial elite consensus about the desirability of continued membership to safeguard essential national interests. Does membership still make sense however in terms of domestic politics? The earlier disagreement between Labour and the Conservatives on the desirability of membership reflected different estimates of the gains and losses from entry. The defensiveness of the Labour movement sprang from a desire to protect the arrangements which had guaranteed full employment and collective welfare. It was a specific national political economy which they saw as the achievement of the 1945 Labour government which was threatened by the free market ethos of the Common Market. The Conservatives however believed that membership of the European Community would help to sustain prosperity and expansion, and that although there were some costs in the form of higher food prices, these would be easily outweighed by the faster rate of economic growth which being a full member of the Community would be expected to promote. This standpoint was that taken in the other member states. Transfers of sovereignty in building the European Community were acceptable if they helped promote the domestic policies on which the post-war political order was based (Milward 1996).

In Britain the Conservatives' post-war electoral strategy of seeking to align themselves with the growth sectors of the economy and society consistently gave them the edge over Labour. This difference became a chasm after 1979 when Labour became identified with declining regions and sectors of the economy. The puzzle remains however. It is easy to see why the national protectionist strategy which Labour adopted in the 1970s and which was already implicit in its earlier suspicion of the Common Market was a weaker electoral strategy than the strategy of the Conservatives. But why then did so much of the Conservative Party and its media allies begin to turn away from that strategy in the 1980s and 1990s? In the 1960s only the *Daily Express*, still wedded to the ideal of the British Empire, opposed the application to join the common market. In 1996 *The Times*, the *Daily Telegraph*, the *Daily Mail*, the *Sun*, and the *Daily Star* had all become strong critics alongside the *Express* of the policies of the European Community. The vehemence of their criticism has begun to cast doubt on Britain's continued membership of it.

One explanation is that the balance of costs and benefits had altered, particularly as a result of the long recession which had affected Britain and the rest of Europe (Gamble 1995). The costs of the common agricultural policy continued to loom large and were only just offset by the benefits from increased trade and increased inward investment. The anti-European wing of the Conservative Party increasingly argued that there was an alternative political economy to the one associated with membership of the European Union, which was capable both of guaranteeing British security and of obtaining greater prosperity than could be secured within the Union.

They believe that as a result of changes in the global economy and the policies adopted by the Thatcher government in the 1980s Britain has an opportunity to become the Hong Kong of Europe, with a policy regime which emphasizes deregulation, low taxation, flexible labour markets, and open trade and investment (Spicer 1992; Holmes 1996). This policy regime is contrasted with that likely to be imposed through the supranational institutions of the EU—regulation, high taxation, inflexible labour markets, and restrictive policies on trade and investment. Europe's position, it is argued, has changed. From being one of the powerhouses of the growth of the world economy in the 1950s it has become relatively stagnant. The fastest growing markets are in other parts of the world, particularly East Asia. Britain's policy should not therefore be to tie itself to an inward-looking bloc whose instincts are restrictive and protectionist, but to pursue its traditional open seas policy of seeking the most rapidly growing markets and the cheapest sources of supply. Such a policy would also be Atlanticist in continuing to entrust Britain's security to NATO and the Atlantic Alliance rather than any arrangements within the European Union. It would also renew Britain's close relationship and understanding with the United States on the organization of the world economy. In this connection membership of NAFTA is seen as more relevant to Britain's interests than membership of the EU.

This alternative political economy is what makes the divide within the Conservative Party so serious. The majority of the party and its media allies is swinging behind this alternative strategy, even if its business allies for the most part remain unconvinced. But the alternative is plausible enough to give the political elite pause, and the resonance with popular chauvinism against Europe orchestrated by the Conservative tabloids makes it look electorally attractive also. The free market nationalist right calculates that there is now a gulf between how the elite perceives the European Union and how the people do. This populist tactic however ignores the ambivalence in the electorate. The European Union is less popular in Britain than in most other member countries, but that did not prevent the referendum result in favour of continued membership and the hard-headed calculation by many voters that although they may not like Europe they still regard it as the best option for maintaining employment, growth, and living standards. The emotional attachment to the pound sterling will be of less significance in the evaluation of a single currency than whether it is likely to make certain outcomes which voters want such as low inflation more likely. The political economy of currency union may well be more complex than many of the anti-Europeans allow. They portray it as an issue of elites versus the people, but really it is another question of elites versus elites, and which elite the people will trust more. The credibility of the alternative political economy of the right then becomes crucial, against the more tested political economy of the left. The present division in the Conservative leadership makes it very difficult for the free market nationalists to persuade the electorate that a radical shift is either safe or sensible.

It has been argued in this chapter that in recent decades the European issue has had a greater capacity to split British political parties more than any other. This is because there are key strategic political economy choices involved. The opponents of European Union have tried to formulate an alternative political economy which would both command the support of the policy elite and of the electorate. The success of the European Union in the past is because the European project secured both. The question for the future is whether a new elite consensus on the desirability of further European integration which can command popular support will become established, or whether the balance will swing to new national-populist elites which will favour a much looser association between the European nations if they favour one at all.

2

The Cauldron:
Conservative Parliamentarians and European Integration

Steve Ludlam

The British Conservative Party once prided itself on being Britain's party of Europe (George 1994). It also enjoyed the incalculable advantage of facing a Labour Party riven from end to end over EEC membership. Even during the 'Thatcher decade', the party's supporters favoured membership more strongly than those of the main opposition parties, and their backing for British membership actually strengthened across the decade.[1] Since the mid-1980s, however, the Parliamentary Conservative Party has been convulsed by divisions over European integration. A succession of Cabinet ministers, and Prime Minister Thatcher, resigned or were ejected from office following disputes over Europe. Indeed, the subsequent rebellion of backbenchers against the Maastricht Treaty ranks among the most bitter and damaging ever suffered by the party, with several former Cabinet ministers including Thatcher involved. In July 1993 over the Social Protocol, it produced the most serious Conservative parliamentary defeat during the twentieth century. In November 1994 John Major voluntarily became leader of a minority government by expelling eight Eurorebels from the parliamentary party. He lost an important budget vote as a result, and later had to readmit the 'Gang of Eight' unconditionally. Factional activity in the party became so unrestrained that by the summer of 1995 Major was stung to resign his leadership mid-term, challenging his critics to 'put up or shut up'. Cabinet critic John Redwood put up, but certainly did not, after Major's victory, shut up, launching another Eurosceptic think-tank.

---

[1] 67 per cent favoured membership in 1983, 79 per cent in 1991.

Redwood's frequent interventions compelled other would-be party leadership contenders to issue coded signals on Europe to the party, while EU fishing quotas, the 1996 'Maastricht II' IGC, the 'beef crisis', and the activities of Goldsmith's Referendum Party, prompted open rebelliousness. The possibility of withdrawal also re-emerged. When Norman Lamont hinted at withdrawal at the 1994 party conference he was roundly condemned by heavyweight Eurorebel Norman Tebbit. By 1996, Europeanists were taking withdrawal extremely seriously, and even Cabinet ministers were obliged to engage in debates on the prospects for Britain outside the Union. This wider debate was partly the result (as he had feared) of Major's concession of a single currency referendum, permitting the rebels to move on to other targets during the sabre rattling of the 'beef war'.

By 1996, factors that had stood in the way of a catastrophic formal split in the party seemed to be weakening. Unlike their European equivalents, right-wing anti-marketeers had had no effective parliamentary vehicle to the right of the Conservative Party. The arrival of the Referendum Party not only brought the financial resources of one of the world's richest men, but also the possibility of a single issue campaign that did not require defiance of the rest of the party's general platform. The Referendum Party's threat to stand against Europeanist Conservatives provided a rationale for Eurorebels to issue sceptical personal manifestos at the general election especially in marginal seats. In April 1996 around a hundred sitting MPs were said to be intending to issue such manifestos. When unrelenting Eurorebel Bill Cash moved a 'who governs?' Referendum Bill in June 1996, his co-sponsors included a broad spectrum of Eurosceptic opinion including members of the 'Gang of Eight', Redwood, Lamont, Jonathan Aitken (the last three all ex-members of Major Cabinets), and John Biffen. In an unwhipped vote, seventy-four Conservatives voted for Cash's bill. The perception that Cash was in harness with Goldsmith infuriated Europeanists, and party managers demanded that Cash stop accepting campaign funds for the European Foundation from the Referendum Party leader. Cash conceded, but Margaret Thatcher immediately covered the loss, declaring the Foundation to be 'vital to the Conservative Party and to the country', and offering her personal financial support for 'those who seek to preserve British sovereignty' (*European Journal*, June 1996).

The second factor was the resuscitation of the Europeanist lobby, combating the rebel publicity machine (Davies 1996; Whitney 1996), and issuing occasional tactical denials that a group of disillusioned Europeanist MPs might defect. These developments were backed up by the emergence during 1995 of the Action Centre for Europe and the relaunch of the European Movement both funded by Europeanist businesses (Action Centre for Europe 1995; *European Campaigner*, Autumn 1995). One Europeanist MP announced that he would not vote for the sceptic Conservative candidate in the constituency to which he was retiring at the 1997 election. At the end of 1995 the recently elected Vice-Chair of the European Movement, Emma Nicholson MP, defected to the Liberal Democrats citing Europe as the key issue in her defection. During the 'beef war' in 1996, by which time the government's majority was vulnerable to a single defection, another retiring MP threatened to resign the whip in protest at the government's obstruction of EU business, and in July 1996 a Treasury minister resigned from office in order to campaign against the single currency.

With time running out before a general election, Major's long struggle to suppress parliamentary divisions had clearly failed. The unwhipped Cash Referendum Bill in June 1996, which attracted seventy-four backbenchers, revealed that the larger group of Conservative sceptics apparent in the attitude survey analysis in this chapter, remained intact, providing powerful evidence of Major's failure. One by one, three vital thresholds were being crossed that had led from internal division to outright split in the historic Tory disputes over Corn Law repeal and Tariff Reform: cabinet division, parliamentary rebellion, and defection to other parties (Baker et al. 1993*b*).

This chapter addresses four key questions raised by this extraordinary collapse of party unity and discipline. Why have the divisions erupted so violently in recent years, given that European integration had been controversial in the party for more than thirty years? What has been the balance of opinion among Conservative parliamentarians during the recent turmoil? What do the divisions imply for our understanding of contemporary conservatism? And finally, what are the implications for British policy on Europe?

THE TREATY TOO FAR

The question of European integration has always caused tension in the Conservative party (Ashford 1980; Berrington 1973; Finer et al. 1961).

Macmillan feared it would split the party (Macmillan 1973: 27), and it made Edward Heath's backbenches more rebellious than any since the war, culminating in Enoch Powell's dramatic resignation and call for a Labour vote to secure a referendum on Community membership in 1974 (Norton 1978). Macmillan and Heath launched high-profile and high-risk campaigns to secure party support for British entry, and Heath was also obliged to rely on rebel Labour MPs. In the earliest disputes MPs committed to Britain's imperial role opposed MPs who saw Europe as the more effective platform for British economic strategy and as a bulwark against Soviet expansionism. For many early Eurosceptics, traditional suspicion of continental entanglements was compounded by the explicit threat to the legislative sovereignty of the Westminster Parliament. The emergence of a neo-liberal critique of British economic policy in the 1970s directed hostility towards the economic interventionism said to characterize EEC policy. Such concerns translated into repeated, but limited rebellions against Heath and high-profile factionalism during the 1975 referendum on Europe (Goodhart 1976). Yet none of the earlier manifestations of dissent match the scale and intensity of the rebellion under Major.

Figure 2.1, which charts key backbench Conservative rebellions since Britain's first application, indicates the crucial political trend.[2] What is striking is the scale of dissent from 1992, both the numbers of rebels, defined as those cross-voting against the whips or deliberately abstaining, and the percentages of backbenchers involved in rebellions. Even more striking is the number of rebellions actually defeating

---

[2] The votes charted: 1961, Conservative government (Cg) motion supporting EC entry application. 1967, Labour government (Lg) motion supporting EC entry application. 1971, Cg motion supporting EC entry application. 1972i, Cg European Communities Bill 2nd Reading. Heath's vote of confidence. 1972ii, rebel pro-referendum amendment. 1972iii, Cg European Communities Bill 3rd Reading. 1975, Lg Motion accepting 'renegotiated' entry terms. 1978, European Assemblies Elections Bill Third Reading. 1986, EC Amendment (Single European Act) Bill Third Reading. 1992i, EC Amendment ('Maastricht') Bill 2nd Reading. 1992ii, EC Amendment ('Maastricht') Bill Paving Motion. 1993i, EC Amendment ('Maastricht') Bill, Council of the Regions amendment. 1993ii, EC Amendment ('Maastricht') Bill referendum amendment. 1993iii, EC Amendment ('Maastricht') Bill Third Reading. 1993iv, Postponed Social Chapter vote, 22 July 1993v, confidence vote, 23 July, on Social Chapter. 1994i, confidence vote, 28 November, EC (Finance) Bill Second Reading. 1994ii, Labour amendment to Finance Bill to abandon stage 2 of imposition of VAT on fuel. 1995i, Labour motion rejecting government European policy. 1995ii, motion noting government position on EU fishing policy.

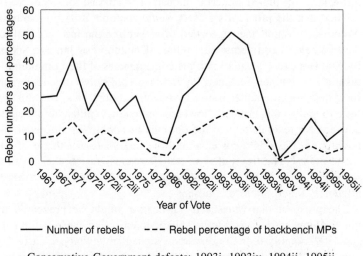

Year of Vote

——— Number of rebels   – – – Rebel percentage of backbench MPs

Conservative Government defeats: 1993i, 1993iv, 1994ii, 1995ii
Conservative confidence votes: 1972i, 1993v, 1994i; free vote 1971

FIG. 2.1. Key Conservative rebellions on European integration 1961–1995

Major's government, an outcome that even Heath's uncompromising advocacy avoided.

Without doubt the key factor underlying these developments was the Maastricht Treaty and the supranationalist model of European integration it appeared to represent. The 'irrevocable' aspects of the third stage of EMU undermined the oft-used argument of Conservative leaders that Britain's participation in any particular integrationist development did not imply any longer term commitments (Ridley 1992: 160). It was to avoid such a treaty that Thatcher had promoted the Single European Act (Thatcher 1993: 547–9). The single currency and independent European Central Bank (ECB) were seen as threatening not only economic policy independence in general, but the very monetary policy instruments that unreconstructed monetarists saw as the essential tools of national anti-inflationary struggle. The extension into new policy areas of QMV procedures that overrode national vetoes incensed sceptics already horrified by the subordination of Westminster to EC law. Thatcher's promotion of QMV as a tactic to overcome protectionist opposition to the single market had backfired spectacularly (Thatcher 1993: 550–3). Almost all Conservative MPs naturally agreed that the social protocol must be resisted as a throwback to pre-Thatcherite industrial relations, but the rebels insisted that the protocol's effects would soon hit Britain in spite of the opt-out. Major had succeeded in preventing the incorporation of the two new intergovernmental pillars (Common Foreign and Security, and Home and Justice) into the competencies of the Community's institutions. Unlike Thatcher, he had also confronted the single currency and social chapter issues by negotiating opt-outs. But this did little to mollify his critics. They regarded the new pillars as a tactical advance for federalists, and the opt-outs as confirming the federalist threat from the single currency and the interventionist threat of EU social policy. The treaty demonstrated conclusively to Conservative sceptics that the drift of European integration was inexorably towards a federal United States of Europe.

The prospect that Maastricht ratification might be prevented by popular opposition was another factor intensifying the rebellion. In June 1992, eighty-four Conservatives signed an unwhipped early day motion (EDM) in the Commons demanding abandonment of the treaty when the first Danish referendum returned a 'no' vote. The collapse of the government's economic strategy soon after, as Britain fell out of the ERM, unleashed even more fury against the Monetary Union at the heart of the treaty. Discontent at Britain's membership of ERM was first inflamed by the humiliation of 'Black Wednesday' in September 1992, then apparently justified by the economic revival that followed. The subsequent dismissal of Chancellor Lamont added an influential voice to the rebellion (Lamont 1993). When Major moved in November 1992 to resume the passage of the Maastricht Bill, he secured a tiny Commons majority only with Liberal Democrat support (Baker et al. 1993*a*).

Other, internal factors help account for the explosion of rebelliousness. By far the most important was the belief that Thatcher's achievements were no longer safe in the hands of her preferred successor. Thatcher, and three of her recent party chairmen, Lords Tebbit, Parkinson, and Baker, openly joined the rebellion and attacked both the treaty and Major's leadership. Former Party Treasurer Lord McAlpine donated a house in Westminster for a rebel headquarters, and Conservative businessmen donated money to fund the rebel campaign. Rebel bitterness now found a focus that Major's otherwise dogged pursuit of Thatcher's policy agenda had hitherto denied them. Backing for the rebels by key Tory newspapers was another vital factor. By the time of Major's leadership election challenge in July 1995, only one national Tory paper still supported him.

Also of significance was the reluctance of local Conservative associations to discipline rebel MPs, probably reflecting the growth of rank-and-file scepticism revealed in academic and party surveys (Whiteley et al. 1994: 57; *Financial Times*, 28 March 1996).

A crucial factor that frequently placed Major at the mercy of his rebels was that out of office for so long Labour's parliamentary party displayed unexpectedly tight discipline in key votes. That Labour MPs were privately just as divided over the treaty simply rubbed salt in this political wound.

The story of the Maastricht rebellion has been told elsewhere (Baker et al. 1994*a*; Gorman 1993). Parliamentary opposition to the treaty ended with the rebels' capitulation in the confidence vote of 23 July 1993, and the subsequent withdrawal of a legal challenge to ratification. Tensions eased further when, in an *Economist* article, Major prominently re-emphasized his commitment to a 'Europe of nation states', and his scepticism at the prospects of EMU (Major 1993). Elements of the government's 'British agenda', stressing enlargement, deregulation (combined with opposition to the social chapter), fiscal conservatism, free trade, subsidiarity, and intergovernmentalist management of the EU based on national vetoes, appealed to many backbenchers, as did the treaty opt-outs, but Major's humiliating QMV U-turn in February 1994 revived dissent. Rebels took care not to break ranks during the April 1994 European Parliament elections, but in November Major expelled the 'Gang of Eight' anti-marketeers, who made the most of their new parliamentary liberty. His attempt to put a stop to factionalism over Europe by resigning the party leadership and successfully standing for re-election, though a short-term success, failed to quell dissent. Nor did it postpone the long-expected retaliation by the Europeanists, whose fear of Portillo entering a second round secured Major's re-election.

As the single currency timetable advanced, and the 1996 IGC approached, rebel demands for a referendum commitment on the former, and a White Paper on the latter, were both conceded by the Cabinet, with the predictable effect that the rebels voiced ever more demands. During and after the Maastricht rebellion, commentators frequently speculated on how far the bulk of the parliamentary party sympathized with the rebels, and how far Major was being pushed around by a small group of dissidents. The Members of Parliament Project ESRC-sponsored survey of 'Conservative Parliamentarians and European Integration' carried out during the 1994 European election campaign revealed the true state of opinion on the Conservative benches in both London and Strasbourg.[3]

THE BLUE MAP OF EUROPE

Among both back and frontbench MPs, the survey demonstrated a considerable degree of Euroscepticism, including support for important rebel positions rejected by the Cabinet, and the existence of large minorities on both Euro-wings of the party that suggested that Major's 'British agenda' for Europe might not, after all, satisfactorily perform one of its functions, that of uniting his party. Table 2.1 offers simplified responses to about one-quarter of the survey statements.

Responses to statements 1.1 and 1.2 indicated that Conservative MPs supported EC membership by a significant majority. Yet other results pointed to deep-seated suspicion of pooling sovereignty, a clear majority favouring the passing of a new 'Act of Supremacy' to reassert the legislative sovereignty ceded in the Treaty of Rome (1.3, 1.4). There was strong support for the suggestion that both agricultural policy should be repatriated, and that immigration control should not be shared (1.5, 1.6). On EMU the majority of MPs were similarly, or even more intensely sceptical. A two-thirds majority disagreed with joining a single currency simply to avoid the economic consequences of not doing so; an absolute majority agreed with the rebel demand for a referendum; and majorities agreed that Britain should never rejoin the ERM, and that joining a single currency would undermine UK sovereignty (1.7–1.10). There was also virtual unanimity in favour of the opt-out from the Social Chapter (1.11).

On issues before the 1996 IGC, MPs opposed further supranationalism in favour of strengthening national parliamentary scrutiny of EC business (1.12, 1.13). Not only did MPs strongly oppose the alternative means of closing the 'democratic deficit' by making the European Parliament a genuine legislature, they supported the rebel demand to strip the Commission of its right to initiate legislation (1.14, 1.15). On an issue of even more explosive potential, the trend

[3] The joint Sheffield and Nottingham Trent universities' survey (ESRC Award R. 000231298) was conducted at the University of Sheffield by the author with the other members of the Members of Parliament Project. The survey data sets are available from the ESRC Data Archive. Fuller discussion of results can be found in Baker et al. (1995, 1996).

TABLE 2.1. *Conservative parliamentarians' attitudes to European integration* (*n=90*)

	Statement	Status	Strongly agree or agree %	Neither %	Disagree or strongly disagree %
1.1	The disadvantages of EC membership have been outweighed by the benefits	MP	60	8	32
		MEP	77	0	23
1.2	People who believe in free trade cannot support the EU as it has turned out	MP	32	10	58
		MEP	4	0	96
1.3	Sovereignty cannot be pooled	MP	62	7	31
		MEP	27	9	64
1.4	An Act of Parliament should be passed to establish explicitly the ultimate supremacy of Parliament over EU legislation	MP	50	17	33
		MEP	5	10	85
1.5	Agriculture should be handled under subsidiarity at the national level	MP	68	6	26
		MEP	24	9	67
1.6	Immigration should be handled under subsidiarity at the national level	MP	81	4	15
		MEP	25	10	65
1.7	Britain should never rejoin the ERM	MP	48	16	36
		MEP	18	14	68
1.8	Britain should join a single currency if it is created because of the economic consequences of remaining outside	MP	27	7	66
		MEP	86	5	9
1.9	The establishment of a single EU currency would signal the end of the UK as a sovereign nation	MP	48	11	41
		MEP	9	5	86
1.10	There should be a national referendum before the UK enters a single currency	MP	50	5	45
		MEP	23	14	63
1.11	Britain should adopt the Social Protocol	MP	5	3	92
		MEP	5	14	81
1.12	The 1996 IGC should not increase the supranational powers of EU institutions	MP	87	5	8
		MEP	32	14	54

TABLE 2.1. *Continued*

	Statement	Status	Strongly agree or agree	Neither	Disagree or strongly disagree
			%	%	%
1.13	The key to closing the 'democratic deficit' is strengthening the scrutiny by national parliaments of the EU legislative process	MP	79	11	10
		MEP	41	9	50
1.14	The European Parliament should be given the right to initiate EU legislation	MP	31	6	63
		MEP	82	0	18
1.15	The Commission should lose the right to initiate legislation	MP	60	6	34
		MEP	18	9	73
1.16	Britain should block the use of QMV in the areas of foreign and defence policy	MP	85	9	6
		MEP	73	9	18
1.18	A single European army would undermine rather than underpin the security of the UK	MP	73	12	15
		MEP	29	19	52

Note: MEP means sitting MEP at time of EP elections in June 1994.

Source: Conservative Parliamentarians and European Integration Survey, University of Sheffield 1994. ESRC Award R. 000231298

to integrated military command structures, Conservative MPs strongly opposed pooling sovereignty, seeing a single European army as a threat to British security (1.16, 1.17).

Backbench minorities on contentious issues, of either Euro-enthusiasts or Eurosceptics, are arguably as serious for party managers as the sympathy with rebel positions. Table 2.1 shows that on a range of issues encompassing sovereignty, EMU, subsidiarity, QMV, and the powers of EU institutions to be discussed at the IGC, potentially dangerous minorities of both Eurosceptics and Euro-enthusiasts could be mobilized. The image of disunity resulting from public display of such divisions in publications and in the media has arguably been more damaging to the party in the long run than the occasional defeat caused by them in the Commons.

Conservative MEPs were frequent targets of Eurosceptic criticism. Thatcher called them the 'residue of Heathism' (Thatcher 1993: 749).

The substance behind this jibe was the long service of many MEPs, often dating back to the unelected European Assembly of the mid-1970s to which they were appointed before Thatcher could influence the selection process. Table 2.1 offers substantial evidence that Conservative MEPs, at least the large group that sat before the 1994 EP election rout, were indeed much more Europeanist. On the benefits of membership, on the social protocol, and on QMV in EU foreign and defence policy, the MEPs take the same line as MPs. But on the question of sovereignty, on subsidiarity, on EMU, and on the powers of EU institutions, and even on the implications of a single European army, they come into direct conflict with their Westminster colleagues. Such differences have attracted several explanations. To the charge that Conservative MEPs 'go native' on taking office in Europe the most convincing reply from the MEPs themselves has been that on surveying the harsh ideological atmosphere of Thatcher's party at Westminster, they found the prospects of a political career in Europe more congenial. Certainly a large proportion of Conservatives becoming MEPs in the 1970s and 1980s had prior political, military, family, or commercial links with Europe.

The party's candidates at the 1994 EP election were revealed by the survey to be far closer to Major's sceptical backbenches than to the pre-1994 set of MEPs. Yet, in spite of the considerable change of Conservative personnel at that election, the BSE crisis in 1996 revealed a group of MEPs generally out of sympathy with the government's confrontation with the EU and alarmed at the accompanying jingoism in the party and the national press.

NATIONAL SOVEREIGNTY: ABSOLUTISTS AND POOLERS

Like the disputes over Corn Law repeal and Tariff Reform that split the party in the past, European integration poses the question of Britain's role in the world economy; but it also poses a direct threat to Britain's political sovereignty whose defence has so often been at the heart of the party's mass appeal (Baker et al. 1993*b*). The notion of national sovereignty has become ever more complex, both as British influence as an imperialist power has declined and as economic internationalization has intensified. It is further complicated by the subordination of Westminster to European law. However unsatisfactory sovereignty may have become as a concept in political science

(Bulpitt 1992), it nevertheless remains a crucial concept for Conservatives. Broadly, Conservative MPs have fallen into two camps on national sovereignty: 'absolutists', and 'poolers'.

Absolutists focus on the legislative supremacy of the Westminster Parliament. They point out that unlike most European Parliaments, Westminster is not obliged by a written constitution to share power with either an executive, or a supreme court, or subnational bodies, and it can abolish legislation at will. This parliamentary supremacy is said to have protected liberty in Britain, not least against the twentieth-century challenges of communism and fascism, and to have come to embody the legitimacy of modern democracy itself. To undermine the sovereignty of parliament is not only to threaten legislative independence and the tradition of liberty, but to threaten the very consent to the law that rests on the legitimacy endowed by elected lawmakers. No such legitimacy, it is argued, can be provided by European institutions, elected or unelected, that can never claim the allegiance that rests on national identities embedded in nation states. The 'democratic deficit' is said to be exacerbated with every intrusion of European law into people's working and social lives. Michael Spicer MP illustrates the content of such absolutist arguments:

In the United Kingdom it [the Maastricht Treaty] would have the profoundest possible consequences for the very foundations of the constitution. This rests above all on the notion that the people exert their sovereignty through a Parliament which is the supreme authority in the land. An essential element of this supremacy is that Parliament can effect whatever changes it chooses, including, often especially, amending the laws passed by a previous Parliament. The commitment at Maastricht to the 'irrevocable' is in direct contradiction to this. However, the fact is that the irrevocable powers have not yet been transferred, and sovereignty is an absolute: you either have sovereignty or you do not. (I have never been able to understand the ideal of 'pooling sovereignty'.) In this sense, Maastricht is a torpedo aimed but not yet fired at the keel of British democracy. (Spicer 1992: 13–14)

By contrast, the poolers tend to judge sovereignty by its usefulness as a policy resource to be bargained with in international policy arenas in pursuit of national security and prosperity. In the same way as pooling sovereignty in NATO is said to have enhanced Britain's military security, sharing sovereignty in the EU is said to enhance the prosperity of British industry and commerce. Such pooling is said to permit Britain to 'punch above its weight'. This approach concentrates on what is said to be the real purpose of possessing sovereignty—the good life. Achieving this end is held to be more important than obsolete constitutional means. The following formulation of Geoffrey Howe illustrates the pooling argument:

> My purpose is to explain how I believe sovereignty is not some pre-defined absolute, but a flexible, adaptable, organic notion that evolves and adjusts with circumstances. It is to explain how sovereignty constitutes a resource to be used, rather than a constraint that inhibits or limits our capacity for action . . . . [Sovereignty] might be summarised as a nation's practical capacity to maximise its influence in the world . . . . it may be a relatively weak country, which uses co-operative arrangements with others as a means of enhancing its otherwise marginal role, seeing sovereignty above all as a resource to be traded rather than guarded in a way that limits its potential influence on others. (Howe 1990: 678, 687)

If the absolutist/pooler distinction were clear-cut, Whips could make reasonably accurate calculations about parliamentary behaviour. It is not, however. Most explosively, supporters of power-sharing to achieve the single market have divided bitterly over monetary policy integration. Geoffrey Howe has recorded the 'three-way split at the heart of the British Cabinet': Thatcher opposed UK membership of the Exchange Rate Mechanism (ERM) and opposed a single currency; her two pioneering monetarist Chancellors Howe and Lawson supported ERM membership; yet only Howe supported the single currency (Howe 1994: 534). Kenneth Clarke, on the other hand, in spite of being the Cabinet's staunchest supporter of single currency membership, has opposed the very notion of independent central banking (Clarke 1993). Table 2.2 gives examples of ambivalence of this kind.

At the level of aggregate opinion, Table 2.2 reveals both absolutist and pooler majorities on different aspects of similar issues. General positions on pooling sovereignty in relation to the ECJ and the European Commission are significantly modified when their powers to police the single market are considered. A similar free market commitment is apparent in support for a supranational strategy for business deregulation, but not a supranational *dirigiste* strategy for industrial investment. Conducted just weeks after Major's notorious QMV U-turn the survey found clear majorities for 'undemocratic' supranational legislation to combat drug trafficking and terrorism

TABLE 2.2. *Ambivalence over sovereignty among backbench Conservative MPs (n=90)*

Statement	Strongly agree or agree	Neither	Disagree or strongly disagree
	%	%	%
on the European Court of Justice			
The continental system of jurisprudence as practised by the European Court of Justice is a threat to liberty in Britain	55	19	26
The increased powers of the European Court to enforce the Single Market are welcome	67	15	18
on the European Commission			
A strong Commission is vital for the success of the Single Market programme	47	9	44
The Commission should lose the right to initiate legislation	61	4	35
on supranational industrial strategy			
In principle there should be a Union strategy on deregulation	54	9	37
In principle there should be a Union strategy on industrial investment	16	14	70
on the national veto			
QMV should be used to advance EU policy against terrorism and drug trafficking	59	22	19
Britain should block the use of QMV in the areas of foreign and defence policy	87	6	7

Source: Conservative Parliamentarians and European Integration Survey, ESRC/University of Sheffield 1994. ESRC Award R. 000231298.

through the intergovernmental Home and Justice pillar, but against the use of QMV in the intergovernmental Foreign and Security pillar. Even Thatcher and the leading Eurosceptic Bill Cash continue to defend the use of QMV to establish the Single Market, and as Cash put it, 'for specific purposes relating to co-operation in the commercial field which will enable free trade to develop within Europe' (Thatcher 1993: 550–3; George and Sowemimo 1996: 250; William Cash, Hansard (Commons), col. 939, 13 January 1993). Such examples suggest a further distinction might usefully be made between attitudes to policy interdependence and attitudes to constitutional sovereignty.

The disputes over sovereignty, complex and intellectually messy though they may be, are thus clearly central to understanding the divisions in contemporary Conservatism, but appear to remain complicated by more traditional right–left, liberal–collectivist dimensions. Apart from those in Ashford's studies (Ashford 1980, 1992), academic typologies of Conservative thinking have neglected the importance of a national sovereignty/interdependence dimension and have been little help in analysing the party's near fatal divisions over European integration, not least the dramatic disintegration of the Thatcherite right wing (Baker et al. 1994b).

The survey data enable analysis to be carried out that takes account of the structuring of attitudes across a range of issues, and is more sensitive to strength of feeling.[4] Table 2.3 shows the four-factor model that resulted from conducting a factor analysis of responses to all the issue statements in the survey.[5]

The first factor to emerge links scepticism about the benefits of EU membership (historically, and in the face of globalization), a very marked defence of national parliamentary sovereignty (not least at the IGC), and an irreconcilable opposition to EMU.[6] Even the cohesion fund statement is fundamentally an EMU item, representing compensation for the dislocation anticipated from a single currency regime.

---

[4] Likert-style scale responses were sought to sixty-five statements framed to illuminate the sovereignty/interdependence and limited/extended state dimensions. The statements were derived from qualitative analysis of relevant documentation, from the published views of politicians, and from a series of unattributable interviews with Conservative parliamentarians representing a range of opinion on European integration. The cooperation of these individuals is gratefully acknowledged.

[5] Orthogonal rotation of factors, the method used here (using the Varimax technique with pairwise deletion of cases, in SPSS for Windows), identifies independent factors. Exploratory principal component factor analysis was carried out using all the issue variables in order to identify superfluous variables. Variables with low loadings (less than plus or minus 0.45) or that 'noisily' reproduced results of similar variables were progressively excluded. A Kaiser-Meyer-Olkin measure of sampling adequacy (MSA) of 0.80 or more is preferable (Walsh 1990: 331). In the thirty-three variable model used here the MSA is 0.90 when only MPs are included. Kaiser himself has described measures in the 0.90s as 'marvellous' (Norusis 1993: 52). Allowing all 'meaningful factors', those incorporating at least three variables, to emerge, provides the most complete factor analysis and this approach was followed here (Walsh 1990: 334). There is some concern at the use of ordinal data for factor analysis. This may be justified statistically, where scientifically sophisticated predictions are to be made on the basis of factor scores. There is no such intention here, where the purpose is to identify attitudinal linkages and clustering. The author is grateful to Professor Paul Whiteley for technical advice.

[6] Positive values indicate agreement with a survey statement, negative values disagreement.

TABLE 2.3. *Factor analysis of Conservative MPs including ministers: orthogonally-rotated factor matrix (n=106)*

Survey statement	Absolutist factor	Pooler factor	Harmoniser factor	Right Nationalist factor
Eigenvalue	15.27	2.20	1.50	1.36
Percentage of variance explained	44.9	6.5	4.4	4.0
The establishment of a single EU currency would signal the end of the UK as a sovereign nation	.80327			
People who believe in free trade cannot support the EU as it has turned out	.77775			
Britain should never rejoin the ERM	.75742			
The globalization of economic activity makes European Union (EU) membership more, rather than less necessary for the UK	−.74591			
An Act of Parliament should be passed to establish explicitly the ultimate supremacy of Parliament over EU legislation	.72042			
Britain should never permit its monetary policy to be determined by an independent European Central Bank	.71576			
Sovereignty cannot be pooled	.70560			
Britain should join a single currency if it is created because of the economic consequences of remaining outside	−.70154			
There should be a national referendum before the UK enters a single currency	.61693			

Survey statement	Absolutist factor	Pooler factor	Harmoniser factor	Right Nationalist factor
Cohesion funds should be phased out	.54956			
The increased powers of the European Court to enforce the Single Market are welcome	−.54541			
In principle there should be a Union strategy on industrial investment		.75645		
The EU's budget should be enlarged		.70709		
Britain should block the use of QMV in the areas of foreign and defence policy		−.66099		
Britain should adopt the Social Protocol		.65000		
Personal taxation should be harmonized within the EU		.62922		
The 1996 IGC should not increase the supranational powers of EU institutions		−.61496		
The UK should use the 'Luxembourg Compromise' to prevent imposition of a maximum 48-hour week in Britain		−.57132		
A single European Army would undermine rather than underpin the security of the UK		−.56837		
The European Parliament should be given the right to initiate EU legislation		.56022		

Table 2.3. *Continued*

TABLE 2.3. *Continued*

Survey statement	Absolutist factor	Pooler factor	Harmoniser factor	Right Nationalist factor
The extension of 'social dialogue' through the institution of works councils is a necessary component of economic progress in the EU		.53769		
VAT should be harmonized within the EU			.74827	
Environmental taxation should be harmonized within the EU			.72357	
The Commission should lose the right to initiate legislation			−.61121	
The UK should incorporate the European Convention on Human Rights into law			.52141	
The continental system of jurisprudence as practised by the European Court of Justice is a threat to liberty in Britain			−.50743	
Reduction of the burden of social costs placed on employers is essential to job creation in the EU				.65405
Immigration policy should be handled under subsidiarity at the national level				.65227
Trade union rights should be handled under subsidiarity at the national level				.59126

Note: Factor loadings <±.5 excluded.

Source: Conservative Parliamentarians and European Integration Survey, University of Sheffield 1994. ESRC Award R. 00023129.

Monetary policy has been the issue most frequently linked to sovereignty in party debates since the mid-1980s. The support for passing a new Act of Supremacy to proclaim Westminster's superiority to European law represents a willingness to defy the Treaty of Rome. This factor, by far the most significant of the four, might legitimately therefore be designated an Absolutist factor.

In the second factor statements predominate that represent a clear willingness to pool sovereignty in key policy areas such as defence and foreign policy, military integration, and to grant the European Parliament the right to initiate legislation (which further weakens national parliaments). A number of key statements implying support for an integrated fiscal and social policy regime also receive positive support in the second factor, including the most controversial (personal) tax integration statement. This can be called a Pooler factor.

The third factor combines pro-European responses on three key EU constitutional reform issues all three concerned with legislative and judicial processes, together with support for two other tax harmonization suggestions. This variant of the pooling approach might be termed a Harmonizer factor.

The fourth factor incorporates neo-liberal responses on trade union policy, and towards the alleged burden of social costs added to European production in the face of globalization, with a nationalist response on immigration control; this appears to be what might be called a Right Nationalist factor.

This allocation of labels to factors is not entirely satisfactory, but it helps to highlight three crucial features about the structure of MPs' attitudes raised by the factor analysis, which go beyond the general clash between Eurosceptics and Europeanists. First, there clearly are dimensions distinguishing absolutists from poolers. We see this most clearly in the issues clustered in the Absolutist and Pooler factors. Second, as noted earlier, one of the contrasts between the two Eurosceptic factors, as well as the two Europeanist factors, is between constitutional sovereignty and policy interdependence. The factor analysis confirms the importance of this distinction. Thirdly, within the factor model there remains a significant presence of 'wet' and 'dry' attitudes on fiscal, industrial, and social issues. The strongest Europeanist factor, the Pooler factor, contains a set of positively *dirigiste* attitudes; the fourth, Eurosceptic Right Nationalist factor structures anti-*dirigiste* attitudes.

Recalling that the purpose of factor analysis is to identify independent structures of responses, it becomes clear that what we are looking at are two strong sovereignty dimensions separately structured around the agendas of the absolutist nationalist and pooling integrationist wings of the parliamentary party, and two similarly structured dimensions that are interlinked with the agendas of its pro- and anti-interventionism wings. This four-dimensional model thus powerfully confirms that a sovereignty–interdependence axis of ideas and attitudes has become a key feature of contemporary parliamentary Conservatism, that it includes some complex distinctions between constitutional supremacy and policy independence, but also that it remains entangled with the more traditional right–left dimension focused on the role of state intervention. The argument that the sovereignty issue is now the most important fault-line in modern Conservatism is strongly supported. The complexity of the party management problem on Europe is also confirmed. There is certainly no factor that corresponds neatly to the content or stance of Major's 'British agenda'. EMU emerges as the policy issue most closely linked to the explosive sovereignty question, but the other factors that emerged, as independent dimensions, also included both constitutional supremacy and policy independence issues. Given the modest and declining size of Major's Commons majority throughout his premiership, can the factor analysis shed any light on the scope of potential disorder?

Table 2.4 shows the distribution of MPs along the four-factor model dimensions, showing percentages measuring +1.0 or more or −1.0 or more standard deviations from the mean average (a measure, in this case, of strong dissidence) and suggesting an approximate equivalent number of MPs taking up strong Eurosceptic or Europeanist positions in relation to the groups of issues structured by the factor analysis. In terms of measurable parliamentary behaviour on key occasions, there are some pleasing mathematical coincidences. The percentage of sceptics measuring −1.0 or more on the Absolutist factor translates into approximately forty-seven MPs, the percentage measuring +1.0 or more on the Pooler factor translates into forty sceptic MPs: forty-six rebelled against the third reading of the Maastricht Bill, forty-four rebelled and defeated the government on the Committee of the Regions amendment (the government's only defeat during the passage of the bill). The equivalent of forty-four MPs are strongly dissident at the Euro-enthusiastic end of the scale. Fifty-two MPs presented a Positive Europe group statement to Major in early 1995 calling for a more Europeanist policy.

TABLE 2.4. *Distribution of dissident MPs including ministers (n=106): percentages located at more than 1.0 and 2.0 standard deviations from mean factor scores, and approximate equivalent numbers of MPs*

	end of axis	<−2.0 sds	<−1.0 sds	>+1.0 sds	>+2.0 sds	end of axis
Absolutist factor MPs	pro-sovereignty	0% 0	14% 47	11% 37	3% 10	pro-interdependence
Pooler factor MPs	pro-interdependence	3% 10	9% 30	5% 18	1% 3	pro-sovereignty
Harmonizer factor MPs	pro-interdependence	5% 17	13% 44	12% 40	0 0	pro-sovereignty
Right Nationalist factor MPs	pro-sovereignty	0 0	11% 37	14% 47	4% 13	pro-interdependence

Source: Conservative Parliamentarians and European Integration Survey, ESRC/ University of Sheffield 1994. ESRC Award R. 000231298

The other striking feature of Table 2.4 is that at the extremes of the parliamentary party (signified here by respondents lying more than two standard deviations from the mean), it is among the Europeanists that there most clearly exists a hard-core group of around ten to fifteen MPs, a significant number given the government's majority. This is counter-intuitive given the media emphasis on the rebels, but will not surprise analysts who have spoken to known Eurofederalists in the party, observed the dilemmas of Europeanists considering leaving the party, or observed the revival of militant Europeanism since 1995. Major's most ardent Europeanists are further from the centre of contemporary party opinion than are his Eurorebels. And, whereas the Eurosceptics have only the single issue Referendum Party as an alternative parliamentary platform, of dubious viability, a Europeanist not determined to fight for the soul of the Conservative Party has both the Liberal Democrat and New Labour parties to choose from. Not surprisingly, therefore, both the complexity and intractability of party divisions made Major the only viable leadership contender in the 1995 party leadership election: no candidate strongly committed for or against the single currency could have held the parliamentary party together and thus preserved it in office. His victory was above all a measure of the fundamentally irresolvable nature of the party's divisions. His platform then was one of no change in policy. At the time, and since, the accusation has been made that British policy towards Europe has been skewed by party management considerations. How valid is this accusation?

POLICY IMPLICATIONS

It is clear from the survey results that, contrary to the cruder accusations, Major's scepticism is not the result of his being bullied by the relatively small number of hard-line rebels; rather his scepticism reflects majority opinion in the parliamentary party. On some issues, his agenda is closer to the Europeanists on matters such as the abolition of cohesion funds, or of the European Commission's right of legislative initiative. Further, and more seriously, it is hard to make out a convincing case that Conservative government policy on Europe has been derailed by the party's Euro-divisions, in spite of the obvious attraction of such a case for opposition parties and for Europeanists in the media and elsewhere. Under Major, the principal change of European policy, the abandonment of ERM membership and the refusal to contemplate re-entry, was not ascribable to party divisions, however much these may have been exacerbated by Thatcher's reluctant entry and Major's reluctant exit. Apart from this enforced policy shift, Major's stance has been remarkably consistent. His denunciation in *The Economist* of supranationalism and monetary integration (Major 1993), made soon after ratification of the treaty, did no more than repeat views he had expressed in an interview before the climax of the Maastricht rebellion (*Financial Times*, 26 May 1993), and in any case was fully in line with his 'intergovernmentalist' stance during the Maastricht negotiations, and with his opt-outs. Major's dramatically intransigent stance on QMV weightings in early 1994, widely blamed on the influence of his rebels, did no more than repeat the previous public positions of the then Foreign Secretary, Douglas Hurd, a prominent Europeanist. Neither did the party's European Parliament election manifesto offer any new concessions to the rebels, taking care even to leave room for manœuvre over QMV (George and Ludlam 1994). The controversy surrounding Major's Leiden speech in September 1994 had more to do with preceding policy statements by German politicians than with the speech's content, which did little more than rehash the EP election manifesto's 'flexible co-operation' as 'variable geometry' (Conservative Party 1994; Major 1994*a*, 1994*b*).

Even when Major then resigned his leadership in mid-1995, complaining that, 'One issue, above all others created this cauldron, Europe', he was careful to make no further concessions to his Euro-rebels (*Daily Telegraph*, 3 September 1995). He continued to refuse to rule out membership of a single currency, the demand of the Redwood camp, and did not budge at that time on the possibility of a referendum. The only new policy emphasis to emerge was Major's positioning of the UK as a future leader of the majority of member states who, he assumed, would be unable or unwilling to enter the single currency with the first group. Major's subsequent pursuit of this issue at summits was entirely consistent with pragmatic diplomacy, and was increasingly acknowledged to be a legitimate issue demanding attention by other member states (Major 1995). This development was cited as an example of the way in which Britain's pragmatic craftsmanship proved its worth in the face of visionary excesses. And, while it may be argued that Major's agreement to publish a White Paper on the UK's IGC stance was a response to party pressures, the same cannot be argued of its content. Even the one new policy that the White Paper contained—curtailing the interventions of the judges of the European Court of Justice—was more obviously an irritated response to recent rulings of the court on workers' rights than to any of the blueprints for change published by the rebels. The British proposals for reforming the court, moreover, soon became much more modest.

With some obvious exceptions, Major's policy platform on Europe differed little in substance from that of Blair's New Labour party (George, 1996). One discernible change has been over a single currency referendum—but the commitment remained hedged around with qualifications designed to hold the party together, and would be triggered only if the Cabinet decided to recommend entry, so there was to be no automatic vote on the 'Euro' currency.

More striking, paradoxically, than any strong evidence of the adoption by Major of the rebel policy platform, was evidence that the mildly sceptical, official 'British agenda' for a 'Europe of Nations' was gaining currency in Europe, not least in the wake of the popular sentiment revealed during the Maastricht ratification process, and of the virtual collapse in August 1993 of the Exchange Rate Mechanism. Increasingly, Major's government was able to claim with some credibility that other key member states were moving towards the British position. Indeed, there were many signs that, irrespective of the domestic politics of member states, the 'British agenda' was being acknowledged as legitimate and even endorsed. The widening or deepening debate appears to have been settled, for now, in favour of the British insistence that enlargement take precedence over integration of existing members, the 'variable geometry' position. This can be explained by the inability of many new members to meet the obligations of the 'acquis communitaire', and the unwillingness of existing members to contemplate funding policies like the CAP or cohesion funds in potential eastern European member states. Even the Delors White Paper on Employment and Growth looked forward to reduced social costs on employers and greater downward wage flexibility at the lower end of the labour market (European Commission 1994). In Italy, Spain, Sweden, France, and Germany, the alleged burden of welfare provision in the face of demographic change and of competition from low wage, low social security economies in the Far East has seen elite opinion moving somewhat closer to British policy positions.

Arguably, the impact of Conservative divisions on British policy, and the status of British policy in Europe, has been more significant in terms of its expected impact on the outcome of the 1997 general election. The Conservatives have never recovered from the dramatic loss of public confidence in their economic competence that followed the ejection from the ERM on Black Wednesday (Pattie and Johnston 1996: 56–61). Nor can the image of disunity be underestimated. It is certainly not underestimated by party leaders and strategists. What was clear, and increasingly the subject of unguarded comment in Europe, was that many policy actors looked forward to working with what was expected to be a less troublesome Labour government in London. The slow pace of the IGC during 1996 was widely interpreted as resulting from such sentiments.

The extraordinary 'beef crisis' of mid-1996, however, might require a reappraisal, as the governments' concessions, at the Florence Summit, to achieve a framework for easing the export bans on British beef prefaced a more protracted retreat from non-cooperation, but one no less obvious than Major's 1994 QMV U-turn. Yet when the deal was presented to parliament, it did not face a sceptic rebellion. Major's ability to discipline his rebels in key votes strengthened as the general election approached. The unwhipped vote on Bill Cash's Referendum Bill and the subsequent kerfuffle over James Goldsmith's financial support for the rebel European Foundation provided relatively harmless outlets for rebel energy. Major declared that he had had a 'bellyful' of party divisions, but none of these noises off interrupted acting on the policy stage. If anything, they induced business organizations to fund anti-rebel groups like Action Centre for Europe, and the revived European Movement, and to prompt the Confederation of British Industry to take a more public stand in support of the Prime Minister's agenda. The BSE crisis otherwise did little to change the political balance within the party, even if louder voices emerged contemplating withdrawal from the EU. What did appear to change as a result of the BSE/veto crisis was the broader diplomatic balance over the IGC. From a position of treating Major's agenda as a legitimate model for EU development, attitudes, especially in Germany, hardened perceptibly. By July serious commentators were reporting that German leaders had despaired of Britain's stance and would take a confrontationist line against British diplomacy in the autumn (Stephens 1996; Davidson 1996). The prospects for partial success for the British government's cautious deregulatory 'variable geometry' policy model for the future of the EU may, in time, be seen as having suffered a serious setback as a result of the BSE/veto crisis. In so far as the veto tactic was made inevitable, by Major's need to pacify his sceptical backbenches, policy outcomes as well as policy stances may thus come to be regarded as having been conditioned by the party's fratricidal struggle over European integration.

CONCLUSIONS

This chapter has argued that the Eurorebellion in the Parliamentary Conservative Party since 1992 has been so bitter and so persistent because of two principal factors: the over-ambitious integrationism of the Maastricht Treaty, and the legacy of bitterness at Thatcher's sacking. The survey revealed, however, that this rebellion reflected very widespread scepticism on the Conservative backbenches, far wider than the numbers of MPs prepared to defy the whips would suggest. To that extent, in so far as Major has adopted a sceptical stance, it has been argued here that it has not been to satisfy a minority of die-hard anti-marketeers, but has been consistent both with his own attitudes and with majority opinion in his parliamentary party, however unpalatable that may have been for the Europeanist establishment in British politics. The survey also revealed how badly divided that parliamentary party has become over Europe. In the face of the divisions, Major has enjoyed the dubious advantage of being the senior party figure who, as leader, has been least likely to trigger a catastrophic split. The survey also established that disagreements over the essential nature and the immediate future of British national parliamentary sovereignty have displaced older divisions as the San Andreas fault of Conservative politics. Or rather, on closer inspection, as a series of fault-lines; since the survey and other evidence presented here suggest that the widening range of policies affected by supranational decision-making has seen MPs become absolutists on some issues, but poolers on others.

British policy, in the form of the 'British agenda' for a Europe of nation states, remained remarkably consistent throughout the turmoil in the Commons. At least until the beef crisis, nationalist posturing for domestic audiences could be discounted in other member states, where the business-like virtues of Major's neo-liberal economic agenda gained considerable currency. The beef crisis, and the proximity of the British general election, however, reduced the impact of British diplomacy as Europe awaited a new, and inevitably less confrontationist government in London. As would-be successors to John Major positioned themselves on European integration it was equally clear that the IGC, the approach of the single currency, judgements of the European Court of Justice, and other integrationist developments, would continue to spark discontent and rebellion in the party. Who might claim the succession, how serious rebellions might be in future, not least whether they would finally provoke a formal split, would be mainly determined by the complexion of the Conservative benches after the 1997 general election which Conservatives would fight more bitterly disunited than at any time in living memory.

3

A 'Rosy' Map of Europe? Labour Parliamentarians and European Integration

David Baker and David Seawright

The raw nerves of division within the Conservative Party over European integration, with consequent problems for party management, are well documented in this book and elsewhere (Baker et al. 1994*a*). Labour divisions over European integration clearly exist, but what is the extent of those divisions and how might they obstruct a Labour government? Tony Blair was quick to denounce Tory claims of greater division within Labour ranks: 'Of course, Conservatives are fond of pointing out that there are divisions in the Labour Party too. This is a glib line . . . the Labour divisions, unlike the Tory ones, are largely part of the past.'[1] A shadow frontbench spokesperson agreed: 'There is no way we ever look like the bastard tendency, there is no way such views would enter into the hierarchy of the party . . . there is no way you will find the venomous hatred of Europe that you will find if you scratch Mr Lilley or Mr Portillo . . . '.[2]

Are Labour's divisions of such marginal significance that a Labour government should not fear being derailed by them? Using our survey data[3] from 1995–6 this chapter asks: can we accept this view of a 'rosy' future for Labour over Europe, and does this outlook emanate

---

[1] 'Britain in Europe', address by the Rt. Hon. Tony Blair MP, Leader of the Labour Party, to the Royal Institute of International Affairs, Chatham House, London, 5 Apr. 1995.

[2] Interviewed as part of an extensive range of interviews carried out at the Palace of Westminster in the summer of 1995. Some interviewees expressed a wish that their comments be non-attributable and of course we respect their wishes; where appropriate we shall cite these conerned.

[3] Members of Parliament Project, ESRC funded, Award No: R000221560, 'Labour Parliamentarians and European Integration'.

from a party led by 'modernizers' of a 'rosy' hue, as distinct from the 'red' stamp of traditional socialism?

Post-war conflict over Europe has been seen as more damaging for Labour than any other party. So bitter was the rift in the 1960s, that the Tribune group put Reg Prentice on its slate, ignoring his right-wing views because he was a passionate opponent of the Common Market, a decision which led to the resignation of some Tribune members (*Guardian*, 24 October 1990). Europe also lay behind Harold Wilson's problems of government and party management. Wilson's famous 'zigzags' on Europe (no in 1962, qualified yes in 1966, no in 1971, yes in 1975) were largely motivated by whether the party was in or out of power at the time, while the 1975 referendum was principally designed to keep a party deeply divided from splitting. The depth of division emerges from the fact that sixty-nine Labour MPs defied a three line whip to vote for the second reading of the 1971 Treaty of Accession Bill, with a further twenty abstaining. This act of defiance exceeded even the Conservative rebellion over the Maastricht Bill; where Labour, it should be noted, also had sixty-six third reading rebels. Indeed without the 1971 revolt, the PLP and thirty-nine Tory rebels could have defeated Heath. Serious divisions within and between the Labour Party National Executive Committee (NEC) and Cabinet became public in the 1975 referendum campaign. Moreover, following the 1976 conference decision to oppose direct elections to the European Parliament, the Callaghan government had to rely on Conservative support to steer the European Assembly Elections Bill through the Commons.

Labour finally split in 1981. After the 1979 election the party conference immediately voted to withdraw from the Community without a referendum, provoking the damaging departure of the future leaders of the SDP, followed by many ardent pro-marketeers. The high water mark of anti-European sentiment was reached with the 1983 manifesto pledge to withdraw from the Community. But Neil Kinnock's leadership effected a slow reversal of this position. One Labour sceptic summed it up thus:

By 1984 we were not for withdrawal any longer but for a renegotiation of the Treaty of Rome and Neil Kinnock brought out a socialist commentary to that effect in *New Socialist*, from that positive enthusiasm which was largely a product of Kinnock's own conversion, which was perhaps his start on his road to Brussels and his Commissionership . . . that meant that increasingly pro-Europeans could emerge from cover, that the stance of the party shifted, it was helped by Jaques Delors' visit to the TUC, the trade unions saw this as a way forward for them, Downing Street was closed for beer and sandwiches and Europe was a way forward for them, and they turned to that. The drift was quite gradual, 1987 we were pro-Europe, by 1992 we were enthusiastic about Europe, and now positively bubbling with enthusiasm . . .[4]

Others view the conversion as genuine, that MPs have become convinced that Europe is the only game in town which has left the sceptics embittered but largely marginalized. One Labour peer, Baroness Tessa Blackstone, insisted that Labour may have 'its Euro-sceptics but they are mainly extinct volcanoes with little or no influence' (*Observer*, 15 May 1994). However, one of those volcanoes, the Labour Common Market Safeguards Committee (subsequently the Labour Euro-Safeguards Campaign) was far from extinct, claiming to have just under a quarter of the parliamentary party as paid-up members in 1990 (*Guardian*, 30 October 1990). They publish a regular newsletter and acknowledge parliamentary influence both in the Lords (Jay and Stoddart) and in the Commons (Benn, Mitchell, Shore, Spearing, and Davies) and even in the European Parliament (Megahy and Seal). Consequently, there appears a detectable unease in Labour's efforts to balance the role of the nation state with that of European integration.

This chapter uses our survey results to analyse the extent of division over European integration amongst Labour parliamentarians, both within and between front and backbench MPs, and European MEPs. We also analyse a 'cohort effect' which compares the attitudes of MPs elected to parliament before and after the high water mark of Euroscepticism in 1983. In Tables 3.1 to 3.5 we view the responses, of MPs, both backbenchers and shadow frontbenchers, along with those of MEPs, to issue statements on Europe. Finally in Table 3.8 and Table 3.9 we show the results of factor analysis applied to the data.

TO LEAVE OR NOT TO LEAVE?

Labour policy on Europe has zigzagged between membership of the club of Europe and a desire to withdraw. The underlying argument has concerned sovereignty, parliament's role *vis-à-vis* European institu-

---

[4] Austin Mitchell, interviewed at the Palace of Westminster, July 1995.

TABLE 3.1. *Membership and sovereignty*

		Status	Strongly agree or agree	Neither	Disagree or strongly disagree
			%	%	%
1.1	Britain should withdraw from the European Union	MP	7	3	90
		MEP	7	0	93
		Back	9	5	86
		Front	0	0	100
1.2	The disadvantages of EC membership have been outweighed by the benefits	MP	52	11	37
		MEP	59	0	41
		Back	55	11	34
		Front	38	14	48
1.3	The EU should be replaced by a Commonwealth of Europe based on sovereign nation states	MP	14	12	74
		MEP	10	4	86
		Back	19	11	70
		Front	0	10	90
1.4	The globalization of economic activity makes European Union (EU) membership more, rather than less necessary for the UK	MP	88	2	10
		MEP	86	0	14
		Back	83	3	14
		Front	100	0	0
1.5	Sovereignty cannot be pooled	MP	30	11	59
		MEP	14	14	72
		Back	34	10	56
		Front	20	15	65
1.6	An Act of Parliament should be passed to establish explicitly the ultimate supremacy of Parliament over EU legislation	MP	18	18	64
		MEP	12	11	77
		Back	23	19	58
		Front	0	17	83
1.7	Subsidiarity reinforces the federalist tendency in the EU	MP	36	32	32
		MEP	32	22	46
		Back	40	35	25
		Front	30	25	45

Source: Labour Parliamentarians and European Integration Survey, ESRC/ Nottingham Trent University 1995/96.

tions. In 1983 the party took the view, still elaborated by its Euro-sceptical wing, that the European treaties strike at the heart of British parliamentary sovereignty. They believe that, not only an incoming Labour government, but any government, will now be bound by a previous parliament's actions, particularly those concerned with European policy; a fundamental deviation from parliamentary sovereignty. On the other hand Labour's enthusiasts are quite sanguine about the notion of federalism, they don't view the developments in the treaties as undermining the idea of the nation state; for them, the idea is one of dispersing power downwards.

Just how striking the success of the slow reversal policy of the 1980s was is clearly seen when viewing Table 3.1.

We see an overwhelming majority against withdrawal and an overwhelming majority believing that membership is even more necessary in a global economy. But this is tempered by a more cautious outlook suggesting that they are only just convinced of the overall historical advantages of membership (statements 1.1, 1.2, and 1.4). On the thorny issue of sovereignty (statement 1.5) a majority believe it can be pooled but significantly a substantial number of backbenchers were more circumspect, more so than MEPs or frontbenchers. However, there appears to be no substantial support for explicitly reasserting the legislative authority of Westminster (statement 1.6).

Periodically, Tony Benn presents a Commonwealth of Europe Bill in the House '. . . which would set up a European community covering fifty-one countries. It would have a charter of rights, a council of ministers, it would have an assembly and it would harmonise by consent. It would be a mini United Nations. I think it would really work, but this [EP institutions] won't work.'[5] However, most of his colleagues do not agree with such a position (statement 1.3).

As noted above the federalist term has been incorporated into the pejorative lexicon of British political discourse. Our survey reveals that the party is evenly split over the idea that subsidiarity will reinforce the federalist tendency within the EU (statement 1.7), with 40 per cent of backbenchers agreeing with this supposedly Eurosceptic shibboleth.

EMU: TAKING FLIGHT OR DEAD AS A DODO?

Tony Blair referred to EMU as *the* hard EU issue, with monetary union an important step on the road to integration. For Blair there is only one immediate question on EMU, 'is it inconsistent with the

---

[5] Tony Benn, interviewed at the Palace of Westminster, July 1995.

nation state?'[6] If it is, then the Labour Party would reject it, even if it were economically prudent to join. If it is not, as Labour believes, then government should participate fully in the formulation of its institutions and its structures, whilst deciding finally on whether to join on the basis of our national economic interest. These caveats reveal unease in Labour's efforts to balance the role of the nation state with that of European integration, made strikingly apparent from the equivocation practised by the leadership over the question of a national referendum on a single currency.

Of further interest are the different priorities placed upon EMU by both its protagonists and its opponents. Supporters of monetary union point to its beneficial aspects, for example, currency stability militating against currency speculation. But its opponents voice acute concern over the constraints placed upon an incoming Labour administration by monetary and fiscal limits, particularly from a Central Bank. Their argument raises the possibility of Labour being unable to legislate if it had a future opportunity comparable to that of the 1945 Attlee government. In the words of the Eurosceptic 'Safeguards Campaign': 'There will be no escape route out of a single currency, like there was from the ERM. Britain would be truly trapped; and the Labour Party, in any remotely socialist form, redundant. We would not be able to function as a democratic socialist party' (Labour Euro-Safeguards Campaign 1995: 72)

Judging from Table 3.2 a majority of parliamentarians, in line with their leader, do not believe that the establishment of a single currency is inconsistent with UK sovereignty (statement 2.1).

Moreover, most Labour parliamentarians regarded EMU as not only realizable but desirable, and this is reflected in the attitude of the number believing that some sort of ERM membership is necessary in the fight against currency speculation and the small number which ruled out any possibility of rejoining the ERM (statements 2.3, 2.8, and 2.9). Although support for what some may term Peter Shore's 'halfway house' of a common currency (in effect John Major's hard ecu) is in a minority, it is interestingly a substantial one, with the majority of respondents in the undecided bracket (statement 2.6).

The acute concerns being voiced by the sceptics over monetary and fiscal limits placed in the hands of a Central Bank are plainly per-

---

[6] Speech by the Rt. Hon. Tony Blair MP, leader of the Labour Party, to the Friedrich-Ebert Stiftung, Bonn, 30 May 1995.

TABLE 3.2. *Economic and Monetary union*

		Status	Strongly agree or agree	Neither	Disagree or strongly disagree
			%	%	%
2.1	The establishment of a single	MP	21	5	74
	EU currency would signal the	MEP	18	4	78
	end of the UK as a sovereign	Back	28	6	66
	nation	Front	0	0	100
2.2	There should be a national	MP	50	10	40
	referendum before the UK	MEP	28	31	41
	enters a single currency	Back	56	10	34
		Front	35	15	50
2.3	EMU is: (*a*) not realizable	MP	24	12	64
		MEP	14	7	79
		Back	28	11	61
		Front	15	15	70
	(*b*) not desirable	MP	16	18	66
		MEP	14	7	79
		Back	23	17	60
		Front	0	21	79
2.4	The UK should not seek to	MP	78	16	6
	meet the EMU convergence	MEP	64	20	16
	criteria if the result is increased	Back	81	13	6
	unemployment in Britain	Front	71	24	5
2.5	A single currency as set out	MP	29	33	38
	in the Maastricht Treaty will	MEP	24	21	55
	institutionalize neo-liberal	Back	31	37	32
	economic policy in Britain	Front	29	19	52
2.6	Britain should accept a common	MP	26	39	35
	European currency but not a	MEP	11	33	56
	single currency	Back	32	38	30
		Front	10	37	53
2.7	Britain should never permit its	MP	42	20	38
	monetary policy to be	MEP	21	18	61
	determined by an independent	Back	44	22	34
	European Central Bank	Front	40	15	45

TABLE 3.2. *Continued*

		Status	Strongly agree or agree	Neither	Disagree or strongly disagree
			%	%	%
2.8	Membership of some sort of	MP	66	13	21
	ERM is essential in the fight	MEP	78	4	18
	against currency speculation	Back	64	9	27
		Front	71	24	5
2.9	Britain should never rejoin the	MP	12	7	81
	ERM	MEP	14	11	75
		Back	15	8	77
		Front	5	5	90

Source: Labour Parliamentarians and European Integration Survey, ESRC/ Nottingham Trent University 1995/96.

meated throughout the parliamentary party (statements 2.4, 2.5, and 2.7). A substantial minority of MPs, not far short of a third, believed that the Maastricht criteria for a single currency would institutionalize neo-liberal economic policy in Britain, with another third taking a neutral position on the statement. However, this concern is clearly not reflected on the front or European benches. A substantial majority of all parliamentarians offer the important caveat that we should not bother to try and meet the EMU convergence criteria if the result is increased unemployment. This concern is also reflected in the two-fifths of MPs believing that Britain should never permit its monetary policy to be determined by an independent Central Bank. Only half that figure of MEPs take a similar line.

The equivocation over a national referendum on a single currency is readily explained by viewing statement 2.2 in Table 3.2. There is not only a clear division between a majority of backbenchers who wanted a referendum and their frontbench team but also between them and their European counterparts who were far cooler on such a proposition. Little wonder that the leadership is not easily drawn on such a proposal.

THE SOCIAL DIMENSION

Labour parliamentarians would regard this area as part of their 'sphere of influence', where both protagonists can be as vociferous in their

TABLE 3.3. *The social dimension*

		Status	Strongly agree or agree %	Neither %	Disagree or strongly disagree %
3.1	Harmonization of social policies should not be an EU objective	MP	9	8	83
		MEP	0	7	93
		Back	9	6	85
		Front	10	14	76
3.2	Britain should support the Swedish proposal to make the pursuit of full employment an EU Treaty obligation	MP	91	6	3
		MEP	100	0	0
		Back	92	5	3
		Front	85	10	5
3.3	Convergence of working standards should be a key objective of EU integration	MP	80	17	3
		MEP	90	3	7
		Back	81	14	5
		Front	85	15	0
3.4	Reduction of social costs placed on employers is essential to job creation in the EU	MP	4	16	80
		MEP	4	24	72
		Back	6	17	77
		Front	0	14	86
3.5	Inflexibility in European labour markets is the principal cause of unemployment	MP	3	7	90
		MEP	3	14	83
		Back	5	3	92
		Front	0	14	86
3.6	Removing obstacles to workers' freedom of movement in the single market should be a priority	MP	58	23	19
		MEP	96	4	0
		Back	60	19	21
		Front	53	31	16
3.7	Third-country nationals legally resident in an EU member state should be entitled to social benefits available wherever they work or live in the EU	MP	72	14	14
		MEP	83	10	7
		Back	70	11	19
		Front	84	16	0
3.8	The extension of 'social dialogue' through the institution of works councils is a necessary component of economic progress in the EU	MP	83	7	10
		MEP	83	7	10
		Back	81	8	11
		Front	90	5	5

Source: Labour Parliamentarians and European Integration Survey, ESRC/ Nottingham Trent University 1995/96.

display of a 'social conscience'. Table 3.3 reveals near unanimity on harmonization of social policy (statement 3.1) and working standards (statement 3.3), while rejecting the supply side notion that reducing employers' social costs is essential to job creation (statement 3.4). These responses place the Labour party well to the left of the core positions of EU policy.

There is strong support for the controversial works council directive (statement 3.8) and a strong rejection of the view that labour market inflexibility is the main cause of joblessness (statement 3.5), which is paradoxically linked to support for the CBI's demand to remove national obstacles to a competitive market in labour (statement 3.6). Moreover, the Labour party supports the controversial position that non-EU nationals should enjoy full social benefit rights wherever they work or live in the EU. Not surprisingly, and in line with their EP leader's call at the 1995 party conference, the Labour Party also strongly supports the Swedish proposal to make full employment a treaty obligation (statement 3.2).

A DIRIGIST PROJECT?

The extent of support for an active social dimension revealed above suggests a broader adherence to an interventionist position. However, the disquiet within the party is not only one of European institutions entrapping Labour but, more importantly, of Labour inculcating free market mores to such an extent that it has decoupled itself from its social ideology. For instance, we saw above that Labour parliamentarians supported the removal of obstacles to workers' freedom of movement in the single market (statement 3.6), Tony Blair, in line with CBI proposals, endorsed this in his 'Bonn' speech:

Europe must become more competitive so that our peoples can become more prosperous. We must remove barriers to fair competition within the Union. Distorting Government subsidies should be removed and we need to examine the proposal—which I know is favoured here—of the establishment of an independent European competition agency, based on the example of the German cartel office.[7]

---

[7] Speech by the Rt. Hon. Tony Blair MP, leader of the Labour Party, to the Friedrich-Ebert Stiftung, Bonn, 30 May 1995.

For some, this is just glorification of competition, à la Thatcher: the 'bike' may now be replaced in the new refrain, 'get on your plane', but nevertheless it is the same sentiment. Unsurprisingly, Tony Benn has reservations:

The story the newspapers won't print is that the Labour movement hasn't changed at all, but we have a leadership that is not Labour, not just socialist, but not Labour. It has abandoned its pride in its own history and it has abandoned its vision for its own future and it is now committed to run capitalism which is why the British establishment wants a Labour victory, to destroy the Welfare State and introduce a fully capitalist society.[8]

Other MPs, like Austin Mitchell, are more relaxed about the leadership's advocacy of competition but question the redundancy of national economic management. So where does Labour now stand in relation to an interventionist project?

Judged by Table 3.4 there still appears to be a certain ambiguity over the level of interventionism that should be applied by a social democratic government. Most agreed that membership was not incompatible with national economic management (statement 4.1). However, sizeable minorities both on the backbenches and more surprisingly, in the European parliament, believed that membership was incompatible with national economic management. Labour parliamentarians favoured a wide range of EU-level strategic economic intervention, on 'infrastructure', 'training', and 'industrial investment'. Although, we do see a dip in such enthusiasm for 'deregulation', in fact MEPs were more or less evenly split on this; a marked exception being that of a Union strategy on 'privatization', where only the frontbench clearly disagreed with the statement, all others being evenly split (statements 4.3a–e).

However, they were far more reticent on the electorally sensitive subject of taxation, with a clear division between the PLP and EPLP on harmonization of 'company tax' and VAT within the EU (statements 4.4a, b). MPs didn't agree with harmonization, while the MEPs did; interestingly, the frontbenchers were far more inclined to accept such harmonization in the case of company tax but not for VAT. Both PLP and EPLP objected to having personal taxation harmonized within the EU (statement 4.4c). But, majorities in both camps favoured harmonization of environmental tax and customs and excise,

---

[8] Tony Benn, interviewed at the Palace of Westminster, July 1995.

TABLE 3.4. *Dirigisme*

		Status	Strongly agree or agree %	Neither %	Disagree or strongly disagree %
4.1	People who believe in national economic management cannot support the EU as it has turned out	MP	34	16	50
		MEP	39	7	54
		Back	38	17	45
		Front	25	15	60
4.2	Public ownership remains crucial to the achievement of social justice	MP	68	9	23
		MEP	76	14	10
		Back	69	9	22
		Front	70	10	20
4.3	In principle there should be Union strategies on:				
	(*a*) infrastructure	MP	88	7	5
		MEP	92	4	4
		Back	92	3	5
		Front	81	14	5
	(*b*) training	MP	77	13	10
		MEP	96	0	4
		Back	84	8	8
		Front	62	24	14
	(*c*) industrial investment	MP	82	8	10
		MEP	84	8	8
		Back	85	7	8
		Front	70	15	15
	(*d*) deregulation	MP	61	10	29
		MEP	48	8	44
		Back	64	7	29
		Front	57	14	29
	(*e*) privatization	MP	42	13	45
		MEP	40	12	48
		Back	46	11	43
		Front	33	15	52
4.4	The following forms of taxation should be harmonized within the EU:				
	(*a*) company	MP	32	22	46
		MEP	50	15	35
		Back	31	24	45
		Front	42	16	42

TABLE 3.4. *Continued*

		Status	Strongly agree or agree	Neither	Disagree or strongly disagree
			%	%	%
	(b) VAT	MP	24	26	50
		MEP	50	11	39
		Back	24	27	49
		Front	28	22	50
	(c) personal	MP	17	26	57
		MEP	12	12	76
		Back	16	29	55
		Front	22	17	61
	(d) environmental	MP	47	20	33
		MEP	69	4	27
		Back	45	21	34
		Front	58	21	21
	(e) customs and excise	MP	49	18	33
		MEP	73	12	15
		Back	49	19	32
		Front	53	16	31
4.5	EU regional funds should be paid directly to the Regions	MP	70	12	18
		MEP	76	10	14
		Back	70	13	17
		Front	67	9	24
4.6	The EU's budget should be enlarged	MP	34	25	41
		MEP	78	11	11
		Back	41	23	36
		Front	15	25	60
4.7	An increase in Cohesion Funds is essential for enlargement of the EU	MP	84	8	8
		MEP	82	7	11
		Back	82	11	7
		Front	86	0	14
4.8	The Labour Party's association with the Party of European Socialists is more of a political liability than an asset	MP	12	10	78
		MEP	17	0	83
		Back	16	12	72
		Front	0	5	95

Source: Labour Parliamentarians and European Integration Survey, ESRC/ Nottingham Trent University 1995/96.

although, once again, Westminster MPs were not as supportive of the statements as their European colleagues (statements 4.4*d*, *e*). Moreover, there appeared to be contradictory attitudes to EU fiscal policy in general, with a majority of the PLP opposed to enlargement of the EU budget (but with an overwhelming majority of the EPLP for such enlargement) but juxtaposed to this, majorities for enlargement of Cohesion Funds (statements 4.6 and 4.7).

There was a large majority in support of public ownership to ensure social justice (statement 4.2). On this evidence the 'rosy hue' resonates a deeper red. MEPs were slightly more in favour of the Clause IV dimension of public ownership but this is hardly surprising given the *Guardian* letter from thirty-two 'disaffected' MEPs attacking the proposals to omit the term 'common ownership' from the Labour Party's constitution. A rash of rhetoric followed and Ken Coates spoke of his 'contempt for shits' of modernizers (*Guardian*, 10–14 January 1995, *passim*). Glenys Kinnock MEP replied:

It seems odd then that, having recognised some of the major changes since Clause Four was written 77 years ago, he glibly asserts any change to our constitution is unacceptable. And it is equally odd that, if 'common ownership' is the phrase that is critical to any definition of socialism, none of our fellow socialist parties in the EU is committed to it' (*Daily Telegraph*, 14 January 1995).

None may now be committed to it but our data suggests that Labour parliamentarians still support it, although this appears to have no adverse effect in their relations with their PES colleagues (statement 4.8).

THE IGC AND THE DEMOCRATIC DEFICIT?

Some in the EPLP may wish to put a pro-European Red Sea between themselves and Tory Euroscepticism, but their Westminster leadership continually offers caveats of not rushing headlong into federalism. This is summed up in the 1995 Conference Report on the 1996 IGC which stated: 'Labour in government will adopt a pragmatic approach. We will act to defend and advance our national interests in Europe. We will seek to reform the institutions of Europe where we consider that to be necessary. But unlike the Tories we will act in accordance with our positive vision of Europe' (Labour Party 1995).

TABLE 3.5. *The IGC and democratic deficit*

		Status	Strongly agree or agree	Neither	Disagree or strongly disagree
			%	%	%
5.1	The 1996 IGC should not increase the supranational powers of EU institutions	MP	38	24	38
		MEP	18	11	71
		Back	42	22	36
		Front	28	24	48
5.2	There should be a referendum on any proposals from the forthcoming IGC that changes the constitutional position of UK citizens	MP	47	16	37
		MEP	30	26	44
		Back	51	16	33
		Front	30	20	50
5.3	The Commission should lose the right to initiate legislation	MP	25	14	61
		MEP	31	10	59
		Back	27	18	55
		Front	20	0	80
5.4	The European Parliament should be given the right to initiate EU legislation	MP	78	8	14
		MEP	82	4	14
		Back	75	8	17
		Front	85	10	5
5.5	All proposed EU legislation should be voted on by the European Parliament	MP	71	13	16
		MEP	93	0	7
		Back	70	11	19
		Front	70	20	10
5.6	The European Parliament should share control with the Commission over policy areas subject to QMV	MP	55	27	18
		MEP	75	18	7
		Back	53	29	18
		Front	60	20	20
5.7	The Council of Ministers should be the supreme institution in the EU	MP	16	16	68
		MEP	10	7	83
		Back	14	16	70
		Front	20	20	60
5.8	The 1996 IGC should abolish QMV	MP	14	18	68
		MEP	7	0	93
		Back	16	19	65
		Front	10	16	74
5.9	Britain should block the use of QMV in the areas of foreign and defence policy	MP	44	13	43
		MEP	31	10	59
		Back	34	15	51
		Front	65	10	25

TABLE 3.5. *Continued.*

	Status	Strongly agree or agree	Neither	Disagree or strongly disagree
		%	%	%
5.10 A single European army would undermine rather than underpin the security of the UK	MP	27	24	49
	MEP	30	22	48
	Back	31	19	50
	Front	16	37	47
5.11 Britain should not participate in the lifting of border controls as specified in the Schengen agreement	MP	26	21	53
	MEP	14	4	82
	Back	25	21	54
	Front	30	15	55
5.12 The UK should incorporate the European Convention on Human Rights into law	MP	89	8	3
	MEP	97	3	0
	Back	86	11	3
	Front	100	0	0
5.13 The continental system of jurisprudence as practised by the European Court of Justice is a threat to liberty in Britain	MP	7	22	71
	MEP	4	4	92
	Back	10	26	64
	Front	0	10	90
5.14 The strength of national identities rules out parliamentary democracy on a European scale for the foreseeable future	MP	35	8	57
	MEP	22	0	78
	Back	34	7	59
	Front	40	15	45
5.15 The key to closing the 'democratic deficit' is strengthening the scrutiny by national parliaments of the EU legislative process	MP	73	16	11
	MEP	29	25	46
	Back	74	15	11
	Front	67	19	14
5.16 Regional devolution offers the best way to close the 'democratic deficit' in an integrated Europe	MP	63	24	13
	MEP	57	18	25
	Back	62	24	14
	Front	62	29	9

Source: Labour Parliamentarians and European Integration Survey, ESRC/ Nottingham Trent University 1995/96.

Table 3.5 suggests that MPs, in some instances, were even more cautious than their leaders. They are split down the middle on being prepared to see the IGC increase supranational powers of EU institutions but were far less inclined than their frontbench colleagues to accept such a development, while the EPLP were strongly in favour (statement 5.1). Again, only the frontbench MPs and their European counterparts showed a majority disagreeing with holding a referendum if IGC proposals have constitutional implications for the UK (statement 5.2). This is significant as Labour take the view that presently there is insufficient accountability built into existing decision-making structures of the EU, in conjunction with a less than desirable level of transparency. This has major implications for the legitimacy of an EU governmental agenda, and Mr Blair has continually stressed that what the Maastricht process revealed across Europe was that European elites were moving too far ahead of opinion in the member states and the corollary of such an argument is allowance for the people to decide directly.[9]

Addressing the 'democratic deficit' of European structures, a majority of surveyed parliamentarians would not oppose the European Parliament sharing legislative initiative with the Council of Ministers, in conjunction with a powerful legislature, while agreeing to remove such rights from the Commission (statements 5.4, 5.5, and 5.3). This is in line with the Party of European Socialists' (PES) suggestion that the EU structures should resemble more the norm of a liberal democracy with the Council as executive and EP as a scrutinizing legislature.[10] Indeed, a majority do not believe that the strength of national identity rules it out on a European scale for the foreseeable future and also oppose the idea that the ministers of the national governments should be the supreme institution of the EU (statements 5.14 and 5.7). However, certain ambiguities remain: the PLP overwhelmingly viewed the strengthening of their legislature as being the key to closing the democratic deficit, opposed not surprisingly by the EPLP, while all believed that subnational government is the best way forward (statements 5.15 and 5.16).

Such sentiments on accountability and legitimacy encroach upon QMV. All parliamentarians, although more so the EPLP, accepted that the European Parliament should share control with the Commission over policy areas subject to QMV (statement 5.6). Just what pillars, holding aloft the EU edifice, should be subject to QMV-able decision-making is amongst the most contentious areas of European

---

[9] Rt. Hon. Tony Blair, the Friedrich-Ebert Stiftung, Bonn, 30 May 1995, op. cit.

[10] Parliamentary Group of the Party of European Socialists, 'An Initial Approach to the 1996 Treaty Review Conference', 29 Mar. 1995.

integration. Labour often criticize the Conservatives on their intransigence on this issue, yet Tony Blair has asserted: 'We will maintain the veto vigorously in areas such as security and immigration.'[11] This cautious ambivalence is also reflected in official policy (see Labour Party 1995).

A majority of all parliamentarians support the retention of the principal of QMV (statement 5.8) but in light of Labour's official policy to protect the national veto in CFSP our data offers extremely interesting results. The PLP splits in half over the issue but importantly a majority of backbenchers did not follow the official party line. They appeared to accept the common foreign and security policy sphere as QMV-able, while the shadow frontbench overwhelmingly supported the retention of Britain's veto in this area (statement 5.9). The fact that the EPLP do not accept official party policy in this field is unsurprising given the revolt by fourteen MEPs in May 1995. This revolt included Pauline Green, the leader of the EP socialist group, who voted in favour of a resolution limiting the veto rights of national governments ignoring a frontbench directive (*Guardian*, 20 May 1995).

QMV is apparently not the only area of contention between parliamentarians' attitudes and the official line. Against the official line (Labour Party 1995), Labour parliamentarians surveyed were not hostile to a single European army and favoured participation in the Schengen agreement (statements 5.10 and 5.11).

Views expressed on the judicial arena were near unanimous with overall support for the incorporation of the European Convention of Human Rights into law (statement 5.12) and no apparent concern that the European Court of Justice's retrospective jurisprudence threatened British liberties (statement 5.13).

THE COHORT EFFECT

Our survey identified when an MP first entered parliament allowing for cohort analysis of MPs elected before and on the high water mark of scepticism, i.e. 1983, in comparison with those from our 'slow reversal period', 1987–92.

---

[11] The Rt. Hon. Tony Blair MP, 'Britain in Europe', Chatham House, London, 5 Apr. 1995, op. cit.

TABLE 3.6. *The cohort effect?*

		Cohort	Strongly agree or agree	Neither	Disagree or strongly disagree
			%	%	%
6.1	Britain should withdraw from the European Union	1950–83	15	0	85
		1987–92	0	4	96
6.2	The establishment of a single EU currency would signal the end of the UK as a sovereign nation	1950–83	33	3	64
		1987–92	11	6	83
6.3	Sovereignty cannot be pooled	1950–83	36	3	61
		1987–92	27	13	60
6.4	Subsidiarity reinforces the federalist tendency in the EU	1950–83	43	24	33
		1987–92	33	36	31
6.5	The globalization of economic activity makes European Union (EU) membership more, rather than less necessary for the UK	1950–83	79	0	21
		1987–92	98	2	0
6.6	EMU is: (*a*) not realizable	1950–83	35	12	53
		1987–92	13	13	74
	(*b*) not desirable	1950–83	26	16	58
		1987–92	9	17	74
6.7	The EU should be replaced by a Commonwealth of Europe based on sovereign nation states	1950–83	24	9	67
		1987–92	4	13	83
6.8	An Act of Parliament should be passed to establish explicitly the ultimate supremacy of Parliament over EU legislation	1950–83	29	6	65
		1987–92	7	25	68
6.9	The European Parliament should be given the right to initiate EU legislation	1950–83	68	6	26
		1987–92	89	9	2
6.10	A single European army would undermine rather than underpin the security of the UK	1950–83	38	18	44
		1987–92	16	31	53

TABLE 3.6. *Continued*

	Cohort	Strongly agree or agree	Neither	Disagree or strongly disagree
		%	%	%
6.11 Britain should not participate in the lifting of border controls as specified in the Schengen agreement	1950–83 1987–92	35 22	21 20	44 58
6.12 Britain should block the use of QMV in the areas of foreign and defence policy	1950–83 1987–92	56 37	10 15	34 48
6.13 The Labour Party's association with the Party of European Socialists is more of a political liability than an asset	1950–83 1987–92	20 2	12 11	68 87

Source: Labour Parliamentarians and European Integration Survey, ESRC/ Nottingham Trent University 1995/96.

In his speech to the Friedrich-Ebert Foundation in Bonn, Mr Blair asserted that, on Europe, 'the centre of gravity in the Labour Party is moving convincingly in my direction'.[12] Judging by Table 3.6, he may well be right. MPs elected after 1983 were far more inclined to be enthusiastic about Europe than colleagues elected on or before 1983, with all figures for our 'sceptical indicators' 1950–83 being far more pronounced than 1987–92 and usually double for that found in our previous tables. No MP from the 1987–92 cohort would contemplate withdrawal (statement 6.1) and twice the number of those elected on or before 1983 believed a single currency heralded the end of the UK as a sovereign nation state (statement 6.2). The 1950–83 cohort were more sceptical on the notion of sovereignty being pooled; more inclined towards the belief that subsidiarity would reinforce the federalist tendency in the EU; more inclined to suggest that EMU is not realizable, even more so that it is not desirable; and less likely to believe that a global market necessitates our membership of the EU (statements 6.3, 6.4, 6.6, and 6.5). Moreover, Tony Benn received greater support for his Commonwealth idea while there was

[12] Rt. Hon. Tony Blair, the Friedrich-Ebert Stiftung, Bonn, 30 May 1995, op. cit.

greater support for reasserting the legislative authority of Westminster and not surprisingly they were less than enamoured about the idea of allowing the EP to initiate legislation (statements 6.7, 6.8, and 6.9). There was also greater scepticism for the European Army proposal and signing up to the Schengen agreement, with a majority of those in the 1950–83 cohort advocating the blocking of QMV (statements 6.10, 6.11, and 6.12). We also find more circumspection in this cohort compared to 1987–92 about the benefits of association with the PES (statement 6.13). However, it should be reiterated that this table in most respects shows more scepticism across cohorts than within them.

SOVEREIGNTY DIMENSION

We conducted factor analysis to confirm the hypothesis suggested by the descriptive statistics, that the sovereignty dimension cuts across the age-old party divide of 'social market/state interventionism'.[13] Our qualitative research alerted us to this when we found MPs taking up diametrically opposed positions on the sovereignty dimension while being commonly thought of as sharing a 'right'/'left' position on the party's ideological spectrum. MPs like Radice on the pro-market right of the party believing that the EU is the only way forward clash with right-wingers like Shore arguing that it is tantamount to surrendering British sovereignty, while on the left old allies like Benn and Sedgemore are deeply divided over their stance on Europe. In our analysis we allowed for all meaningful factors, i.e. those with at least three variables, to emerge (Walsh 1990: 334). Table 3.7 shows the resulting four-factor model, in which variables loading below 0.5 are excluded.

The principal component with an Eigenvalue (8.33) and accounting for 29.8 per cent of the variance is quite clearly a sceptical 'Constitutional Sovereignty factor'. In scrutinizing the EU legislative process we find loadings for the constitutional supremacy of the Westminster

---

[13] Factor analysis is a method of reducing data to reveal underlying dimensions from a data set. Orthogonal rotation of factors, the method used here (using the Varimax technique with pairwise deletion of cases, in SPSS for Windows), identifies independent factors. Good factor analysis depends on adequate representativeness of the sample. We are satisfied that ours is a representative sample, for reasons set out in the Appendix to this chapter.

TABLE 3.7. *Orthogonally-rotated factor matrix for all MPs (N=81): Four-factor model, excluding factor loadings <.5*

Survey statement	Factor 1	Factor 2	Factor 3	Factor 4
Eigenvalue	8.33	3.28	2.45	1.61
Percentage of Variance Explained	29.8	11.7	8.8	5.8

Factor 1

A single European army would undermine rather than underpin the security of the UK	.73562			
Sovereignty cannot be pooled	.71788			
Britain should block the use of QMV in the areas of foreign and defence policy	.69831			
The continental system of jurisprudence as practised by the European Court of Justice is a threat to liberty in Britain	.68182			
The European Parliament should be given the right to initiate EU legislation	−.63671			
An Act of Parliament should be passed to establish explicitly the ultimate supremacy of Parliament over EU legislation	.60572			
Britain should withdraw from the European Union	.59735	.53917		
The globalization of economic activity makes European Union (EU) membership more, rather than less necessary for the UK	−.59162			
The key to closing the 'democratic deficit' is strengthening the scrutiny by national parliaments of the EU legislative process	.56465			

Factor 2

The UK should not seek to meet the EMU convergence criteria if the result is increased unemployment in Britain		.79979		

TABLE 3.7. *Continued*

Survey statement	Factor 1	Factor 2	Factor 3	Factor 4
There should be a referendum on any proposals from the forthcoming IGC that change the constitutional position of UK citizens		.67952		
Public ownership remains crucial to the achievement of social justice		.67064		
Britain should support the Swedish proposal to make the pursuit of full employment an EU Treaty obligation	.60732			
Britain should never permit its monetary policy to be determined by an independent European Central Bank		.58797		
Britain should never rejoin the ERM		.58609		
The establishment of a single EU currency would signal the end of the UK as a sovereign nation	.50909	.58428		
A single currency as set out in the Maastricht Treaty will institutionalize neo-liberal economic policy in Britain		.57750		
There should be a national referendum before the UK enters a single currency		.52181		
Factor 3				
Personal taxation should be harmonized within the EU			.90566	
VAT should be harmonized within the EU			.85840	
Company tax should be harmonized within the EU			.76676	
In principle there should be a Union strategy on privatization			.58305	
Factor 4				
Reduction of social costs placed on employers is essential to job creation in the EU				.70601

TABLE 3.7. *Continued*

Survey statement	Factor 1	Factor 2	Factor 3	Factor 4
Britain should not participate in the lifting of border controls as specified in the Schengen agreement				.58439
Inflexibility in European labour markets is the principle cause of unemployment				.58297
Britain should accept a common European currency but not a single currency				.54807
The UK should incorporate the European Convention on Human Rights into law				−.52008
The Council of Ministers should be the supreme institution in the EU				.51249

Factor 1 = Constitutional Sovereignty
Factor 2 = Left Scepticism (Democratic Socialist)
Factor 3 = Policy Harmonization
Factor 4 = Right Scepticism (Social Democrats)

Parliament and the strengthening of national parliaments. We see that policy independence variables are found in the second and third components. The highest loading of nearly 0.8 in 'Factor 2' delineates opposition to EMU if the convergence criterion results in higher levels of unemployment. We also find loading on this factor, our 'Clause IV' statement on public ownership, along with support for the Swedish proposal on pursuing full employment. Quite clearly this is a left interventionist factor. But the opposition to a European Central Bank, and the ERM, in conjunction with the proposed referendum on any IGC proposals for constitutional change, marks it out as representative of the sceptical wing of the state interventionists. We can safely call this factor the 'Left Scepticism' factor.

Our third factor in this four-factor model has four variables loading on it, one more than the 'required rule of thumb'. This factor is definitely a policy factor. But significantly, the loadings are now comprehensively in favour of tax harmonization within the EU and in favour of a Union strategy on *privatization*. This factor is representative of the 'right-wing' Euro-enthusiasts within the party, the

MPs who share a similar position with Austin Mitchell on the 'pro-market' end of the right–left ideological spectrum *but*, as Mitchell disapprovingly points out: are 'now positively bubbling with enthusiasm'.[14] This third factor we can call the 'Policy Harmonization' factor. However, the last component of our four-factor model contains statements that Austin Mitchell may well agree with. It is certainly a 'pro-market' factor to the extent that it is supportive of a supply side economic strategy, but it is also Eurosceptic, opposing *Schengen* and supporting institutional control by the Council of Ministers. Clearly, we can name this factor 'Right Scepticism'.

Our four-factor model has been extremely useful. The divisions within the parliamentary party, particularly within its left wing, have become apparent. The signing of the first factor suggests it is predominantly sceptical, but the second and fourth, while still predominantly sceptical, suggest contrary positions on the 'level of state interventionism', while the third is a Euro-enthusiastic factor on policy harmonization. The signing of the loadings in the unrotated matrix confirms that these orientations are the result of MPs responses, not the geometry of the rotation. Similar to the findings in the previous chapter's factor analysis, what we are looking at are two sovereignty dimensions, but this time separately structured around the pro-nation-state and supranationalist wings of the Labour Party, and two state intervention dimensions structured around the agendas of more or less state intervention. In general, the factor analysis, in terms of the factors that emerged, and of the factor scores, reinforced the picture presented in the descriptives of a party with the potential for serious division on Europe. This begs a summary of just where the divisions within the Labour Party actually remain on the issue of European integration.

CONCLUSION: CLEAR DIVISIONS?

Evidently Labour has moved some considerable way along the road of European integration since 1983. Mr Blair may feel confident that the centre of gravity is moving in the direction of a man 'who voted for Britain to remain inside the EEC in 1975 and who fought to persuade his Party to become a party of Europe'.[15] But, our survey also

---

[14] Austin Mitchell, interviewed at the Palace of Westminster, July 1995.
[15] Rt. Hon. Tony Blair, the Friedrich-Ebert Stiftung, Bonn, 30 May 1995, op. cit.

TABLE 3.8. *Clear divisions?*

Issue statement		MPs seriously divided (30+ v. 30+)	Back and frontbench opposite majorities	MP and MEP opposite majorities
1.2	Impact of EU membership	Yes	Yes	No
1.5	Sovereignty–not pooled	Yes	No	No
1.7	Subsidiarity/federalist	Yes	Yes	Yes
2.2	EMU/Referendum	Yes	Yes	Yes
2.6	Common Currency	No	Yes	No
2.7	European Cent-Bank/ power	Yes	Yes	Yes
4.1	National econ- management	Yes	No	No
4.3	Union strategy/ privatization	Yes	Yes	No
4.4	Tax harmonization	Yes (Company Environment Customs)	No	Yes (Company VAT)
4.6	EU's budget/enlarged	Yes	Yes	Yes
5.1	The 1996 IGC no supranational powers	Yes	Yes	Yes (MPs evenly divided)
5.2	Referendum on IGC	Yes	Yes	Yes
5.9	Britain block the use of QMV	Yes	Yes	Yes
5.14	National identity/ Democracy	Yes	No	No
5.15	National parliaments key to democratic deficit	No	No	Yes

Source: Labour Parliamentarians and European Integration Survey, ESRC/ Nottingham Trent University 1995/96.

revealed that it would be a serious mistake for Mr Blair to feel overconfident. The statements on our social dimension (Table 3.3) reveal that Labour remains a party with strong collectivist and interventionist values. In fact, this was the only dimension where we found almost unanimity on attitude statements. There is therefore potential for conflict between a party leadership, whether forced or willingly, accepting free market policy emanating from Europe.

This potential cleavage is evident in Table 3.8, which demonstrates that there are several issues from our previous tables that are or will become central to the debate on European integration, over which both the PLP as a whole, its back and front benches, and the EPLP, are divided.

We see this in the statements on interventionist policy from our Table 3.8 (4.1, 4.3, 4.4, and 4.6). MPs were seriously divided having 30 per cent or more supporting each side of the issue. In two of the statements (4.1 and 4.4) there was a clear division between frontbench and backbench attitudes, with further confusion added as MPs and MEPs have opposite majorities for statements (4.1 and 4.3). This potential for division is clearly evident when looking at the responses to the call for a Union strategy on the neo-liberal clarion call of privatization (statement 4.1). The parliamentarians are divided almost straight down the middle on this.

We see this circumspection reflected in attitudes to membership and sovereignty (statements 1.2, 1.5, and 1.7). On subsidiarity re-inforcing federalism we find a slight majority of MPs supporting this option; an option commonly identified as a core sceptic position. More importantly, we find the divisions reflected in the potentially explosive electoral issues of EMU and the consequences of the 1996 IGC. For example, there are divisions in all three cells over a refer-endum on EMU, with similar findings for the statements on a refer-endum for any proposals from the forthcoming IGC which had constitutional implications and over the issue of blocking the use of QMV in foreign and defence policy (statements 2.2, 5.2, and 5.9).

Table 3.9 confirms the descriptive findings, the distribution of MPs along the four-factor model dimensions, showing percentages mea-suring +1 to +2 standard deviations and −1 to −2 standard devia-tions from the mean, a measure in this case of strong dissidence from party policy.

What is striking about Table 3.9 is the presence it reveals of both hard-line Eurosceptics and Euro-enthusiasts who measure one, or in some instances two standard deviations, from the mean. In the four-factor model, we find on the Constitutional Sovereignty factor, that 5 per cent of MPs from our sample are two standard deviations from the

TABLE 3.9. *Distribution of MPs (n=64): selected standard deviations from the mean factor scores*

	End of axis	<−2.0.sds	<−1.0sds	>+1.0sds	>+2.0sds	End of axis
Four-factor model						
Constitutional Sovereignty factor	pro-sovereignty	5%	13%	14%	0	pro-integration
equivalent number of MPs		13	33	35	0	
Left Scepticism factor	'Bennite'	0	20%	14%	2%	'Sedgemore'
equivalent number of MPs		0	50	35	5	
Policy Harmonization factor	pro-harmonization	6%	13%	17%	0	anti-harmonization
equivalent number of MPs		15	33	43	0	
Right Scepticism factor	'Shoreite'	3%	17%	19%	2%	'Radice'
equivalent number of MPs		7	43	48	5	

mean. Significantly, this translates into thirteen MPs with outright hostility to any further supranational proposals emanating from the IGC.

Our four-factor model highlights how the sovereignty dimension now cross-cuts the old right–left ideological positions. Crucially, we find the left just as split on Europe as the right. Potentially, we have fifty MPs from the 'Bennite' wing of the left, taking a hard-line sceptical position, faced by forty on the left taking an equally hard-line pro-integrationist stance. Again, we see this potential for serious division matched on the right with a split of fifty sceptics against fifty-three enthusiasts.

The diversity of the sovereignty dimension was confirmed by our factor analysis and the importance of the sovereignty dimension was confirmed by its predominance in all the exploratory analyses. Labour sceptics are quick to denounce 'Tory nationalism' and declare that Tory scepticism is much more concerned with the nation state, while Labour scepticism and hostility to EU integration is based far more on the constraints and restrictions imposed upon national economic management policies. But whatever the underlying ideology, if anything, sovereignty seems more important to the mindset of Labour MPs than is traditionally believed and the results certainly suggest that there is scope for a revision of traditional typologies. Our four-factor model also revealed the depth of division within the party, with twin sovereignty and state interventionism factors apparently reflecting alternative agendas, none more so than on the left of the party.

The party management problem over Europe, then, is all too apparent. Mr Blair was aided considerably by the fact that 'power' at Westminster appeared a tangible possibility for Labour by the winter of 1995/6. The reality of this situation certainly helped discipline the parliamentary party and reduced the extent of rebellion. Our evidence clearly shows the potential for future eruptions within the party. The open letter signed by fifty MPs demanding a single currency referendum may only be the beginning (*Guardian*, 28 March 1996). It is therefore evident that New Labour still has potential for party fissures on the issue of European integration.[16]

---

[16] The authors would like to give special thanks to Dr Steve Ludlam for his invaluable assistance with the Factor Analysis in this chapter.

APPENDIX

The survey questionnaire contained 59 questions on European integration. The survey was conducted by four mailings between 10 November 1995 and 27 February 1996. The questionnaire was sent to all Labour MPs and MEPs. Excluding non-respondents to identification questions, 33 per cent of backbench MPs responded, and 29 per cent of the shadow frontbench, giving an overall response rate of 33 per cent for MPs and 47 per cent for MEPs. We also analysed respondents in terms of their cohort, i.e. which general election brought them into parliament or followed their entry in a by-election and were reassured by this criterion of representativeness.

We further tested our known respondents by two measures of parliamentary behaviour over Europe. Questionnaires were anonymous but four-fifths of MPs also returned a separate identity-coded postcard, enabling such tests. We know that Labour had sixty-six third reading rebels on the Maastricht Bill; the remaining sixty-three 'rebels' now in the House of Commons make up 23 per cent of the PLP; we identified 21 per cent of those rebels in our survey. Moreover, the remaining ninety Labour signatories to Peter Mandelson's 'enthusiastic' early day motion of 16 December 1992 now constitute 33 per cent of the PLP; we identified 24 per cent of those signatories in our sample. Furthermore, we tested for ideological bias with the known members of the most active left-leaning 'Campaign Group' of Labour MPs. This Campaign Group constitute 11 per cent of the PLP and our survey had 12 per cent of known Campaign

TABLE 3A.1. *Representativeness in terms of cohorts*

	%PLP	%respondents
1950	1	1
1964/6	7	8
1970	6	2
1974/I/II	9	5
1979	10	12
1983	14	12
1987	23	21
1992	30	39

members. All in all, taking into account the extent of the Labour whips' circumspection[17] over the controversial nature of the issues covered, we obtained a satisfactory degree of representativeness from the tests we deployed.

[17] Added to the general problem of questionnaire fatigue, we were informed by some MPs that both MPs and MEPs were advised not to reply to our questionnaire. See also the *Tribune* tax survey of 24 November 1995: 'Tribune has since learnt that the questionnaire succeeded in stirring anxieties in the Labour leadership and all Labour MPs were ordered to have nothing to do with it by the Whips' Office'. And the *Independent* survey on the future of the monarchy, 18 Feb. 1996: 'The majority of Labour MPs were silent. Of the 183 we spoke to, 120 refused to answer any questions. Several said that the party whips had ordered them not to take part.'

4

The Liberal Democrats and European Integration

Scott Clarke and John Curtice

'We are part of the community of Europe and we must do our duty as such.'

W. E. Gladstone 10 April 1888

INTRODUCTION

When the Liberal Democrats were formed in 1989, the party inherited from the Liberal Party a long tradition of consistent and enthusiastic support for European unification. The Liberals were amongst the first in Britain to back the European Coal and Steel Community, a European Defence Community, the Western European Union, the European Free Trade Area, and the European Economic Community (EEC). This chapter asks why this should be so. Although support for closer European integration was not inconsistent with the party's ideological and historical traditions, neither did these point unambiguously towards such a position. Further, there is little evidence that its position has been electorally advantageous to the party or that it has come under strong pressure from its membership to maintain a strongly pro-European stance. We will suggest that a key influence on the party's position was its long absence from the corridors of domestic power. Europe, in contrast, offered a more enticing prospect of both influence and resources.

Of course a Liberal MP has not occupied a ministerial limousine since 1945, so we might question whether the Liberals' pro-Europeanism has been of any consequence. We shall argue that because of the splits on the issue in both the Conservative and the Labour parties, the

Liberals' attitude has occasionally been vital to the development of Britain's links with Europe, not only directly in votes in the House of Commons but also indirectly through the role Europe has played in changes in the party system. It is with this argument that we begin.

DOES THE LIBERALS' POLICY TOWARDS EUROPE MATTER?

For most of the time since 1945, the Liberals have been reduced to political impotence. Not only have they only had little more than a handful of MPs, but apart from the period between 1976 and 1979 the government has always enjoyed a parliamentary majority. Which way they trooped through the division lobbies has thus rarely mattered. But, thanks to the divisions which Europe has generated within the Conservatives and Labour, on two occasions Liberal votes have been of vital importance in determining Britain's relationship with Europe.

The first occasion was when Britain initially entered Europe. When Parliament voted on the necessary legislation, the Liberals found themselves with the balance of power. True, when the principle of whether Britain should enter Europe on the terms negotiated by Edward Heath was first debated in the Commons in the autumn of 1971, the Conservative government had an easy majority of 112, thanks to a widespread rebellion against a three-line whip instructing Labour MPs to vote in opposition. But when it came to the passage of the necessary, legislation, most of Labour's pro-European MPs decided to follow the official party line, while the government's own anti-EEC MPs often abstained or voted with Labour. As a result the votes of the five of the six Liberal MPs who backed Britain's entry could be decisive.[1] In particular, the second reading of the European Communities Bill, secured by a majority of just eight on 17 February 1992, would have been lost without those votes. Moreover, during the detailed committee stage, at which the passage of any amendment would have required the renegotiation of Britain's terms of entry, the government's majority fell to as low as four. In short, in the absence

---

[1] A sixth Liberal MP, Emlyn Hooson (Montgomery), dissented with the official party line and voted against the government. Hooson took the view that Britain should have entered the Community at the outset and now the timing was not right for Britain to obtain satisfactory terms of entry.

of Liberal support, Britain might never have joined the Common Market in the first place.

The second occasion was during the passage of the legislation implementing the Maastricht Treaty. Due to severe internal divisions over the party's European policy coupled with a small parliamentary majority, the Conservative government could not guarantee the Maastricht Bill safe passage through the House (Baker et al. 1993a). On several occasions, Liberal Democrat support helped Major's government to carry the day. In particular, in November 1992 the government only won by three votes a crucial debate designed to give it authority to proceed with the bill. Without the support of nineteen of the twenty Liberal Democrats that vote would clearly have been lost.[2]

The Liberals' position on Europe has also mattered indirectly. The Liberals played a leading role alongside pro-European Conservative and Labour enthusiasts in the Britain in Europe campaign during the 1975 referendum. True, the Liberals' contribution to the overwhelmingly successful pro-European campaign was hardly vital. But that campaign acted as a catalyst for subsequent developments in the party system (Bradley 1981). For it was within the 'Britain in Europe' campaign that the Liberal Party first established positive relations with Labour's pro-European MPs including Roy Jenkins. Six years later these relations helped to encourage these MPs to split with the Labour Party and form the SDP in alliance with the Liberals, in part because of Labour's increasingly anti-European stance (see Jenkins 1991). And that split in Labour's ranks helped to ensure its defeat in the 1983 election, by which time the party was committed to withdrawing from the European Community if it had attained power.

The Liberals' attitude towards Europe has then been an influence in determining Britain's role in Europe.[3] Indeed, the Liberals have

---

[2] The only Liberal Democrat to vote against the Maastricht Bill was Nick Harvey (North Devon).

[3] There have been other less dramatic occasions in recent years when the Liberal Democrats have exerted a degree of influence over Britain's European policy. During the passage of the Maastricht Bill, the Liberal Democrats supported a Labour amendment which required that the United Kingdom's representatives on the Committee of the Regions should be elected by local authorities rather than nominated by government. The government was defeated by 22 votes. Meanwhile, the Liberal Democrats were instrumental in the passing of the European Union Finance Bill in 1994. Labour attempted to destroy the spirit of the bill by proposing an amendment not to sanction any increase in the United Kingdom's contribution to the EU budget without action by the government to curb fraud and waste in Europe. However, the Liberal Democrats refused to back Labour's move and the government secured a majority of 27.

probably played a more important role in this area of government policy than any other in the post-war period. Understanding why the Liberal Democrats have been so keen on Europe is then essential to any understanding of Britain's relations with Europe.

IDEOLOGICAL INHERITANCE AND HISTORICAL TRADITION

The most obvious place to start to look for an explanation of the Liberals' enthusiasm for Europe is the party's philosophy and historical tradition. How far do these suggest that the modern party's support for Europe grows naturally from its ideological and historical inheritance? In this section we examine that inheritance and then in the next section consider its implications for the party's position on Europe.

The heart of Liberalism is a preoccupation with the rights and happiness of the individual. The principal goal of a political system is the attainment of individual happiness (Bullock and Shock 1956). Moreover, ruled by reason and conscience rather than by habit, prejudice, or blind obedience to external authorities, the individual is considered to be the best judge of what will contribute to that happiness (Bradley 1985: 14–15). The role of the state is simply to provide the order, security, and peace which are needed to protect individual liberty and enable the individual's true potential to be realized (Bradley 1985). [4] What the state should avoid is both war and needless interference in economic activity, including not least the imposition of tariffs.

From these premises flow an enthusiasm for both free trade and internationalism. Free trade encouraged division of labour and thus economic prosperity. And economic prosperity could remove the most potent sources of economic suffering and discontent which otherwise limited human potential (Abel 1954). Moreover, increasing the economic interreliance of nations also helped to make war less likely (Sidorsky 1970: 1–28). Moreover, for nineteenth-century British liberals such as Richard Cobden and John Bright war was undesirable not

---

[4] However, the liberal concern for the development of human liberty does not involve the freeing of people to do what they would like regardless of the consequences, but rather the enabling of them to make the best of themselves and contribute to the well-being of the community of which they are part.

least because it involved the immediate suspension of individual liberty.

Liberals regularly put the principle of free trade into practice. They were vocal opponents of Joseph Chamberlain's Tariff Reform campaign in favour of Protection (Searle 1995: ch. 3). The party opposed the coalition government's decision to abandon free trade in favour of Imperial Preference following the Ottawa Agreements of 1931. And Liberals gave full support to the agreements reached at Hot Springs and Bretton Woods as well as the signing of the Atlantic Charter in August 1941, the aim of which was 'to bring about the fullest possible collaboration between all nations in the economic field with the object of securing for all improved labour standards, economic advancement and social security'.

A key feature of all of these stances was the rejection of regional trading blocks. Such blocks might facilitate free trade between their members, but for Liberals this was not sufficient. For example, Liberal leader Archibald Sinclair justified his party's support for the Atlantic Charter with the following words:

We must broaden the whole basis of commerce and industry by breaking down the barriers to foreign trades by making economic agreements with the US and by forming with the countries of the British Empire, with America if she will come in, and with France, Belgium and Holland the Scandinavian countries and anyone else who will join a low tariff group of nations who will trade with one another on terms of the greatest freedom that can be arranged. (*Liberal Magazine*, November 1944)

The reason for Liberal suspicion of regional blocks was expressed clearly by the MP Percy Harris writing in the *Liberal Magazine* in 1944:

Economic federations on a regional basis may serve as a stepping stone towards a wider intercourse but in proportion as they are exclusive in character, must contain a threat to international harmony . . . Trade with the British Commonwealth should be developed in the framework of a global economy and not of empire isolationism . . . The realisation of an integrated and harmonious world economy can only be achieved in an atmosphere of confidence and co-operation and by a sustained and deliberate international effort in which the country should take part second to none.

Liberal support for internationalism flowed from the belief that the rights of the individual transcended national borders. Human beings had more in common with each other than their apparent national differences would indicate. It was not 'human' for an Italian only to be an Italian or a German only to be a German. Their common humanity was more important than their nationality. It followed that the spread of liberalism would reinforce the spirit of cosmopolitanism and internationalism and bring the civilized peoples of the nations of the world closer together (Bernstein 1986: ch. 8).

But how Liberals should put their internationalism into practice was not so clear-cut. For Liberals often accepted that for freedom to be achieved internationally, individuals must first achieve freedom at home. Thus Gladstone championed the efforts of numerous nationalist movements across the European continent as well as loosening the bonds of colonial dependency in granting independence to the Cape of Good Hope, Cyprus, and Jamaica and allowing Australia and New Zealand to set their own level of tariff.

Unsurprisingly, support for national self-determination and international peace were not always easy bedfellows. For some Liberals, at least, some nations were better able to contribute to international order than others. Even Gladstone in his support for a Concert of Europe reflected a belief that Europe had a special role in the maintenance of peace and civilization in the wider world, describing the Concert as 'a tribunal of paramount authority, the general judgement of civilised mankind'(Gladstone 1879: 249). Although never precise about the institutional form which the Concert should take he appears to have regarded it as an arbitrator, court of justice, and international peacekeeper (Bradley 1985: 63). It would be the primary purpose of the Concert to 'check aggression and oppression in any part of the world' (Hansard, 3rd series, 1876: 184).

But the belief amongst Liberals that international order could best be achieved through the supremacy of some nations over others reached its height with the move towards Liberal Imperialism in the late 1880s and 1890s. Liberals such as Roseberry, Asquith, Haldane, and Sir Edward Grey clashed with more traditional sectors of the Liberal hierarchy by arguing the need to make support for the maintenance of the Empire part of the modern Liberal creed (Matthew 1973). In so doing they reflected a belief in Britain's cultural supremacy and ability to bring good order to the world. Far from being based on a narrow consideration of Britain's own interests, imperialism was characterized by 'a real sense of responsibility and duty to the subject peoples, and the idea of developing our state for the good of the native peoples as well as the good of Britain' (Douglas 1971: 5).

It is only after the First World War that Liberals converted their internationalism into support for forms of international collaboration which recognized the equality of the peoples and nations of the world (Butt Philip 1983: 18). Under the leadership of Lloyd George it played a central role in the organization of the League of Nations Union in Britain. By the late 1940s several key Liberals including Clement Davies and William Beveridge had become active members of 'Federal Union', whose objectives included securing support in Great Britain and elsewhere for 'a federation of free peoples under a common government elected by and responsible for their common affairs, with national self-government for national affairs'. Writing in the organization's official publication *Federal News*, in 1950, Clement Davies said:

I believe that the world will not know absolute peace, will not be able to free itself completely from the fear of war, until there is established, as someday it will be established, one world government; one world government with effective power to maintain law and order and administer one rule of law to which all, strong as well as weak, shall be subject.

In short, by this time many Liberals were prepared to accept the demise of the nation state. This was the natural response of a party which had watched in horror as the foundations of modern liberalism nearly collapsed under the hammer of National Socialism. Davies wanted to safeguard the liberal ideas of individualism and liberty from the forces of nationalism by introducing, 'a new supranational entity with a scope and powers belonging to each man and nation that no nation ever had' (Clement Davies in the *Liberal Magazine*, January 1945). And in response to the argument that the nation state was irreplaceable, Liberal activist Miss A. Galbraith Piggot wrote:

Would it not be correct to say that devastated Europe has discovered that all mankind has the same needs and hopes and fears which constitute modern life . . . Has there ever before been such an opportunity for European races (and others) to come together in a common understanding of the rehabilitation effort and detestation of oppression . . . Let us keep our loyalty to our nations whether republican, composed of Soviets, or an enlightened monarchy, but add to them a Supra-nation and be loyal to that also. (*Liberal Magazine*, January 1945)

IDEOLOGY, HISTORY, AND EUROPEAN UNIFICATION

So, given the party's inheritance, what might we expect the Liberals' attitude towards Europe to be? In many respects, we might expect Liberals to be natural supporters of European unification. The European Union has two characteristics of particular importance to Liberals. First it aims to remove trade barriers between its members. Not only has it eliminated tariffs between members but it has also attempted to remove indirect discrimination against overseas goods by means of taxation and regulatory policies. Second, it has provided a bulwark against the threat of nationalism by moving towards closer political integration.

But the European Union also has one major disadvantage for Liberals. It is a regional trading block which the party might have been expected to view with much the same scepticism as it had previously regarded Imperial Preference. For although the Union has promoted the reduction of tariff barriers between its members, it has done so within a 'Common External Tariff' (CET). Indeed, joining the Common Market required Britain to raise barriers against some of its fellow members of the British Commonwealth. It could be argued that the Market was no more than a protectionist cartel which was exemplified by its agricultural policy, aimed to fix and maintain prices for the advantage of industry and the disadvantage of the consumer.

This tension between two potential alternative stances towards Europe was clearly evident within the party in the early post-war period. True the party assembly passed a series of motions welcoming further European cooperation. In 1950 the party openly endorsed the Schuman initiative for the integration of European coal and steel production. Speaking to the party assembly the following year, Clement Davies welcomed the creation of the European Coal and Steel Community and called for further steps towards the integration of Western Europe (*Liberal Magazine*, November 1951). And at the 1954 assembly a resolution was carried giving full support to the creation of a European Defence Community (EDC), arguing that such a development was vital to the continued security of Western Europe.

But throughout this period the party leadership faced continuous pressure to change its European policy from those in the party who believed it should stick to the principle of free trade. Led by Oliver

Smedley, S. W. Alexander, and Roy Douglas, the traditional free trade wing of the party suggested that the true nature of the Schuman Plan had been to create an international European cartel to fix and maintain prices. Smedley wrote to the *Liberal News* in the summer of 1954 arguing that 'a single market is a cartel market which can only be maintained by excluding competitive enterprise. Supranational economic planning can only function as a totalitarian monopoly' (*Liberal News*, 23 July 1954). What Smedley and his colleagues wanted was free trade without a common external tariff.[5]

This debate reached its height in the mid-1950s following the collapse of the EDC initiative in 1954 (Butt Philip 1983: 221). The 1956 Assembly called for British participation in the Common Market but once the Treaty of Rome was signed in March 1957 without Britain, the Liberal Party backed the government's decision to embark upon negotiations to set up a European Free Trade Area (EFTA) as an alternative to UK membership of the Common Market. Butt Philip (1983: 221) suggests that the main reason for the oscillation in the party's European policy at this time was the change in party leadership from Davies to Grimond, but this is to ignore the wider climate of opinion in the party in favour of free trade rather than a customs union.

Still, this oscillation did not last for long. Once negotiations between EFTA and the Common Market broke down at the end of 1958, the party returned to its position of favouring British membership of the latter. For Euro-enthusiasts, including the influential Mark Bonham Carter, who won the Torrington by-election in March 1958 (Butt Philip 1983: 222), the crucial missing ingredient in EFTA was that it was unlikely ever to bring about political integration or develop institutions of a supranational character and thus be able to provide Europe with the security it needed against the threat of war. Although the Common Market had its shortcomings, these could best be overcome by Britain working to improve it as a member. In particular it was the only organization that looked

[5] The Liberal Free Traders also disagreed with the pooling of national sovereignty believing that only a unity of free, strong sovereign powers, united by common ideals and dangers could successfully maintain world peace. See the contribution of Air Vice-Marshall Bennett in *Liberal News*, 17 Sept. 1954. Some of the Liberal Free Traders subsequently left the party and founded the Institute for Economic Affairs a think-tank which subsequently became one of the intellectual power houses of Thatcherism within the Conservative Party.

capable of developing a supranational character. (See Arthur Holt in *Liberal News*, 13 July 1959; and Mark Bonham Carter in *Liberal News*, 22 Feb. 1959.)

Thereafter, and uniquely amongst Britain's political parties, the Liberal Party never wavered in its support for Britain's membership of the Common Market. That support has however not been an uncritical one. Liberals have regarded the European Union as only an essential first step along the path of closer political integration and economic cooperation. As the Liberal maverick Michael Meadowcroft wrote in 1980, 'Liberalism's international dimension and its commitment to the European ideal can only be reconciled if the European Community is seen as being a first step—albeit a crucial first step towards a broader international grouping' (Meadowcroft 1980: 15). In practice this has meant the party has been keen on moves to create a democratic federal Europe in which, for example, the European Parliament is strengthened and the Council of Ministers weakened. The Liberal Democrats are to date also the only party to pledge unequivocal support for a single European currency and a European Central Bank. At the same time the party has been keen to see the European Union expand its borders, not least into Eastern Europe. For Liberals these steps are essential if the European Union is to achieve the goals of multilateral free trade and global security.

Thus despite the consistency of Liberal support for Britain's membership of the European Union, that position is far from being the inevitable consequence of the party's ideological and historical legacy. The Union violated the party's commitment to free trade and only imperfectly met its internationalist aspirations. The party's expressed desire for a more open-trading, democratic Europe differs substantially from the reality of an intergovernmental organization whose decisions are often made behind closed doors and without political control (Dahrendorf 1972). We evidently need to consider whether there might have been further reasons for the party to have taken the stance it did.

ELECTORAL BENEFIT AND MEMBERSHIP PRESSURE

If the party's stance towards Europe cannot simply be accounted for by the party's ideological and historical traditions, how else might it be? Perhaps the party has pursued Europe for electoral advantage?

Certainly, ever since the emergence of the Labour Party at the turn of the century the Liberal Party has struggled to differentiate itself ideologically from its two nearest competitors. The reluctance of both Labour and the Conservatives to embrace the Common Market in the 1950s meant that Europe was one issue at least on which the party could avoid being the centre party. Instead, the Liberals could strike a stance which placed it at one end of the continuum and both its opponents on the other.[6]

However, from the very beginning the Liberal Party struggled to translate its European identity into significant electoral gains. In fact, the European issue failed to feature in any of Britain's general election campaigns during the 1950s. Reduced to minor party status the Liberal Party was not in any position to catapult the question of EEC membership on to the main political agenda. For example, during the 1959 general election, half the Liberal candidates mentioned Britain's relationship with the European Community in their election addresses (Butler and Rose 1960: 132). However, despite the efforts of the Liberal Party to make Europe an issue, the election was fought and eventually won and lost on the issues of taxation, employment, and social expenditure (Butler and Rose 1960: 132). The Liberals were forced by their very position within the political system to fight elections on the issues preferred by the two more dominant parties.

Even the distinctiveness of the Liberals' position was threatened when in July 1961 Macmillan announced that Britain would be opening negotiations for EEC membership. However, Europe has proved the most divisive issue in British politics ever since, giving the Liberals the chance at least of exploiting the divisions within both major parties over the terms on which Britain could join the EEC. These divisions have meant that the Liberals have been able to project themselves as the only major party in Britain fully committed and united behind the European ideal.

Nevertheless, the party appears to have derived little or no benefit from this stance. If it did, one thing that we would expect to find is that Liberal and Liberal Democrat voters would be more likely to adopt a pro-European stance. Yet evidence from the British Election Study conducted immediately after the 1992 election shows that

---

[6] According to directional theory, being at the end of the continuum on an issue helps to motivate voters to vote for a party even if they themselves would prefer a smaller move in that direction (Rabinowitz and Macdonald 1989).

despite forty years of campaigning for Europe, Liberal Democrat voters are barely more pro-European than their Conservative or Labour counterparts.

Consider, for example, answers to a range of statements designed to get at underlying attitudes towards the European Community (EC) rather than support for particular policy proposals. As Table 4.1 indicates, the attitudes of Liberal Democrat voters are almost indistinguishable from those of Conservative and Labour voters. Only around half of Liberal Democrats think that the EC is making Britain more efficient, as do around a half of Conservative and Labour voters. And while only four in ten Liberal Democrat voters think that lots of good traditions might have to be given up if Britain stays within the EC, only around four in ten Conservative and Labour voters think the same way.

True, when we consider more specific policy options, Liberal Democrat voters do appear somewhat more pro-European than their Labour and Conservative counterparts but even then only marginally so. For instance, Liberal Democrat voters are more prepared to replace the pound with a single currency, than are Conservative and Labour voters. Just 18 per cent of Conservative and 23 per cent of Labour voters take this view but even amongst Liberal Democrat voters barely a third (32 per cent) are in favour.

Meanwhile, as Table 4.2 demonstrates, Liberal Democrats are no

TABLE 4.1. *Attitudes towards Europe*

Agree	Reported vote in 1992		
	Con %	Lab %	Lib Dem %
If we stay in the European Community, Britain will lose control over decisions that affect Britain	54	51	53
The competition from other EC countries is making Britain more modern and efficient	54	48	53
Lots of good British traditions will have to be given up if we stay in the EC	43	45	40

Source: British Election Study 1992.

TABLE 4.2. *Views on Britain's policy towards Europe*

Britain's long-term policy should be . . .	Reported vote 1992		
	Con %	Lab %	Lib Dem %
to leave the European Community	9	13	9
to stay in the EC and try to reduce its powers	42	23	30
to leave things as they are	16	19	11
to stay in the EC and try to increase its powers	27	33	36
to work for the formation of a single European government	7	13	14

Source: British Election Study 1992.

keener on the idea of a single European government than are Labour voters. Indeed, over one in three Liberal Democrat voters wish to reduce the powers of the EC or leave the organization entirely.

Perhaps the most striking testimony to the lack of electoral reward which the Liberals have derived from their pro-European standpoint is their record in elections to the European Parliament. During the Lib-Lab pact in the late 1970s, the party had tried to ensure that these elections were conducted under a regional list system of proportional representation. However, in the decisive vote in November 1977 only 147 out of 308 Labour MPs voted in favour. As a result all four rounds of European Parliament elections to date have been held using the single member plurality electoral system. Due to the geographically even spread of its vote, this system usually does the Liberals few favours in any election. With European constituencies containing approximately half a million voters, the Liberals found it difficult to muster enough strength to win anything at all. Indeed, Britain's most pro-European party failed to secure any representation in the European Parliament until it finally won two seats in 1994.

However, it is not just the party's haul of seats which has been a disappointment. Its share of the vote has failed to match expectations as well. This can be seen in Table 4.3 which compares the party's share of the vote in each Euro-election with that in elections which in

TABLE 4.3. *Liberal Alliance and Liberal Democrat performance in European elections*

	% share in Euro-election	% share in previous election[a]
1979	13.1	14
1984	19.5	22
1989	6.2	18
1994	16.7	27

[a] In 1979 this is the Liberal share of the vote in the 1979 general election. In other years this is an estimate of the equivalent national vote share in the previous month's local elections. For further details see Curtice and Payne 1991.

each case took place just a month before the relevant Euro-election. On all four occasions the party's performance was worse than it was just a few weeks previously. Indeed, in 1989 its vote went into freefall in the wake of the row about the merger between the Liberals and the Social Democrats, leaving the party a poor fourth behind the Greens.

European elections are commonly regarded as second-order elections in which attitudes towards European matters, perhaps, rather paradoxically, play little role in determining how voters vote (Reif 1984). However, it is doubtful whether this is entirely true so far as the Liberal Democrats are concerned. At minimum it seems difficult to rule out the possibility that the party loses votes at European elections because of its strongly pro-European policy (Curtice and Steed 1995). Indeed, there is quite clear evidence that voters who would have been prepared to vote for the Liberal Democrats in a local or general election in June 1994 were reluctant to do so in a European election. The 1994 wave of the British Election Panel Study found that 3 per cent more people would have been prepared to vote for the Liberal Democrats in a general election in June 1994 and 5 per cent more in a local election (Heath et al. 1995). Similarly, an ICM poll conducted immediately after polling day found as many as 5 per cent more willing to vote Liberal Democrat in a general election than actually voted for the party in European elections (ICM 1994).

So if there is little reason to believe that the party has pursued its pro-European stance for electoral advantage, what of internal pressure from the party's membership? According to May's curvilinear law of disparity, typically a party's members are more extreme than either its voters or its leaders (May 1973). As a result, parties are always liable to experience pressure from their activists to move policy further from the centre than most voters might prefer. It has never been clear how we might expect this law to apply to a centre party, but perhaps on this issue, where the Liberals adopted a position at one end of the policy continuum, we might see it in operation. Indeed we might anticipate that it was the keenness of Liberal Party members to adopt a pro-European stance that helped ensure it was maintained despite its lack of electoral popularity.

In order to test this proposition fully we would need evidence of membership attitudes throughout the last forty years. Alas, the first systematic survey of membership attitudes only took place in 1993, although the study in question did survey former members of the Liberals and the SDP as well as current Liberal Democrats (Bennie et al. 1996). In any event the survey gives little support for the thesis. For example, Liberal Democrat members were asked the same question about what Britain's long-term policy towards Europe should be as was asked of voters on the 1992 British Election Study. As Table 4.4 indicates, Liberal Democrat members prove to be no keener than Liberal Democrat voters on strengthening the powers of EC institutions.

Other evidence from the survey is consistent with this finding. Only 55 per cent of members said that the government should make Britain part of a federal Europe, while 35 per cent were opposed. In addition, only 47 per cent favoured either the formation of a single European

TABLE 4.4. *Liberal Democrat voters' and members' attitudes towards Europe*

Britain's long-term policy should be . . .	Liberal Democrat	
	Voters %	Members %
to leave the European Community	9	6
to stay in the EC and try to *reduce* its powers	30	36
to leave things as they are	11	13
to stay in the EC and to try to *increase* its powers	36	30
to work for the formation of a single European government	14	16

Source: British Election Survey 1992: Liberal Democrat members study.

government or an increase in the powers of the EC, while as many as 44 per cent favoured either the withdrawal of Britain from the EC or at least a reduction in the European Union's powers. Further, no less than one in five of those who said they might not renew their membership said that it was because of the party's decision to support the Conservative government at the vital stage in the progress of the bill to implement the provisions of the Maastricht Bill in autumn 1992 (Bennie et al. 1996: 141). Far from pressurizing the leadership to take a pro-European stance, the survey suggests that if anything that stance was capable of losing the party members.

If the membership was not particularly pro-European after forty years of their party adopting a pro-European stance, it seems unlikely that it was pressurizing the leadership to take such a stance in earlier years either. Certainly, the parallel surveys of former Liberal and SDP members which were also conducted suggest that it was the latter who, if anything, were marginally the more pro-European of the two old Alliance parties (Bennie et al. 1995).

EUROPEAN LIBERALS AND POWER

Bereft of influence at Westminster, perhaps one possible attraction of Europe for British Liberals is that it provided them with greater opportunities for political influence. Liberalism is after all one of the principal European families of political parties, along with Christian Democracy and Socialism. Thanks to the opportunities afforded them by proportional representation many European Liberal parties regularly formed part of a coalition government in their own countries, while collectively they could expect to act as the 'hinge' between the Christian Democrats and Socialists in the European Parliament. Closer links with Europe would seem to have afforded British Liberals with an opportunity to escape from the largely powerless ghetto to which they appeared to be confined at Westminster.

Yet collaborating with their European colleagues has also had its potential pitfalls for British Liberals. By the post-war period, the British Liberal Party was very much a 'social liberal' party which accepted that the state had a positive role to play in society and the economy (Curtice 1988). In contrast, many overseas Liberal parties were 'economic liberal' parties whose economic philosophy was much closer to classical liberalism.[7] Thus, cooperation with parties which sometimes appeared even further to the right than the British Conservatives has not always come easily.

Thus, the British Liberal Party was not amongst the original membership of twenty countries that formed the Liberal International in 1947, even though the organization was little more than a debating society. Rather it delayed membership until 1955 at the same time that the party backed Britain's membership of the European Coal and Steel Community. Even so it provided the party with little more than social support, most notably in the form of the appearance of a string of representatives from West European liberal parties at party assemblies.

The British Liberals were however inaugural members of the Federation of European Liberals and Democrats (ELD) founded in Stuttgart in 1976. This was a far more significant development. As the letter of invitation signed by Gaston Thorn (Luxembourg) and Hans-Dietrich Genscher (Germany) made clear, ELD had a firm organizational purpose, viz., to enable West European Liberal parties to fight on a common platform in the forthcoming direct elections to the European Parliament:

In 1978, all citizens of the European Community will directly elect their Parliament for the first time. The Liberal parties in the EC have to face this challenge. The citizens of the European Community expect of the Liberals that they will take decisive steps towards a European Union and that they will present a united and independent front in the first direct elections to the European Parliament.

But membership of ELD was not without its difficulties either. It faced an inevitable debate about the meaning of liberalism and thus which parties should be admitted into membership. Particularly controversial were the attempts of the French Republicans the 'rightist' FNRI led by Giscard D'Estaing to secure membership. When they did so in 1977 the existing French members, the left of centre MRG withdrew. Ironically, this was the group with whom the British Liberals had most in common (Butt Philip 1993: 150). At one stage the ensuing debate within the British Liberals about whether to maintain their membership saw the majority for staying in within the party's national council fall to just one.

---

[7] For an interesting discussion of these two strands of liberalism see von Beyme (1985: 31–46).

Despite these difficulties ELD (subsequently named the federation of European Liberal Democratic and Reformist parties ELDR, in 1986) has had a number of significant advantages for British Liberals, advantages which could help explain the party's continued support for the European Union, despite its shortcomings. One of the main organizational functions of ELD in its early years was to disperse to its members the funds which the European Parliament made to its groups to facilitate the provision of 'information' about the European elections. This money was of vital importance to the British Liberals. Of the party's total budget of £113,000 for fighting the 1979 European elections, no less than £110,000 came from ELD and in 1984 the ELD provided no less than £180,000 (Liberal Party Organisation 1980, 1985).[8] Withdrawal from ELD at this time, either because of its dislike of the French Republicans or because of a tempering of its Euro-enthusiasm, would have been an expensive decision for the British Liberals.[9]

Participation in ELD also gave the Liberals political influence despite their inability prior to 1994 to win any seats in the European Parliament. The organization has a federal structure which invites regular participation in its organizational and policy-forming work by representatives of its constituent political parties. Thanks to the fact that in terms of votes at least, the British Liberals are the largest liberal party in Europe, they have often been able to have a significant influence on ELD's policy, especially if they could secure the backing of the other key player, the German Free Democrats.

Participation in Europe has had then some valuable compensations for Liberals. It has been a source of both material resources and political influence. The party's enthusiasm for Europe has of course not simply been the product of self-interest. But such considerations have not been entirely absent either.

CONCLUSION

Of all Britain's principal political parties, the Liberal Party has undoubtedly been the most enthusiastic about Europe. And that

---

[8] The party's annual report the following year remarked that, 'The grants to the Party from the ELD were of great assistance. Without them most candidates would not have been able to fight and the Party would not have been able to mount the campaign.'

[9] However, following a decision of the European Court of Justice, the flow of information funds for all parties was much reduced by the time of the 1989 election.

enthusiasm has on occasion had a decisive influence on Britain's relations with Europe. But it is a mistake to assume that this posture is the natural result of the party's ideological and historical inheritance. The European Union does promote free trade amongst its members and does provide Europe with a supranational forum that helps insulate the continent against the dangers of war. But it is also a regional trading block operating within a common external tariff, an arrangement which previously has been rejected by Liberals. And it still primarily operates as an intergovernmental organization rather than the democratic, integrated organization Liberals desire.

Why then have the Liberals remained faithful to Europe? In part it was an acknowledgement of reality. Britain's trade with its Commonwealth partners was in decline after 1945, that with Europe growing. The United States showed no inclination to join any wider organization while liberalism in Europe needed as much protection as possible from the threat beyond the Iron Curtain. The Common Market was simply the only show in town.

However, support for European integration was also in the Liberals' self-interest. True, it brought little electoral reward. Nevertheless, one motivation behind the party's pro-European policy appears to be its need for some form of product differentiation from its main competitors. Indeed there are few other issues where the Liberals are clearly separated from both other main parties. The party appears to have used its support for European integration as 'a symbol of its modernity and its distinctive position in British politics' (Butt Philip 1983: 161). This area of distinctiveness has been reassuring to candidates and party activists, that the Liberals are not just a pale shade of blue or red, but something quite different.

Moreover, participation in Europe gave the party an influence in Europe which eluded it at Westminster. Indeed, constantly excluded from the power structures at home, it is hardly surprising that Liberals should have evinced relatively little concern about the loss of British sovereignty entailed by European Union membership. The prospect of power and influence for the Liberals has always seemed closer in Europe than it has at home.

So far as the immediate future is concerned, this picture is unlikely to change. But our analysis suggests that should the Liberal Democrats ever secure a real slice of power at Westminster, Britain's relations with Europe might not change quite as much as is often supposed. Although the substance of their criticisms would be very different, Liberals can find as much ideological justification to be critical of the European Union as any Eurosceptic Conservative. Whether this other side of the Liberal attitude to Europe will ever emerge, however, only time will tell.

5

Member State or Euro-Region? The SNP, Plaid Cymru, and Europe

James Mitchell

INTRODUCTION

Gellner argues that Nationalism is 'primarily a political principle, which holds that the political and national unit should be congruent' (Gellner 1983: 1). Implicit in this is the idea that forces outside the nation have no right to interfere in the nation's affairs. Hence, classical nationalist thinking viewed international organizations with suspicion and supranational organizations as contrary to the natural order. Nationalists of any sort would be expected to be opposed to the process of European integration and 'ever closer union'. Yet, both the Scottish National Party (SNP) and Plaid Cymru (PC) are today strong supporters of the European Union, though, for much of their recent past, the two parties were deeply hostile to European integration. This has roots early in the history of both parties.

The main cleavage inside the SNP has been that between 'fundamentalists' and 'pragmatists' (Mitchell 1996).[1] Since the party's inception, this has been a perennial tension which has occasionally undermined unity. In any party, particularly a radical party, there is likely to be tension between pragmatists willing to compromise and those who adopt a more fundamentalist position. From a pragmatic perspective this tension is about strategy, though fundamentalists

I would like to thank Laura McAllister at the Liverpool Institute of Public Administration and Management for assistance with this chapter.

[1] In an earlier article (Mitchell 1990), I distinguished between fundamentalists and gradualists, the latter being defined as those willing to accept devolution as a stepping stone to independence. It would be more accurate to refer to these SNP members as pragmatists as they would move to independence immediately if circumstances permitted.

often doubt the sincerity of pragmatists' support for the party's stated objectives. The key debates in the SNP since its foundation in 1934 have been about devolution, that is home rule short of independence, whilst in Plaid, there has been a tension between cultural/linguistic nationalism and political nationalism (McAllister 1995: ch. 6). Plaid has generally been willing to cooperate with other organizations and movements, including the Campaign for Nuclear Disarmament, the environmental movement, and, most notably, Welsh language organizations. More than the SNP, Plaid has been relaxed in seeing itself as a pressure group and part of a wider political movement as well as a political party. In neither case could it be said that international or supranational organizations have been central concerns until relatively recently. This is hardly surprising, since the nationalism of the state,[2] or 'official nationalism', such as UK/British nationalism, may be threatened internally by disintegration or externally by supranational organizations (Kellas 1991: 52). On the other hand, given the national context in which they exist, Scottish and Welsh 'secessionist' nationalisms are inevitably more concerned with relations between the 'nation' and 'state'. It might be expected on the issue of European Union membership that fundamentalists would be opposed while pragmatists would support it, at least so long as they saw some benefit accruing from membership, but more often divisions on Europe cut across the key fundamentalist–pragmatist cleavage. In large measure this is because Europe has been of secondary importance. Attaining self-government or protecting the language has been the priority for these parties.

SUPPORT FOR A UNITED EUROPE

Before the 1960s electoral breakthrough, the SNP and Plaid were in favour of a united Europe, however ill-defined. Each party saw international organizations offering a stable environment for small countries in a potentially hostile world. However, with both parties barely significant electorally their views were seen as irrelevant to mainstream political debates. Indeed, in both parties Europe was not

[2] There is a problem in describing the 'official nationalism' of the United Kingdom. Just as there is no agreed name for the nation associated with the government of the UK, as Richard Rose has pointed out (Rose 1982: 11), there is no accepted adjective to describe the nationalism of the state.

particularly important in internal debates prior to the 1960s. None-theless, both parties have uncovered past evidence of support for European integration and membership of supranational organizations to lend legitimacy, particularly for internal party purposes, to recent support for 'ever closer union' in Europe.

Though European integration made little impact on British politics in the 1920s and 1930s, Plaid supported an international role for Wales and expressed support for European integration. The founder of Plaid, Saunders Lewis, who was the 'outstanding personality' in its 'little company of "highbrows"' (Coupland 1954: 374), placed Welsh independence in a European context (Lewis 1926, 1938). This theme was picked up in *Y Ddraig Goch* (The Red Dragon) and the *Welsh Nationalist*, the party's newspapers in the 1930s. Plaid remained committed to supporting European integration after the Second World War but the issue did not become salient until the 1960s. The party played an active role in the International Congress of European Communities and Regions, established by regionalist and decentralist forces following the Hague Congress of 1948, and committed to the establishment of a decentralized, federal Europe. However, it would be wrong to suggest that Europe was central to Plaid's message. Welsh Nationalists would later play up the existence of Plaid's early Europhilia, but not always in context. In fact, European integration was of little significance for Plaid for much of the party's existence.

A similar situation existed in the SNP. The party's support for European integration developed in the 1940s and 1950s with a series of resolutions supporting Scottish membership of the European Coal and Steel Community (ECSC), and European integration. Conference resolutions in 1943 and 1948 committed the party to a position broadly similar to its current stance of independence in Europe (National Library of Scotland (NLS), Acc. 6419). Like Plaid a decade before, the SNP leadership placed Scottish independence within a European framework (Young 1948). This position persisted through-out the 1950s, though the issue was barely significant in British or Scottish politics. The SNP called for separate Scottish representation in the ECSC and was critical of the British government for failing to support the French proposal for a European Defence Community in 1954.

There was still some debate within the parties and concern that European integration would prove detrimental to the causes of Scottish and Welsh nationalism. One internal criticism was that the SNP was removing British government, and replacing it with the European government of Scotland. But an article in the *Scots Independent*, its semi-independent house journal, suggested that 'exchanging one controlling authority for that of a whole set of nations' was less threatening as European integration was 'very different from that of subjection to a single and much greater nation' (*Scots Independent*, 23 April 1955). Being part of a large European authority was deemed less threatening to Scottish and Welsh national identity than being part of a smaller, but more tightly organized British state, a persistent theme amongst pro-integration nationalists. Another theme was the notion that Scotland and Wales were 'European nations'. Saunders Lewis in Wales frequently made this point (McAllister 1995: ch. 5). Scottish nationalists argued that the Roman law base of the Scottish legal system meant that it had more in common with European legal systems than it had with English common law. In 1956, a prominent Scottish nationalist argued: 'We are a European people, and instinct and interest alike should align us with our European kindred . . . Let us stand by the folk with whom we have a genuine common interest—let us create a European authority' (Dott 1956).

In this early period, the hazy notion of European integration appeared less threatening to many Scottish and Welsh nationalists than the reality of British rule. The former was believed to be more pluralist, decentralist, and without a single centre of power. But, again, it should be stressed, debates on Europe amongst Scottish and Welsh Nationalists were of limited significance.

OPPOSING EUROPEAN INTEGRATION IN THE 1960s
AND 1970s

A number of developments combined to turn the SNP and Plaid against European integration. Support for integration in principle in the late 1950s had been relatively painless, and potentially advantageous, but the Treaty of Rome establishing the EEC and the European Atomic Energy Community (Euratom), made the idea more concrete. British governments also came to support membership, removing the possibility of the SNP and Plaid distinguishing themselves on the issue. Indeed, a new criticism was now voiced by the nationalists that British membership would drag Scotland and Wales into the European Communities against the interests and wishes of the Scottish and

Welsh people. The EEC was now portrayed as centralized, bureaucratic, and inimical to self-government.

In addition, the two parties grew in the early 1960s with members joining with a background of anti-nuclear campaigning. There had always been a strong pacifist element within the SNP and Plaid and the foundation of the Campaign for Nuclear Disarmament (CND) had a considerable impact on both parties, especially after Labour abandoned its short-lived unilateralism in the early 1960s. The European Community, and especially Britain's membership of it, was now thought to erode national self-government and operate as a means of extending American influence. In the SNP, many of these new members came to prominence within a decade and ensured that an anti-EEC policy became fairly firmly entrenched. Opposition to the EEC amongst the Scottish and Welsh publics also played its part with the Nationalists able to play a populist card against Europe. In 1971, Scotland had the highest proportion of opponents of EEC membership. A poll showed 81 per cent of Scots opposed to joining the Community and only 14 per cent in favour.

The anti-EEC mood within each party strengthened in the 1970s. Though there were supporters of European integration both parties' leaderships managed the issue sufficiently well to give an impression of unity. Plaid's policy hardened after its 1969 conference focusing on the absence of Welsh representation in negotiations for EEC membership. The CAP was also viewed as a threat to Welsh interests and the notion of the EEC as an American satellite was put forward. The importance of CAP was both economic and cultural. The decline of Welsh agriculture, which CAP was assumed to threaten, would destroy Welsh-speaking agricultural communities.

In 1970 Donald Stewart won the Western Isles becoming the first SNP member returned at a general election. In that election, he had argued against EEC membership largely on the grounds that it would damage the fishing industry (Stewart 1994: 38). The importance of fishing constituencies in north-east Scotland to the SNP in the 1970s meant that the interests of this industry exerted considerable influence. An SNP delegation visited the European Commission and Billy Wolfe, party chairman from 1969 to 1979, articulated the view commonly held at this time:

The SNP delegation which went to Brussels has confirmed our view that it is the aim of the Common Market to establish political domination of the whole of Western Europe and to tolerate no deviations from this line. The Common Marketeers of today are as much doctrinaire centralists as their opposite numbers in the Kremlin in Moscow. Their political philosophy is insidious to those who are steeped in democratic tradition. They say 'To be big is good; to be bigger is to be better; to be biggest is to be supreme. To be centralised is to be efficient; to be a Common Market organisation man is to be one of Europe's chosen people.' It is no accident that the English Parties have indicated their strong wish to go into the Common Market. To do so is the logical continuation of their centralist thinking which has been so damaging to Scotland's people and to Scotland's economy. (Wolfe 1973: 139)

THE 1975 REFERENDUM ON CONTINUED EC MEMBERSHIP

The 1975 referendum on continued membership of the EC was important in the history of both Plaid and the SNP. With Labour and the Conservatives divided over Europe, Nationalists had an opportunity to associate themselves unambiguously with an anti-EC position, something particularly attractive given that most Scots opposed EC membership. In January 1975 only 29 per cent of Scots favoured continued membership and 45 per cent were against (Butler and Kitzinger 1976: 148). The Nationalists hoped that a majority of Scots and Welsh would vote to leave the EC while a majority in England, and thereby perhaps of the United Kingdom, would vote to stay in. This was made possible to test since the count took place within the local government boundaries which allowed Scottish, Welsh, and English results to be known separately. The decision to hold local counts had been a gamble by the Labour government which had paid off. A majority in Scotland and Wales voted for continued membership though by a smaller margin than in Britain as a whole. A UK-wide count would have given the Nationalists the opportunity to suggest that Scotland and Wales had been more hostile than was actually the case. The existence of official figures showing that Scotland and Wales had both convincingly voted for continued membership undermined the Nationalists.

At a special SNP National Assembly meeting in January 1975, the party had voted almost unanimously to campaign for a 'No' vote in the referendum. There was, however, an element of ambiguity in its message. Five of the SNP's eleven MPs were thought to be sympathetic to EC membership. The SNP campaigned under the slogan,

TABLE 5.1. *Result of EC membership referendum, 1975*

Nation	Turnout (%)	'Yes' vote (%)	'No' vote (%)
England	64.6	68.7	31.3
Wales	66.7	64.8	35.2
Scotland	61.7	58.4	41.6
N. Ireland	47.5	52.1	47.9
UK	64.0	67.2	32.8

'No—on anyone else's terms'. Less hostile party members emphasized their opposition to the British terms of entry and suggested that
membership might have been possible if separate Scottish terms were
agreed. The focus of grievance for these members was the British
government. Oil, fishing, and Norway were key themes in the SNP
campaign (Criddle 1978: 57–8). The discovery of North Sea oil, with
its potential to make Scotland extremely wealthy, was an important
element in SNP propaganda. The prospect of an EC Common Energy
Policy was thought likely to undermine the SNP's potent slogan—
'It's Scotland's oil'. The fishing industry was deemed under threat
from a Common Fisheries Policy. The Norwegians had voted against
joining the EC in 1972 and this small, highly successful Scandinavian
country was offered as a model for a future independent Scotland to
follow.

Plaid proved less united than the SNP on EC membership. The
more hostile element within the party attacked the EC itself. The party
campaigned under the slogan, 'Europe Yes, EEC No' but Dafydd
Wigley MP played no part in the campaign as his preference for
independent Welsh membership of the EC was not on offer. Later,
as leader of the party, he was to argue that Plaid had finally come to
accept his viewpoint, though it might be countered that a wholly
different situation prevailed in the 1990s (McAllister 1995: ch. 7).
Added to this, the veteran Welsh Nationalist, Saunders Lewis called
on voters to abstain (Balsom and Madgwick 1978: 78). Plaid produced a volume of study papers on the EC in the run-up to the EC
referendum which demonstrated an ambiguous attitude to EC
membership. The party fought two quite distinct campaigns in the
referendum. As part of the 'Wales Get Britain Out' campaign, the
party forged some links with Welsh trade unionists. In rural, Welsh-

speaking Wales it campaigned more as an independent body (Balsom and Madgwick 1978: 79).

What became clear in the referendum was that support for continued membership of the EC was fairly uniform across Britain as a whole. Pro-EC forces in Scotland targeted SNP constituencies where it was assumed there was the greatest prospect of a 'No' vote, and only the Western Isles and Shetland voted against continued membership. In Wales, Plaid's support was much more concentrated. The official figures suggested that the party was out of step with its electorate. Rural, Welsh-speaking Wales appeared to be at least as strong in its support of continued EC membership as any other part of Wales. Gwynedd, the heartland of Plaid support, voted overwhelmingly in favour of continued membership. Part of the explanation lies in the strong support found amongst Welsh hill farmers for the EC, seen as a lucrative source of funds through the CAP.

The EC referendum was a salutary experience for the Nationalists. It demonstrated that support could dwindle in the course of a referendum campaign. There was little change in attitude amongst SNP supporters. However, between 20 and 40 per cent of those who had voted SNP at the previous general election failed to follow the party's

TABLE 5.2. *Result by Scottish region*

Region	Turnout (%)	'Yes' vote (%)	'No' vote (%)
Borders	63.2	72.3	27.7
Central	64.1	59.7	40.3
Dumfries and Galloway	61.5	68.2	31.8
Fife	63.3	56.3	43.7
Grampian	57.4	58.2	41.8
Highland	58.7	54.6	45.4
Lothian	63.6	59.5	40.5
Orkney	48.2	61.8	38.2
Shetland	47.1	43.7	56.3
Strathclyde	61.7	57.7	42.3
Tayside	63.8	58.6	41.4
Western Isles	50.1	29.5	70.5

TABLE 5.3. *Result in Wales by county*

County	Turnout (%)	'Yes' vote (%)	'No' vote (%)
Clwyd	65.8	69.1	30.9
Dyfed	67.5	67.6	32.4
Gwent	68.2	62.1	37.9
Gwynedd	64.3	70.6	29.4
Mid Glamorgan	66.6	56.9	43.1
Powys	67.9	74.3	25.7
South Glamorgan	66.7	69.5	30.5
West Glamorgan	67.4	61.6	38.4

Source: F. W. S. Craig, *British Electoral Facts, 1885–1975* (London)

lead, thus weakening the link with its new found electoral support (Butler and Kitzinger 1976: 153).

While pro-EC activists were working together and forging important links for the future, in Scotland few valuable contacts were made with Eurosceptics in other parties during the cross-party campaigning of the referendum. In Wales, some links were established with the trade unions but these were insufficient to win the 1979 referendum on devolution.

In Scotland, one of the most significant developments was the emergence of the Scottish Labour Party (SLP) in 1975. The SLP broke from Labour over devolution and though commanding little support it articulated the case for independence in Europe. Jim Sillars, its founder and a Labour MP from 1970, had been an opponent of EC membership campaigning vigorously for a 'No' vote in the referendum. In 1973, Sillars founded the Scottish Labour EC 'watchdog

TABLE 5.4. *SNP supporters during 1975 referendum (%)*

	28 Jan.–5 Feb.	25 Feb.–5 Mar.	27 Mar.–4 Apr.	28 Apr.–2 May	26–30 May
Pro	25	26	22	21	20
Anti	55	58	58	59	58
DK	20	16	20	20	21

Source: Butler and Kitzinger 1976: 151.

committee' to monitor developments as they affected Scotland. However, Sillars had argued from the early 1970s that if Britain was to join the EC it would be in Scotland's interests to seek independent membership. In 1973 he insisted that if Britain stayed in Europe he would become a Scottish Nationalist (Benn 1989). The SLP was short-lived, but it planted the idea of Scottish independence in Europe more firmly than any pro-EC SNP member did at the time and was a precursor of SNP policy a decade later.

In the mid-1970s, both parties claimed to see EC membership as a threat to Scottish and Welsh identity and 'sovereignty'. On Europe, both parties appeared to have adopted hard-line, fundamentalist positions, whereas on devolution both parties were quite pragmatic at that time. On the other hand, opposition to EC membership might be seen as having a pragmatic or strategic, indeed populist, motivation. The issue of European integration was less important for the Nationalists than was the use to which it could be put in pursuit of the goal of independence. It had become much more significant as an issue compared with earlier years but was still only of secondary significance.

THE TRIUMPH OF EUROPE IN THE SNP

In time Nationalists came to accept, indeed embrace, European integration. Developments within the SNP and Plaid, changes in the EC itself, and more particularly changed perceptions of the Community, as well as developments in British politics all played a part in the evolution of policy towards Europe. Plaid recovered more quickly from the problem of losing the 1975 referendum. The SNP could take some comfort from poll findings which showed that 70 per cent of Scots wanted to have independent representation in Brussels. But it was Sillars who took up that theme with greatest skill.

The early 1980s was a period of internal divisions and rancorous debates on strategy. The failure of devolution and the loss of seats at the watershed general election in 1979 provoked intense battles within both parties. The pragmatist-fundamentalist fault-line within the SNP was opened up. The main issue of contention was the party's attitude to devolution. The hard-liners saw devolution as a means of dissipating the party's energies and diluting its message. The pragmatists feared that the party would appear out of step with Scottish public opinion and lose ground if it opposed devolution. In Wales, the heavy defeat of devolution meant that a complete rethink on strategy was necessary. A party inquiry was conducted setting out the alternatives.

As twenty years before, a new wave of members joined in the 1980s, particularly in the SNP and many of the key figures from the 1960s and 1970s lost ground in internal party politics. The demand for a new strategy, focusing more on Scotland's central belt and less on the fishing communities of the north-east, came to be articulated inside the SNP. A new generation came to the fore who were more open in their attitude to European integration. An organized faction, calling itself the '79 Group, was set up in 1979 following the loss of nine of the SNP's eleven seats at the general election. Sillars joined this new group on joining the party in 1980. The group, self-styled socialist and republican, argued for a more radical image for the party. Its main aim was to change the party's strategy and give priority to Scotland's Labour-dominated central belt.

The '79 Group's two leading members—Sillars and Stephen Maxwell—were divided on the issue of Europe, with Sillars a strong supporter of independence in Europe and Maxwell opposed. Equally, the group's main opponents within the party were divided on Europe. While leading opponents of the Group, including veteran Nationalists Robert McIntyre and Winnie Ewing, came to support European Community membership, others including Douglas Henderson and Jim Fairlie (successively deputy leaders in the early 1980s) were against. Yet no clearly defined faction developed on the issue of EC membership. It remained of secondary importance in party debates cutting across the fundamentalist-pragmatist divide. Though some hard-liners argued that devolution and membership of the EC undermined Scottish sovereignty, they represented only a small group within the party. In the late 1980s, Jim Fairlie resigned from the SNP and along with others joined the uninfluential Scottish Sovereignty Movement.

Because divisions on Europe did not correlate with the main fault-line in the SNP, it did not resonate as it might have done in internal debates and failed to result in polarization. Resolutions continued to be passed at annual conference critical of the EC but there was little serious debate until the late 1980s. The party supported a referendum following independence and the renegotiation of Scotland's terms of membership, allowing for sufficient ambiguity to cover differences of opinion.

The SNP were unprepared for the 1983 election. It held its two seats but its vote dropped from 14 per cent to 12 per cent while Plaid held its two seats with 7.8 per cent of the vote. This made both parties highly conscious of the damage that could be done through internal battles. A 'new realism' and desire to find common ground emerged after the 1983 election. Gordon Wilson, SNP chairman from 1979, proposed a reconsideration of its position on devolution, NATO membership, and the European Community. Devolution was the most contentious, dividing the party on its fundamentalist-pragmatic fault-line. Wilson asserted that support for independence gave the party its energy and dedication, but that by appearing intransigent the SNP was not furthering its cause, erecting a barrier between the party and the electorate. From 1983 the party moved away from its hard-line position and the following year the annual conference voted to support a constitutional convention.

The SNP while consistently opposed to nuclear weapons, historically had a more ambivalent attitude towards NATO membership. This ran contrary to the view that international organizations offered small countries protection, but reflected the deep-rooted opposition to nuclear weapons and substantial pacifist wing inside the SNP. For Wilson, NATO offered a means of removing the accusation that an independent Scotland would be vulnerable in terms of its defence. However, though the party moved to some extent, it rejected his proposal.

Wilson proposed that the party should abandon its anti-EC stance. There was some opposition to this but gradually the party adopted a pro-EC position. In 1983, this proved the least controversial of Wilson's proposals. Indeed, many bitter opponents during the days of the '79 Group came to find common ground on the issue of Europe. If anything, Europe helped to heal wounds in the party. As it became more pro-EC, the issue became more salient both in internal and, more significantly, in public debates. In the European Parliament elections in 1984, the SNP sounded more pro-EC than it had done for over twenty years. Its manifesto challenged the notion that the EC would become a centralized superstate, arguing that the enlargement of the Community had 'diluted some of the dangers of centralism'. Echoing the views expressed in the *Scots Independent* thirty years before the manifesto asserted that 'The bigger it gets, the looser it becomes.'

But the change in outlook was not always smooth. In 1986, the party's membership rejected a national executive committee paper which maintained that the SEA did not threaten national sovereignty.

Sillars became particularly active on the issue producing papers, making speeches, and giving leadership to the pro-EC elements within the party. Winnie Ewing, MEP for the Highlands and Islands, had become a passionate Europhile, and still commanded considerable support amongst older and more traditional party members. Sillars and Ewing proved a formidable combination.

External events were also important. The EC had gone through a difficult period after Britain had joined, largely due to the economic malaise which afflicted the international economy, but also because of disputes over Britain's contribution to the EC budget. The resolution of the budgetary disputes and the upturn in the international economy marked an opportunity for further European integration. Within a fortnight of the new European Commission being appointed in 1985, the new President Jacques Delors suggested the removal of all borders inside Europe by 1992 (Ross 1995: 3). From the SNP's perspective, the single most significant aspect of the Delors presidency was the high public profile which European integration attained. The moves towards 'ever closer union' were significant, but the manner in which 'Europe' caught the imagination of Europe's publics, and not only its elites, was notable.

At its 1988 party conference, the SNP launched its 'independence in Europe' policy. The SNP more than any party operating in Scotland, set the European agenda in Scottish politics and forced its opponents to react to it. The Liberal Democrats, who had been more consistently pro-integration than the SNP had difficulty competing. Even some of their prominent members, publicly affirmed their support for Scottish independence in Europe, at least in the long term. The Labour Party struggled to attach a European dimension to their devolutionist proposals. David Martin, Labour MEP for the Lothians, proposed the vague notion of a 'Europe of the Regions'. The idea of establishing a European office of the Scottish Parliament was proposed and some vague proposals to allow representatives from the Scottish Parliament to join the British permanent representation in Brussels emerged. None of these caught the public imagination, all were reactions to the SNP's 'independence in Europe' line and some were unworkable. In office, the Conservatives also found it necessary to 'Europeanize' their policies and proposed the establishment of an information office in Brussels (Mitchell 1995).

Serendipity played its part, but there was an element of strategic thinking in the SNP's new policy. For Sillars, Europe offered a means of making independence both electorally possible and more economically viable (Sillars 1986). The 1988 Inverness conference represented the public proclamation of a change that had been evolving. A few leading figures from the 1960s and 1970s including Isobel Lindsay and Tom McAlpine expressed their dissent. Lindsay argued that only independence outside the EC would give Scotland the opportunity to 'pursue the same strategy as the successful small states in Europe who have remained outside the EC' (*Scotsman*, 13 November 1988). But Lindsay's influence was on the wane and she later defected to the Labour Party.

The Maastricht Treaty caused controversy inside the SNP but in a quite different way from that which occurred inside Labour and Conservative parties. The German government had successfully argued for special institutional arrangements for the Länder, the regional tier of government. The Länder feared that they would be cut out of decision-making with progress towards 'ever closer Union'. A consultative Committee of Regions (CoR) was proposed. The Conservative government, struggling to get the Maastricht legislation through the Commons, needed every vote it could get. The Scottish Secretary Ian Lang negotiated a deal in early 1993 with Margaret Ewing, leader of the three SNP MPs, to give Scotland between six and eight members of the CoR in exchange for SNP support. The SNP MPs joined with the Tories provoking criticism from the media and within the party. The MPs only narrowly won support for winning the 'concession' from the party's national executive committee. The matter did little immediate and no long-term damage to the SNP, in spite of vociferous attacks by the Scottish media. It did, however, remind party leaders that they had to be more anti-Tory than pro-European integration.

The SNP's change of policy and emphasis on the European dimension forced the other parties to reconsider their policies and to push Europe up the political agenda in Scotland. The SNP had become an agent for 'Europeanization', a very different role from that which it had played a decade before.

THE TRIUMPH OF EUROPE IN PLAID CYMRU

Following the 1975 referendum, Welsh Nationalists focused on the case for strong Welsh representation in Brussels. According to Plaid the result changed the debate on Welsh self-government in two respects. First, membership of the EC made 'full national status an urgent necessity to get fair representation' and second, it made devolution 'outmoded . . . Now that Wales is governed by Brussels as well as by London, the importance of London will diminish in the minds of the people' (quoted in Balsom and Madwick 1978: 85). The party claimed to be in a no-lose situation: 'From the very beginning, we have recognised that EEC membership, whilst bad for Wales, is good for Plaid' (quoted in Balsom and Madwick 1978: 80). Plaid joined other European nationalist and regionalist movements to found the short-lived lobbyist 'Bureau of Unrepresented Nations', soon overtaken in 1978 by the European Free Alliance (EFA), which signed a Charter for Europe, calling for a Europe of Regions (Hix 1996: 315). Plaid's involvement with such bodies was always greater than the SNP's, because it had less concern at being associated with parties which demanded self-government short of independence and was more prepared to act as a pressure group than a party aspiring to govern. This reflected the view amongst many in the party that it should be a movement and pressure group and not just a conventional political party.

The devolution referendum in 1979 proved a serious setback for Plaid. Only one-fifth of voters supported Welsh devolution with Gwynedd recording the highest 'Yes' vote at only 34 per cent. At the subsequent general election, Plaid lost one of its seats, leaving it with two MPs, and its vote fell by 2.7 per cent to 8.1 per cent. As with the SNP, Plaid went through a period of introspection. A Commission of Inquiry was held which reported in 1981. This failed to resolve the key problems and tensions facing the party. Plaid needed to break out of Welsh-speaking Wales, but even there the vote for devolution had been limited. Defence of the language remained paramount. The European Community would be judged on this as much as any other matter.

While the SNP progressed to unequivocal support for independence in Europe, Plaid experienced a more tortuous period of European policy formulation reflecting internal party differences over the meaning of independence and the nature of European integration. A reassessment began with the 1983 party conference debating the merits of Welsh membership and the prospect of independence in Europe. The conference adopted a cautious approach at this time, in supporting a referendum on Welsh membership after self-government in which

Plaid would not campaign for or against European involvement (Plaid Cymru 1983). This policy was significant because it was neither pro- nor anti-EC, though it can be interpreted as a step on the way to a pro-European stance.

From 1984 until 1991, Plaid adopted a pro-European policy that had more in common with the 'Europe of the Regions' position of regionalists in Belgium, France, and Spain, and what Labour in Scotland later argued for, than the independence position of the Scottish National Party. The adoption of a regionalist approach to Europe was influenced by the party leader Dafydd Elis Thomas. This reflected an antipathy to the state and ideas of national sovereignty that had roots in the writings of Saunders Lewis. Elis Thomas's views had changed considerably, if gradually, from his earlier fairly hard-line belief in a Welsh nation state. In short, a utopian vision of a Europe without states lay at the heart of the notion of the Europe of Regions to which the leader came to subscribe. This was in line with other aspects of his leadership including the alliance with the Green Party in Wales (Lynch 1995). Plaid members could find common cause with some European institutions, notably the Council of Europe, in the support they gave to minority languages and cultures. In 1988, the Parliamentary Assembly of the Council of Europe approved a draft charter on regional and minority languages (*Agence Europe*, no. 4867, 6 October 1988).

In 1989 with the adoption of a two-stage strategy Plaid's position became clearer, though no less ambiguous. Following the SNP's example, Plaid campaigned around the theme of independence in Europe using independence as a first step towards Welsh autonomy. This would be followed by Wales taking its place within a decentra-lized Europe of the Regions as a regional state (*Welsh Nation*, May 1989). The party was therefore committed to a fundamental, if fairly imprecise, reform of the European Community, involving the aban-donment of the intergovernmental aspects of its organization, including the Council of Ministers and European Council.

Plaid had performed relatively well in the 1979 and 1984 Euro-elections and decided to give greater priority to the 1989 elections. Daffyd Elis Thomas was adopted as candidate in North Wales and considerable effort was put into winning the seat, but the party came third behind Labour and the Conservatives. Overall, the Welsh results were disappointing with only a slight increase in its share of the vote to 12.3 per cent, though Plaid did replace the Liberal Democrats as the third party in Wales. Plaid and the SNP tended to do better in Euro-elections than in elections to Westminster (the SNP scored its highest ever vote of 32.6 per cent in the 1994 Euro-elections), though this may well have had something to do with the electorate's perception that these were not first-order elections.

Dafydd Elis Thomas stood down as leader and was replaced by Dafydd Wigley, MP for Caernarfon, in 1991. Wigley was less utopian and under his leadership Plaid came to support independence in Europe. The notion of a Europe of Regions was not entirely banished from party literature, but Plaid adopted a stance similar to the SNP. The Maastricht debate highlighted one of the main differences between Plaid and the SNP. Plaid also engaged in negotiations with the government over the number of Welsh members of the Committee of the Regions. Whereas, the Scottish media lambasted the SNP for doing this, the Welsh media's treatment of Plaid was more informed and balanced. In part, this reflected the fact that Plaid was not engaged in the kind of trench warfare with Labour as the SNP but it also reflected Plaid's greater willingness to act as a pressure group for Welsh interests even if this undermined its image as a potential party of government.

EURO-REGIONALISTS VERSUS BRITISH NATIONALISTS?

As noted above, Scotland was fairly hostile to European integration in the 1970s. But this has changed. Around the time of the 1992 general election, 83 per cent of people in Scotland were in favour of remaining in Europe, including 83 per cent of Labour voters and 76 per cent of SNP supporters.[3] Though SNP supporters recorded the lowest levels of support for the European Community, there was a considerable change from the past. The Scottish levels of support for the EC were significantly higher than those in England, where 76 per cent of English voters were in favour of remaining in Europe.

In the years between 1974 and 1992, the percentages in each party which favoured withdrawal fell in Scotland. In England, by contrast, the percentage favouring withdrawal went up, both among electors as

---

[3] Data derived from the Scottish Election Study, directed by James Mitchell and Jack Brand, University of Strathclyde. The questionnaire and data are available from the ESRC archive, University of Essex, SN2368.ESR

TABLE 5.5. *Support for withdrawal from the EC by party*

	Con	Lab	Lib/LibDem	SNP
Scotland				
1974	14	32	14	32
1992	12	17	6	24
England				
1974	9	22	12	—
1992	22	27	20	—

a whole and in each party category. The SNP alone cannot be credited for this change of public opinion, but arguably played a significant part in this process. In the late 1980s, the SNP set the European agenda, forcing the other parties to upgrade their European profiles.

Other questions elicit similar conclusions. In 1979 and 1992, voters were asked to signify the degree of their support for the EC. Given the differences between the questions asked, it is not possible to compare the results in terms of magnitudes, but one can compare the ordering of parties in terms of support. The SNP was the most anti-EC party. In 1979, the average scores can be seen from Tables 5.6 and 5.7.

In France, it has been noted that supporters of domestic decentralization are also more likely to be supporters of European integration and vice versa (Dolez 1991). The evidence in Scotland is mixed. Support for European integration corresponds to some extent with a Scottish identity rather than a British identity.

However, support for continuing in Europe was not associated with the constitutional option selected by the voters. Among those who selected the official SNP policy of independence in Europe, 86 per

TABLE 5.6. *Support for the EC, 1979*

Conservative	5.5
Liberals	4.3
Labour	4.1
SNP	3.4

Note: Electors were asked to give the EC marks out of 10 with a high score indicating support for the EC.

TABLE 5.7. *Support for uniting Europe, 1992*

	Scotland	England
Labour	4.4	5.5
LibDem	5.1	6.4
SNP	5.2	—
Conservatives	5.8	6.6

Note: Electors were asked to give a mark on a scale of 1 to 11 but this time a low score indicates support for the EU.

TABLE 5.8. *Strength of Scottish identity and support for the EC, 1992 (%)*

	Scottish not British	Scottish more than British	Equally Scottish and British	British more than Scottish	British not Scottish
Continue	80	83	83	91	73
Withdraw	20	17	17	9	27

cent wanted to continue in Europe, as with 84 per cent of those who supported devolution and 86 per cent of those who favoured the constitutional status quo. In addition, the EC was somewhat less important for SNP voters than for the others and there was a common and high level of agreement that the EC had been good for Scotland; 62 per cent of both Labour and Nationalist voters agreed with this, as opposed to 64 per cent of Conservatives and 66 per cent of Liberals.[4]

Though the SNP has been at the forefront of campaigns for independence in Europe it has not been the exclusive recipient of the increased support for constitutional change. Support for the SNP is not the same as support for independence or home rule, nor does it equate with Scottish national identity. Labour and SNP voters have been remarkably similar (Brand et al. 1994a, 1994b) and support exists across the parties for the different constitutional options. Prior to the 1992 election the greatest impact the SNP's independence in Europe campaign achieved would appear to have been on the debate on Europe rather than on Scotland's constitutional status.

---

[4] Data derived from the Scottish Election Study, directed by James Mitchell and Jack Brand, University of Strathclyde. The questionnaire and data are available from the ESRC archive, University of Essex, SN2368.ESR

NATIONALISTS AND REGIONALISTS IN THE EUROPEAN PARLIAMENT

The SNP was given a seat in the unelected European Parliament and its sitting member Winnie Ewing became the elected Member of the European Parliament for the Highlands and Islands in 1979. She was to be their only MEP until the 1994 European elections when Allan Macartney was elected in North-East Scotland. Plaid have failed to win a seat in Wales despite strenuous efforts to win the North Wales seat. Nonetheless, Plaid's involvement in organizations representing various nationalist and regionalist parties in Europe has been more extensive than the SNP's. The problem for the SNP in the early 1980s was that it had few obvious allies in the Parliament. But it made sense to join a group as it offered greater opportunities for participating in debates and on committees as well as financial support from the European Parliament. In the European Parliament, Ewing initially sat in a grouping which included the French Gaullists and the Irish Fianna Fáil. This caused some controversy inside the SNP because the group was perceived to be right wing.

The European Free Alliance (EFA) had emerged in the early 1980s as a loose collection of regionalist and nationalist parties but with little support in the European Parliament, and as such had little appeal for the SNP. The EFA existed as an extra-Parliamentary coalition with Plaid playing a more active part in its proceedings than the SNP.

The accession of Spain strengthened the regional movement in the European Community. In 1989 a Rainbow Group within the European Parliament was formed, with EFA involvement, which Ewing joined. It largely consisted of regionalist and nationalist parties. The inclusion of the Italian Lega Nord caused some trouble with its anti-immigrant rhetoric, free market ideology, and the possibility of it joining in an Italian government which included neo-fascists. The SNP were attacked for their association with the Lega. Plaid suspended its membership of EFA in April 1994 for a brief period over the matter, causing the SNP even more problems. The situation was defused when EFA suspended the Lega. After the 1989 elections a new regionalist grouping emerged, the European Radical Alliance (ERA) in the European Parliament which did not include the Lega. The six Lega Nord MEPs somewhat embarrassingly joined the European Liberal Democrats, who only a few years before had been attacking the SNP for participating in a group with the Lega. The

ERA was not without controversy either. The largest party within it was the French party, Energie Radical, whose leader Bernard Tappie faced criminal charges in France. The European Parliament's groups are fairly loose and Ewing and Macartney have used membership as a means of maximizing their own impact in the Parliament. To date, they have proved of little significance in internal party politics with most members probably unaware of the name and nature of the group which the SNP MEPs have joined.

CONCLUSION

The European Union presents both challenges and opportunities for the SNP and Plaid. Both parties have come to terms with membership to a greater extent than Labour or Conservative parties. In part this may be because they are secessionist parties and do not face the immediate prospect of forming a government. The real challenge might come if Scotland and Wales were independent. Would the Euro-enthusiasm of the SNP and Plaid remain? On the other hand, many small states in Europe have been better able to come to terms with European integration than the larger states. Constitutional politics, questions of sovereignty, and power are the essence of the politics of both the SNP and Plaid. Hard-liners still exist in each party but they have become a minority. The fundamentalist–pragmatist divide in the SNP is not replicated in their debates on Europe.

The perception of European integration differs in the two parties. The SNP has been more consistent in supporting a Europe of states with some supranational component. Plaid, on the other hand, has been more sympathetic to the idea of a Europe of Regions, involving a very different construction of European integration. Europe is seen as a means of transforming debate on the constitutional status of Scotland and Wales but in different ways. Plaid's more 'utopian' tendency has more often emphasized changes in the European Union as the motor for change in Wales. The EU is now important to the SNP but it does not wish the EU to be anything other than an intergovernmental body with some supranational elements. The SNP is, in this sense, much more of a traditional nationalist party than Plaid with its regionalist tendencies.

During the Delors presidency, efforts were made by the European Commission to win support for 'ever closer union' from a wide range of interests. Regions and regionalist movements were included in this appeal. Fears that European integration would undermine the position of small states and regions within Europe were assuaged. The SNP and Plaid were also receptive to a body which was at odds with the Thatcher government.

Perhaps even more significant than the conversion of the SNP and Plaid in the 1980s was the conversion of Scotland and Wales to the idea of Europe. In this respect, both Nationalist parties played an important role. Plaid's support for European integration had an impact on Welsh politics and played a part in the development of a more positive attitude towards Europe in the Welsh Labour Party. This was particularly significant because the party was strongly opposed to European integration in the past. In Scotland, the SNP had a role as agenda setter on Europe, forcing other parties to 'Europeanize' their policies in the late 1980s. The SNP and Plaid played a significant part in heightening awareness and support for European integration in Scotland and Wales.

6

The Integration of Labour? British Trade Union Attitudes to European Integration

Ben Rosamond

INTRODUCTION

Trade unions have always been important players in British debates about European integration. There are two reasons why this should not be surprising. First the economic emphasis of the integration project has consistently held implications for the largely industrial domain populated by unions. The Treaty of Rome and its successors promised a large scale reordering of economic activity with consequent effects for employment, industrial relations, labour law, social policy, and other areas within the immediate reach of legitimate union concern. Secondly, the engagement of unions in broader political debates has been one of the most notable features of the post-war political economy of the UK. The largely permissive (if tokenistic) incorporation of union elites into the policy process under successive Labour and Conservative governments throughout the 1950s and 1960s afforded some legitimacy to the idea of unions as participants in the public debate about the future of the British economy and society. Moreover, the key role of a large number of unions in the Labour Party made trade union attitudes central to the conduct of political debate on the centre left of the political spectrum. Thus as the 'European question' penetrated the consciousness of the left in Britain, so unions became engaged. Both of these elements conspired to ensure that the trade union movement tended to fashion its responses to European integration in terms beyond either the concerns of specific industrial sectors or, for that matter, the business of an 'industrial' domain separable from wider socio-economic and political concerns.

BRITISH UNIONS AND EUROPE

It is necessary to make a distinction between the approach of the Trades Union Congress (TUC) and that of individual affiliated unions. As a peak association, the TUC exercises limited control over its affiliates and so it is impossible to treat the trade union movement as a unitary actor. It is certainly possible to speak of official TUC policy at any given time and the importance of policy debates within the framework of the TUC should not be underestimated. Some of the most bitter rhetorical exchanges in debates about European integration have taken place on the floor of Congress. At the same time, individual unions have always held distinctive positions on European-related questions. However, this sense of weakness should be qualified slightly. The TUC's resources of information, knowledge, and research capacity have enabled the General Council to accumulate 'European' expertise over time. This expertise has allowed the TUC's leadership to define the nature of the European environment within which unions operate and to act as the main agenda setter within the union movement on questions of European integration.

With the above provisos in mind it is useful to summarize the role played by unions in British debates about 'Europe' since the Second World War (for fuller accounts see Rosamond 1992, 1993*b*; and Teague 1984, 1989*b*). Unions have been most visible as participants in these debates during certain key 'flashpoints': 1962 following the decision of the Conservative government of Harold Macmillan to apply for membership of the European Community (EC); 1971–2 as the Heath government's terms of entry were finalized; 1975 during the referendum campaign; and 1988 following the provocative appearance of Commission President Jacques Delors at that year's Congress. This should not be taken as evidence of union engagement only occurring at points where the 'European issue' stood squarely in the public domain. Such a conclusion would ignore the long-standing research efforts of both the TUC and a number of its affiliates. The TUC's leadership (General Council) tended to frame the European question in terms of the economic costs and benefits which might be associated with membership of the EC and with certain developments at the European level. Many of the more overtly 'political' arguments about Britain and Europe were introduced into trade union policy discussions by representatives of individual unions.

A case in point was the TUC's activity in response to the

Conservative government's plan to set up a free trade area in Western Europe as a rival to the embryonic EEC in 1957. Here the General Council's report emphasized the imperative of economic prosperity defined largely in terms of the free trade area's impact upon employment levels (TUC 1957: 270–6). Similarly, the General Council's 1961 document 'European Economic Unity' made it plain that the peak association was most animated by the extent to which EC membership would advance or retard certain economic aspirations: 'the real test of European economic unity is whether it will promote full employment, economic growth and better living standards' (TUC 1961: 469). This 'wait and see' posture was the dominant motif of official Congress policy until the early 1970s. In a stance which anticipated the Major government's position on economic and monetary union by over two decades, the TUC's leadership held that a position on whether the UK should join the EC could not be made until the product of government-EC negotiations were known. However, in a manner familiar to students of the Conservative Party in the 1990s, this official policy held sway amidst some particularly vituperative debates on the floor of Congress and within the pages of various trade union and left-wing journals.

The TUC's self-consciously 'pragmatic' stance was challenged by a coalition of unions hostile to British membership of the EC and to a lesser extent by a smaller group which took the diametrically opposed view. Both groups, but particularly the anti-membership faction, fought without success throughout the 1960s to bring official TUC policy into line with their respective positions (cf. Rosamond 1992: 314–20). The 'antis' used a range of diverse arguments in support for their position. Membership was often taken to be the antithesis of Britain's national interest. More often than not this interest was defined as synonymous with the retention of the right to make economic policy at Westminster. It was also argued that membership of a narrow European club such as the EC would constitute an abdication of Britain's global role, a view which was frequently articulated with the concept of internationalism. One of the most interesting features of trade union debates in the 1960s and 1970s was the use of nationalist discourse on the 'anti-membership' side of the argument. Concerns for the decision-making autonomy of the British Parliament were developed into elaborate defences of sovereignty. When allied to core concerns for the left, it soon became apparent that the retention of parliamentary sovereignty in the UK was widely understood to be a necessary prerequisite for the development of socialist economic and social programmes in Britain. By definition, the project of European integration became detrimental to the interests of the British left. On the other side of the argument, representatives of pro-membership factions tended to argue that EC membership would allow British industry to have proper access to its fastest growing markets. There were attempts in the course of debates to counter the nation-state socialist position of the 'antis' with a more cosmopolitan, internationalist vision of socialism, but these always fell on deaf ears.

The anti-membership position gained ascendancy within the TUC coalition after 1971. That year's annual Congress saw the first victory for a motion expressing opposition to British membership of the Community and produced the first unequivocal statement from the General Council to that end (TUC 1971: 308–28). The transition from the 'wait and see' posture was accomplished in 1972, when the TUC declared its opposition 'in principle' to British membership (TUC 1972: 446–8). The 'anti' coalition was built in the first instance around the huge combined block vote of unions such as the Transport and General Workers (TGWU) and the Amalgamated Engineering Union (AEU), but also drew strength from the association of EC membership with the neo-liberal urges of the new Conservative government of Edward Heath.

Membership of the Community brought with it seats on a range of advisory committees to the Commission. As a token of continued hostility, the TUC chose to boycott these committees in spite of some significant opposition to this position. The result of the 1975 referendum saw the British union movement commencing its participation in the advisory committee structure, but official policy continued to oppose UK membership of the EC. The final flourish of the anti-membership policy arose in the run-up to the 1983 general election with an argument which drew on the main premises of the so-called alternative economic strategy (AES). The bulk of British trade unions advanced the argument that the reconstruction of the British economy could only be accomplished with the reclamation of full economic sovereignty. Curtailing EC membership would allow both the erection of import controls and the immediate implementation of a recovery programme built around extensive government intervention (cf. TUC 1980: 283–8).

The membership question became less salient on the British left following the Conservative victory in the 1983 general election. The

European issue almost vanished from formal trade union debates, but the apparent silence masked two significant developments which were to influence trade union thinking on European integration in years to come. First, trade union leaders began to explore the strategic possibilities afforded by British membership of the Community. Following the termination of the TUC's boycott of the Commission's advisory committees in 1975, the evidence suggests that British union representatives sought to maximize and extend the influence of these institutions (Rosamond 1992: 193–9). To suggest, as Wendon (1994) does, that the union movement was slow to react to the internal market programme neglects the discussions which took place in the mid-1980s in bodies such as the Economic and Social Council (ESC). It was here that the TUC representatives began to develop the position that the liberalization of the internal market would only be acceptable with the implementation of adequate social protection. The debate within the union movement about the ill-fated 'Vredeling Directive' on the consultation of employees in multinational companies was illustrative of the general strategic reorientation. The preparatory research and lobbying by the TUC on this matter placed European-level company law and workers' rights onto the trade union agenda and the rhetorical dimensions of the TUC's response to Vredeling anticipated later statements which juxtaposed 'positive' developments at the European level with the intransigent tendencies of the British Conservative government (see TUC 1984: 392–404, 517–19).

The second development emerged from the general reorientation of thinking on the British left away from the combination of socialism and national political economy that produced the AES and towards Europe-wide strategies for the advancement of social progress. Volumes such as those edited by Stuart Holland (1983) and Ken Coates (1986) amounted to rebuttals of the nation-state socialist project. Coordinated, transnational programmes were both preferable and more plausible. The opening of this intellectual space was important because it displaced membership as the primary 'European question'. It also dovetailed with the new tendency of the TUC's leadership to think strategically about both the profitable use of available European arenas and the development of transnational trade union cooperation.

The memorable appearance of Jacques Delors at the 1988 TUC Congress was a very public signal of the 'new' trade union approach to European integration. Besides this important intervention by the

Commission President, the General Council presented a report to Congress entitled *Maximising the Benefits: Minimising the Costs* (TUC 1988*b*) and a composite motion with sponsorship across the trade union spectrum was passed. Both the report and the motion developed an agenda for action in the context of the forthcoming single market programme. There was a need to devote trade union research capacity to the task of understanding the important changes in the European environment. Information would need to be disseminated throughout the trade union movement and all of the TUC's activities would need to acquire a European dimension and core matters of collective bargaining would come increasingly under European-level influences. Cooperation between unions at a European level would constitute a vital adjunct to the general reorientation of the work of British trade unions. An important component of these public outputs, and here the contribution of Delors was vital, was the recognition that effective exploitation by unions of the new European agenda could have an important part to play in undermining the dominance of Thatcherism in the UK.

One of the more remarkable aspects of trade union engagement with the '1992' programme was the apparent consensus on the issue across the union movement. The fact that unions with very different basic assumptions about European integration were able to coalesce around a particular policy line, is testimony to both the agenda management skills of the General Council and to the importance placed upon the strategic use of the European dimension by a diversity of unions.

Unions appeared to fall into three groupings within the TUC coalition: 'pro-Commission' unions, 'left sceptics' and 'sectoral pragmatists' (Rosamond 1992: 204–90; 1993*b*: 427–9). The pro-Commission position, expressed by unions such as the AEU and the general GMB union, was supportive of the single market programme, provided that adequate social measures were in place to suppress the worst excesses of market restructuring. It advanced the cause of transnational trade unionism and saw deeper European integration as an opportunity to 'modernize' both the preoccupations and practices of British trade unions. Sectoral pragmatist unions were those with a predisposition to engage with an issue *only* when it had a direct impact upon their industrial sector. The Banking, Insurance and Finance Union (BIFU) became interested in the implications of the single market for the British finance industry.

Left sceptics tended to retain a critical view of European integration
as a project devised to serve the interests of capital. But by the late
1980s, unions such as the TGWU and Manufacturing Science and
Finance (MSF) had come to reject the efficacy of national programmes of economic renewal. Thus a premium was placed upon
the development of European-level strategies to overturn inequalities
in the distribution of wealth and in the labour market.

The policy coalition within the union movement was galvanized
by the emergence for a period of the 'social dimension' as the
central item of contention in British debates about Europe. The
argument canvassed very publicly by Jacques Delors, that the creation of the single market would require a portfolio of complemen-
tary measures to ensure workers' rights and social protection,
meshed well with the British left's developing argument about the
links between social justice and economic efficiency. In addition it
stood in marked contrast to the views of the British government,
which held that measures such as those proposed in the Commission's Social Charter (1989) and later in the so-called Social Chapter
of the Treaty on European Union (1992) constituted costs upon
employers and amounted to the interventionist re-regulation of the
labour market.[1] Lobbying in pursuit of the achievement of the aims
of the social dimension soon became the focal point of union
activity at all levels. Individual unions sought to raise awareness
among their memberships about the benefits of European-level stat-
utory workers' rights, calling upon negotiators to lobby employers at
the level of the shopfloor (cf. GMB 1990; TUC 1991). Elsewhere, as
Wendon (1994) notes, unions pursued a twin-track strategy of lobbying European institutions and seeking to consolidate and widen
transnational trade union linkages. TUC policy also became committed to the deepening of the EU's competence in the area of social
policy with the concurrent widening of the scope for qualified
majority voting in the Council of Ministers on social policy questions. The institutionalization of 'social partnership' at the European
level between unions and employers was also a priority (TUC
1996*b*).

---

[1] The 'Social Chapter' was excluded from the formal text of the Treaty on European
Union at the insistence of the British government at the final negotiations in Maastricht
in December 1991. The other member states (then eleven) signed a 'social protocol'
which allowed them to use the Community's institutions to enact legislation in social
policy and workers' rights.

Official TUC policy also came to support the principle of economic and monetary union (EMU). Support for UK entry into the Exchange Rate Mechanism of the European Monetary System (TUC 1989) was justified by the argument that the management of exchange rate parities would hold positive anti-inflationary and anti-recessionary consequences. Support for EMU was grounded in an acceptance of the argument that such a step would bring economic benefits. The UK should be ready to join (TUC 1996*a*). However, the crucial adjunct to this support was that targets for employment should achieve equal status to monetary targets. Moreover, a deeper 'social union', involving consultation rights for workers, the assurance of minimum incomes and measures to combat racism, should accompany the drive to full EMU (TUC 1996*a*).

The potential for future dilemmas is implicit in such contemporary trade union thinking about the EU. There is a marked dissonance between the formal TUC position, which has developed from the late 1980s and an apparent reorientation of priorities within the European Commission. The alliance with the Commission which has been in place since the late 1980s is beginning to show cracks in the mid-1990s. Formal policy statements from the Commission on Employment (1993, 1995) asserted that employment growth will follow from labour market flexibility. The suggestion that social protection and the promotion of social partnership are secondary aims has been reinforced by the non-interventionist Commissioner for Social Affairs, Padraig Flynn (*Financial Times*, 11 May 1995). Social policy is to be used at the European level, where necessary, to stimulate economic growth; otherwise it is to be regarded as a potential 'cost burden' to business (*Financial Times*, 13 April 1995). The Commission Vice-President and former Conservative Cabinet minister Leon Brittan argues:

The myth of an inexorable march forward of a more and more interventionist Europe is miles from the reality. Europe is cutting back on red tape and adopting a business-driven agenda. When I first went to Brussels my opposition to social legislation meant being looked at as if I wanted to send boys up chimneys in the Victorian era. Today keeping social costs down and a flexible labour market are the accepted watchwords. (*Financial Times*, 16 May 1996)

While the neo-classical tendencies within the Commission appear to foreclose the option of using Brussels as a direct ally in British trade union struggles, one should not anticipate a renationalization of union concerns and strategies. British unions are increasingly familiar with using European-level action as a means to pursue goals. Secondly, union preoccupations have become 'Europeanized'. This is most evident in the apparent cross-union consensus on the need for workplace rights which constitutes a major break with the 'voluntarist' traditions of British industrial relations (Taylor 1994*b*; Wedderburn 1995). Finally, the frame of reference for unions has also acquired a European dimension. These observations by John Monks, the General Secretary of the TUC, are typical:

[W]hen European Union Governments, other than our own, talk about deregulation, they often mean devolving responsibility for regulation to the social partners. That is why for the European Commission the watchwords are 'negotiated flexibility'. Unions and employers are seen as partners in the management of change. For them agreement is preferable to coercion. Developing the role of social partnership in regulating Britain's labour market along European lines is a central objective for the next century. (Monks 1995)

EXPLAINING UNION ATTITUDES TO 'EUROPE'

The most obvious observation is that British trade unions have moved from an anti-European posture, held for much of the post-war period, to a pro-European position. In other words they have migrated from a position which combined labourist goals with an allegiance to the retention of sovereignty in the UK. This 'old' stance emphasized that the virtues of collective bargaining and planning for full employment would be best achieved within a national framework. Accrual of powers by a supranational authority would diminish the ability of both unions and government to achieve economic and social progress in the UK. As a consequence, extensive European-level activity by trade unions was neither necessary nor particularly desirable. The 'new' position appears to recognize value in European-level activity, in terms of both lobbying and transnational trade unionism. It regards British membership of the EU as generally favourable for the UK's economic prospects and as a productive arena for the pursuit of trade union concerns. The latter continue to revolve around the need to promote higher levels of employment in macroeconomic policy, but no longer cherish the laissez-faire aspects of collective bargaining. Rather unions have become champions of the insertion of positive workers' rights into UK law. This is best achieved, goes the argument, with legislation at the European level.

Two further conclusions spring to mind. First, this is nothing less than a radical transformation in terms of their orientations to the European question. Secondly, this transformation is explained by the fact that unions have found good reason to embrace the European cause.

The forlorn experience of unions in the UK in the 1980s and 1990s might easily be advanced as a decisive determinant of changing attitudes. Moreover, domestic embitterment fuelled by a legislative and ideological onslaught at the hands of the Thatcherite Conservative government was readily juxtaposed with a union-friendly European Commission which appeared to espouse attractive ideas such as workers' rights and social partnership.

Arguments of this sort are commonplace (cf. Marsh 1992; Stirling 1991; Taylor 1994*a*) and frequently imply that the new pro-Europeanism of British unions amounts to little more than a cynical reflex to the opening of a window of opportunity. Two further arguments are used frequently. First, there is the suspicion that the deeply ingrained insularity of British trade union thinking remains intact in spite of the new cosmopolitan posturing. Secondly, there is the observation that the wholesale embrace of the social dimension is a dangerous affectation given the underlying neo-liberal thrust of contemporary European integration. Such views are not without merit, but they are not theorized and as such remain assertive. By attributing policy change to opportunism, they fail to address key questions about the broad context in which attitudes and policy choices are formulated. The strategic realignment of actors such as unions in the context of the internationalization of governance is worthy of deeper theoretical reflection. The next section seeks to explore how this might be done. Five structural elements are identified which provide boundaries of trade union thought and action in the area of European integration. This is not to say that union attitudes to Europe are simply determined exogenously, but rather that the setting of these boundaries is related to trade union practice. Moreover, such a framework, which concentrates on the complex interplay between agency and structure, should be useful for the deeper theorization of the relationship between British politics and European integration.

THE THEORETICAL BOUNDARIES OF
TRADE UNION ATTITUDES

A framework is necessary for understanding the evolution of British trade union attitudes to European integration across time. We can establish five 'boundaries' which both constrain and offer opportunities for trade union thought and action. These boundaries may be labelled the British macro-European debate, the European context, the domestic context, perceptions of trade union purpose, and 'knowledge'.

1. The British Macro-European Debate

The changing conduct of the European debate in British politics clearly offered constraints and opportunities for trade unionists. Between 1957 and 1983, trade unions were participants in a debate about British *membership* of the European Communities, which might be termed the 'old politics' of an economic 'club'. Thereafter the debate shifted to the appropriate shape of an economically and *politically* integrated Europe and the place of the UK within such an entity. Henceforth opposition to British membership became a marginal position (Rosamond 1993a). This shift afforded opportunities for the terms of debate to change. The 'new' politics of European integration began from the premiss that the membership issue was settled. Debate came to centre on the future of European integration and the place of Britain within that project.

The shift is important because it created the *image* of a major realignment in the European debate. It is true that actors on one side in the old politics may, of course, find themselves facing the same opponents in the new politics. But it is not enough to say that any given actor has become more 'pro' or more 'anti' European.

The question that needs to be addressed for trade unions is the strategic function of the new assumptions and arguments. Are they simply new discursive strategies to fight old oppositional battles against the Conservative government and proponents of labour market deregulation? Or is it necessary to attend to the *relational* aspects of the debate, so that the repositioning of one actor is intimately linked to the evolving positions of other actors? If the logic of the second question is followed, then it is possible to understand how the new politics helped to open up new terrain for trade union activity.

2. The European Context

Two aspects of the European debate are important. First, the extent to which trade union actors see themselves as legitimate contributors to debates about future British political economy. This is intimately connected to questions of trade union purpose and perceptions of the domestic context discussed under section 3 below. Second, the amount of European-level activity in areas of core trade union concern is discussed here.

Since its foundation, the EU has always had competence in the area of 'social policy' defined largely in terms of workplace-related issues. Articles 117–18 of the Treaty of Rome (1957) charged the Commission with the promotion of cooperation in the 'social field' and advanced the promotion of living and working standards. Articles 119–22 set objectives for equal pay for equal work and equal provision for paid holidays across the Community, and Articles 123–8 established the European Social Fund to promote employment opportunities and to facilitate labour mobility. The key to understanding the role of European social policy was contained in Articles 48–51 which sought to optimize the mobility of labour between member states. Thus, activity in these areas was seen as no more than a mechanism for the standardization of access to the putative common market. Also, as Purdy and Devine (1994) rightly note, the original treaty provisions on social policy did not aspire to denationalize the social and political aspects of citizenship.

Attempts to reactivate and expand EC-level social policy competencies throughout the 1970s were confronted and eventually defeated by widespread national reactions to recession throughout Europe. Therefore, for the bulk of the British trade union movement, solutions to economic crisis lay with national programmes enacted through the Westminster Parliament. Debate about issues such as employment law, social security, vocational training, and occupational health and safety sat beneath this national umbrella.

Activity at the European level had little strategic rationale for trade unions until the mid-1980s. The Single European Act (SEA) added modestly to the Community's social policy competencies, but was followed with the emergence of the Social Charter, the broad idea of 'social dimension' to the internal market programme and the attempt at Maastricht to give a treaty basis to the idea of workers' rights across the EU. The expansion of European-level activity and debate, along with the potential revolution in European labour law which was implied provided clear stimuli for the engagement of the British trade union movement (Bercusson 1992). Moreover, the spillover of new European directives into UK labour law laid the basis for positive connotations of European integration to become embedded in British trade union discourse (Miller and Steele 1993; Rosamond 1996).

The role of the Commission is also significant in the construction of union understandings of the European context. The General Council developed some important lines of dialogue with the Commission prior to the appearance of Delors at the TUC in 1988 (Rosamond 1992). The symbolic, but important, interventions by Delors were central to the emergence of the 'new' politics of European integration in the UK. In addition, the Commission's role as a 'purposive opportunist' (Cram 1994), should not be overlooked. Cram argues that as an institution the Commission has become particularly skilled at creating windows of opportunity for the advancement of its interests. This usually involves the building of alliances with important sectoral interest groups at key moments. In the case of the Directorate General of the Commission, responsible for employment, industrial relations, and social affairs (DGV), officials are constantly engaged in the business of constructing strategies to justify a long-standing agenda to expand the Community's social policy competence. Alliances with trade union actors might be construed as one element of that strategy. Thus, there is an 'intersubjective' component to union attitudes to Europe: perceptions and policies do not derive from a detached and sober analysis of the changing European environment, but from a more complex interplay with other actors and their ideas.

3. The Domestic Context

Much of the literature on British unions and European integration has tended to assume that reorientations of trade union attitudes are caused primarily by altered (and possibly even mistaken) perceptions of the efficacy of national institutions for the achievement of trade union goals (Dorfman 1977; Stirling 1991). The apparent 'Europeanization' of British trade unionism from the late 1980s is generally thought to derive from union perceptions of a developing dissonance between the possibilities of favourable policy enactment at the domestic and the European levels. By the late 1980s, goes the argument, British unions had been severely weakened through a legislative onslaught and union elites had been largely ejected from the policy-making process (for a good critical overview, see Marsh 1992). Indeed this perception was apparently widespread in trade union circles. Ron Todd, then TGWU General Secretary, announced memorably in 1988: 'In the short term we have not a cat in hell's chance of achieving [worker participation and industrial democracy] in Westminster. The only card game in town is in a town called Brussels' (TUC 1988*a*: 572). Such sentiments, juxtaposing the experience of the Conservative government in the UK with the comparatively union-friendly Delors Commission in Brussels, were commonplace in official policy briefings at all levels of the union movement. This successful construction of a positive European image also relied heavily on the polarization of the debate about Europe occasioned by the appearance of the '1992' internal market project. This debate forced the clear articulation of positions on 'Europe's future'. The appearance of a forthright version of Europe, apparently sanctioned by the Conservative leadership which combined anti-interventionist neo-liberal economics with a neo-conservative defence of sovereign statehood, provided a powerful impetus for the development of a plausible pro-European alternative. The slogan devised by the European Labour Forum, which deliberately subverted the message of Margaret Thatcher's Bruges speech, was typical: 'Socialism through the back door. Come in! Don't bother to knock!' (*European Labour Forum*, Winter 1990–1).

It might be that the sheer importance of the '1992' project and its spillovers into the social dimension and EMU, were so important to the recognized sphere of the labour movement, that a trade union response would have been inevitable regardless of the shrill rhetoric of the Conservative government. Such an argument may have some merit, especially if the arguments outlined below about trade union purpose are accepted. However, we should not underestimate the importance of hostile union perceptions of the domestic political economy in both galvanizing responses to developments in European integration and in cementing a policy coalition across the labour movement. Union attitudes in this area are best viewed as a kind of two-level game, where perceptions and interactions of the domestic context are intimately linked to understandings of the efficacy and the desirability of action at the European level.

4. *Perceptions of Trade Union Purpose*

The fourth boundary concerns the role which trade unions and trade unionists assign to themselves. It is important to consider whether unions understand themselves as reactive or proactive in relation to their environment. Do they see their role as gathering information about their environment and then formulating an appropriate response? Or is their role to be a 'shaper' of that external environment? The precise nature of reactivity or proactivity is related to core trade union concerns. In addition, there is the question of how unions define their external environment. The evidence of British unions from the late 1980s onwards is that a major re-evaluation of the external environment has taken place, with 'Europe' becoming a major component of that context.

Trade union purpose also includes whether they construe themselves as primarily 'industrial' or more broadly 'political' organizations. This again has an important bearing upon the European debate. The TUC's General Council and the leaderships of many of the larger trade unions have always understood themselves as significant players in broad national debates. Although for much of the period discussed, the General Council adopted a highly reactive posture to European-level developments. However, some unions consciously define their legitimate realm as not extending beyond the sectoral interests of their members. In the late 1980s, 'sectoral pragmatist' unions, such as the Banking, Insurance and Finance Union, saw their role as *responding* to the externally created European agenda as it affected their sector of industry.

Such narrow conceptions of trade union purpose are reinforced through practice, but are not immune to change. A culture of reaction to external stimuli suggests that the union movement would be sensitive to changes in the European agenda. One argument might be that this sensitivity facilitated a transition in core trade union concerns away from the promotion of British style 'collective laissez-faire' industrial relations towards a more 'continental' rights-based conception of the regulation of the labour market.

5. *Knowledge*

Unions also operate within a prevailing 'knowledge structure'. In other words, attitudes and actions tend to be guided by prevailing assumptions which promote certain strategies and prohibit others. So when confronted with data about European economic integration and the building of European institutions, unions do not have a 'free' choice. Responses depend upon the way in which that information is mediated through the lens of dominant assumptions. For example, the General Council's approach to Europe throughout much of the period under discussion was built around broadly Keynesian criteria for defining economic good. Membership of the Community would be acceptable if it advanced Britain's prospects for economic growth and allowed intervention to rectify market failure. This framework, which is labelled 'naïve Keynesianism' by Teague (1989*b*), imagines that national strategies for economic and social progress are best achieved via the election of a majority Labour government at Westminster, committed to interventionist strategies in pursuit of economic growth and full employment. Meanwhile unions should be allowed to engage in free collective bargaining in the workplace. This 'golden formula' clearly dominated the mindsets of trade union policy-makers for much of the 1950s and 1960s and thereby imposed a closure upon attempts to think otherwise about either the growth of economic and social policy competencies at the European level, or the departure from the British model of collective laissez-faire in the Labour market.

The development of the AES on the British left in the 1970s was built largely around the assumption that 'socialist' programmes for economic and social renewal could and should be accomplished within the boundaries of a protectionist nation state. Membership of the EC did not define the context of trade unionism within such discourse, but a logical corollary of AES thinking was the termination of membership. The Europeanization of AES themes in left-wing thought after 1983 jettisoned the assumption of the primacy of national economic sovereignty. This crisis of nation-state socialist discourse created the space for significant strategic re-evaluation on the part of unions.

The key changes to the trade union knowledge structure since the mid-1980s have occurred in assumptions about the economy and industrial relations. In tune with much thinking on the left, British unions have, for the most part, arrived at the position which accepts that effective national economic planning is no longer feasible in the context of 'globalization' and the development of regional economic institutions in the world economy (Burnham 1996). There has also been something of a settlement with neo-liberal economic orthodoxy so that sound money and low inflation are identified as priorities along with traditional concerns such as the maximization of employment levels (TUC 1990). Allegiance to the traditionally British mode of labour market regulation through immunities has been largely abandoned and replaced with a view which espouses the virtues of positive individual workplace rights.

The argument is not that changes to this knowledge structure have enabled the outlook of British unions to become Europeanized. Nor that changes at the European level have stimulated changes in knowledge. A better approach is to adopt a 'constructivist' view of knowledge. Interaction with the 'European environment' and with other actors generates a set of shared meanings and shared expectations (Duvall et al. 1996).

Simplistic and unidimensional explanations of the reordering of trade union discourses, policies, and activities in relation to European integration are guarded against through the identification of the five 'boundaries' of trade union attitudes. The argument of this chapter is partly that it is difficult to identify single 'causes' for shifts in union policy towards Europe and that a 'relational' model which considers the interplay of different ideational structures provides a richer explanation. For example, to attribute altered policy stances to changes in the domestic context of union activity ignores the interplay between the domestic and the European levels. But it is also dangerous to attribute certain sorts of motivations to trade union actors in the context of the European debate alone. The implicit assumption in much of the literature is that the interests and preferences of trade union actors are given exogenously and that they respond to the European debate in terms of these interests. The position adopted here is broadly in line with structurationist analyses (Bhaskar 1979; Cerny 1990; Giddens 1984) which pursue the reciprocity between agency and structure. Agents may make structures, but are also subject to the behavioural modifications which those structures impose. Having said that, it is clear that structuration theory permits agents to be sufficiently reflexive to operate within these constraints, to the extent that structures may be modified. Action, based upon certain knowledge or in pursuit of certain identities, within structural confines, can create new situations which may challenge or transform that knowledge or those identities. Simple 'cause-effect' explanations are too simplistic. The development of a structurationist explanation contributes to a more sophisticated understanding of changes in trade union attitudes to 'Europe'.

CONCLUSIONS

Union debates have not been confined to the impact of integration upon the workplace and industrial relations. Union actors have been central to arguments on the left about the economic costs and benefits of integration, as well as about the efficacy and desirability of national sovereignty. In the mid-1990s, the bulk of British trade unions perceive the EU as a (perhaps *the*) central component of their external environment. Europe has become vital strategic terrain for the pursuit of trade union concerns. The key issue for unions is the extent to which they will be able to continue to pursue productive strategies through the use of the European dimension. The 'Europeanization' of union activities and concerns looks to be more or less permanent. The intensification of European-level activity by British trade unions is likely to be reinforced through practice, but the ability of unions to strike productive alliances with bureaucratic actors in the European Commission remains in some doubt.

This chapter has also argued for a more thoroughgoing theorization of the interplay between actors in the British political economy and the processes of European integration. Thinking about the interplay between agency and structure offers insights into the motivations and perceptions of domestic actors and the structural environment which may constrain and (or) enable their actions. Such theoretical reflection shows how actors are not necessarily prisoners of their environment. The case study shows very well how the constraining circumstances of Thatcherite domestic hostility towards trade unions could be transformed with the judicious use of a new European discourse.

The case study of British unions and Europe provides an excellent example of the ways in which actors interact with, make, and remake their structural environment. The responses of trade unions are structured in a particular manner, through the five 'boundaries' identified above, which tend to foreclose particular options, while also providing opportunities for action and discourse. This might suggest that unions are either helpless victims of structural constraints or potentially skilful users of structural opportunities. But the case study also shows how unions have contributed to the making of the structure in which they operate.

7

British Business: Managing Complexity

Justin Greenwood and Lara Stancich

There is scarcely any doubt that British business, like its counterparts on the Continent, is positive about Europe. It cannot afford not to be. The single market remains at the core of 'project Europe', with over 370 million customers forming the largest home market in the world and equipping European capital with the means to compete on the global stage. From 1979 to 1992, Britain attracted 44 per cent of all total direct investment in the EU as a base for external capital to participate in the single market. In the first two decades of British membership the proportion of British exports to the rest of the EU has risen from around one-third to one-half. Investment by UK firms in Europe more than quadrupled from 1986 to 1993, while the UK's stock of inward investment tripled in the same period (CBI 1995*a*). Two decades of membership have intertwined the British economy with that of the rest of Europe, while UK firms have, through alliances, take-overs, and mergers taken on the identity of European firms. A recent survey of 1,700 firms conducted by the British Chambers of Commerce (BCC) and the Confederation of British Industry (CBI) found that 90 per cent of firms thought that the interests of UK firms would be best served by staying in the EU, and only 7 per cent that withdrawal would best serve their interests (BCC/CBI 1995). It is no surprise therefore that business contributions largely financed the 'Yes to Europe' campaign in the referendum on British accession (Butt Philip 1992). British firms shared a role in the work of the European Round Table of Industrialists (ERT) in agenda setting, and driving through, the single market project as Europe's response to global competitiveness.

Our interviews with British 'peak' business associations and large firms confirm these positive views. If there is, in Sabatier's terms, a 'government/business policy community' towards Europe (Sabatier 1988), then there is a 'deep core' advocacy coalition in favour of membership.

The advent of QMV has meant that firms throughout Europe have had to rely less upon the 'national channel' of interest representation, and develop their own 'Euro channels', including participation in European-level sector associations. For instance, the Rover car firm (now BMW-Rover) found that a UK minister traded away a cherished standard on lean burn engine technology as part of a deal on fisheries (McLaughlin 1992). Like business elsewhere in Europe, large firms often make their own direct representations to Brussels, and many have established their own Brussels offices. Similarly, sectoral business participates as fully in European-level trade associations as do those from other large EU countries. In many cases this long predates British accession, although in some instances European membership did signal a reorganization of domestic associations (Butt Philip 1992). In sectoral affairs, the UK has a relatively good record of implementing directives, and in 'low politics' domains British involvement in Europe is relatively unproblematic. Here, the main point of contention among British business seems to be a view that it suffers from over-zealous national implementation of EU directives in comparison to elsewhere in Europe, producing an uneven effect in competing in the single market (BCC/CBI). On the whole, however, a 'British' identity is not necessarily discernible in sectoral European business affairs.

Rather than through any cleavages based on purely national affiliation, cross-sectoral 'rich firm clubs' such as the ERT maintain their identity through their status as major European players. The ERT partly works by the spread of ideas through its members, relying upon them to go home and convince domestic governments and business associations of the merit of ERT positions. Thus, one key ERT member took responsibility for 'selling' the ERT report 'Beating the Crisis' to the UK government. President of the Board of Trade Michael Heseltine was reputedly so impressed with the document that he put his pen through a Ministry report on related themes, and told his civil servants to adopt the ERT approach as closely as was possible (Cowles 1995).

Like business elsewhere, British corporate rhetoric strongly supports: a free market evenly and fully implemented; the minimum regulation and bureaucratic cost necessary to achieve it; as much deregulation and simplification as possible; openness in decision-making; better access to markets in Eastern Europe; and further action to reduce public expenditure, including a reduction in the cost of the Common Agricultural Policy and a drive against fraud. However, such support is contextual. Thus, free trade and deregulation are supported provided it is not sector specific. Bureaucratic cost is to be avoided, provided it can accommodate expansion in the Commission's business services, including DG III (Industry), DG XV (Internal Market and Financial Services), and units dedicated to the elimination of fraud and waste elsewhere. Administrative openness is seen as valuable where business interests in Brussels are best able to take advantage of access to documentation. Expansion to the East is welcome, provided it does not mean a drain on the public finances of the present members through the structural funds and Common Agricultural Policy. For British business interests, a single market is welcome provided there are exceptions over production conditions involving employment and environmental costs, and the possibility for a British opt-out on monetary union. Social policy is also acceptable provided it is limited to initiatives on the free movement of workers, employment creation, and labour flexibility, rather than upon improvements in working conditions.

Ultimately, a 'British business' identity in Europe is provided more from the 'high politics' of European integration and in arenas where the British government pursues a distinctive position. This means that the 'peak' organizations representing the cross-sectoral constituency of British interests in 'high-politics' domains is the relevant unit of analysis to investigate a 'British business position towards Europe'.

BRITISH PEAK BUSINESS ORGANIZATIONS AND THE EU

'Peak' organizations of British business include the Confederation of British Industries (CBI), the Institute of Directors (IoD), the Association of British Chambers of Commerce (BCC), the Forum of Private Business (FPB), and the Federation of Small Businesses (FSB). Although all of these associations claim that small businesses account for the majority of their membership, the FPB and FSB are the only organizations dedicated solely to representing the interests of small firms. In common with most peak-level organizations, all four find the diversity of constituencies they represent makes common platform building difficult. As is evident in later sections, some of the positions taken have resulted in turbulence amongst their membership, although this has not prevented them from adopting distinctive styles towards European integration.

The CBI represents 250,000 firms from every sector of UK business, and 200 trade, commercial, and employer associations. Over 90 per cent of the membership of the CBI are small and medium-sized enterprises (SMEs). The mandate of the CBI is based on regular surveys of members, as well as direct consultation with them. Policy is formed by a number of specialist executive committees consisting of individuals drawn from member firms. Drawing on surveys and consultation with members conducted over the past three years, the CBI feels that support for Europe amongst its members is generally increasing, not least because of a view among enterprises that they need to be more vociferous in their support for Europe in the face of uncertain political rhetoric.

With the notable exception of social policy initiatives, discussed later, the CBI and its antecedents have viewed European integration as central to the prosperity of UK businesses since the 1960s (Butt Philip 1992). Prior to UK accession to the EC in 1971 the CBI established an office in Brussels, located within the UNICE (Union of Industrial and Employers' Confederations of Europe) building. The role of the CBI Brussels office today is to keep channels open with the European institutions and with UKREP. It also represents the interests of the CBI within UNICE: to liaise with other member federations; to provide support for and facilitate CBI activity in Brussels; to assist and advise CBI members in dealing with the EU; to contribute to CBI policy work; and act as an 'early warning system' of developments in Brussels (CBI 1995*b*; Eberlie 1993). The full implementation of the Single Market in 1992 encouraged further development of CBI and UK business involvement, with the establishment in Brussels of the British Business Bureau (BBB), funded jointly by the CBI and a number of its supporting federations. Its function is to assist sectoral federations to make use of corresponding EU-level trade associations, to help establish contacts for them, and to provide information and act as a facilitator for UK federations seeking more direct contact with the European level (Eberlie 1993).

While expressing a preference for dealing directly with European institutions on matters of European policy, where the need is perceived, the CBI does seek to influence or change UK government policy, and where necessary, those of other member states through sister organizations. However, it operates at the European level more commonly than through the domestic route of interest representation. In 1988, the CBI recorded twice as many meetings with EC Commissioners as with UK Ministers (Grant 1990).

The Institute of Directors (IoD), with 20,000 members, is somewhat of a rival to the CBI. It takes a more conditional stance to European integration, stating that although businesses are completely committed to membership of the EU, and benefit positively from the Single Market, they are opposed to the 'related baggage' of what is seen as excessive regulation, social Europe, and in particular, to a single currency. Even this position however, reflects something of a shift in direction for this organization, whose director-general once pronounced that '1992 was bound to fail' (Butt Philip 1992: 158). European structures include a working party, an executive committee comprising both IoD staff and IoD members, and a permanent Brussels presence. However, its Brussels office is restricted to the role of a 'listening post' and information point for its UK office. The organization does not seek to influence or participate directly in European-level policy-making and does not act collectively in European-level associations. Instead, it seeks mainly to influence UK government policy for deregulatory stances in European public policy, and has a preference to use the 'national channel' of interest representation in European public affairs.

The Association of British Chambers of Commerce has a membership dominated by small businesses represented via local chambers of commerce, together with a number of business and trade associations drawn mainly from the retailing sector, as a result of the merging of the BCC with the Chambers of Trade. Historically, these organizations have been deeply concerned with export trade and commerce. The development of policy is institutionalized via consultation with members, whose opinions are passed on to a number of standing committees, of which one is the EU Committee. The resulting opinions are collated into a more official format which is then approved by a national council of fifty members. The BCC have very little, if any, contact with the UK government for European public affairs and tend to bypass such channels in favour of the more direct 'Brussels route' of interest representation. Consultation with the UK government tends to occur at the stage of implementing EU policies. BCC's membership of EUROCHAMBRES provides their main mode of influence at the European level, and main channel for conveying their opinions and priorities.

Somewhat independently of the BCC, its EU Committee of the BCC became active in Brussels in mid-1995, facilitating a higher profile for British business interests at the European level. A direct link between British businesses and the EU has been established by the Committee including monthly 'breakfast meetings' with director-generals, allowing UK business executives to network with lawyers, public affairs people, and UKREP.

Our fourth British peak organization, the Forum of Private Business, regards the CBI and IoD more as 'large firm clubs', and less representative of small businesses as a whole. Quarterly surveys of their membership by the FPB suggest that although much of their membership are relatively unaffected by the 'high-politics' agenda of Europe, the single market is seen as a source of vital trading opportunities, and that a positive view of Britain as part of Europe prevails. Like BCC, it places greater reliance upon the 'Brussels route' of interest representation than the national route. However, the organization is consulted regularly by the UK government on European affairs which affect member interests.

A major difficulty identified by both the FPB and BCC concerns the difficulties for their members in taking advantage of the single market because of a lack of information about business opportunities. The need for information about political and economic conditions in the single market has been identified as one of the major rationalities for collective action at the European level (Vipond 1995), and may partly explain the emphasis placed by the CBI, the FPB, and the BCC upon the use of European-level collective structures as routes of interest representation. In part, the UK government was held responsible by some of these organizations for the lack of information experienced by small businesses regarding European opportunities. But the actual structure of British business interest groups may be part of the problem. Dyson has identified the absence of strong local channels of communication between government and business in the UK as a major impediment to the preparation of small businesses for the single market, whereas a higher level of awareness about market opportunities among small businesses in Germany was attributed to the strength and autonomy of networks of local chambers of commerce, and the ability to use these structures as channels for training and communication. In turn the absence of information and training channels in the UK was held responsible for a high prevalence of negative attitudes towards Europe in a survey of enterprises (Dyson 1991).

'Peak' associations, by nature, have a cross-sectoral remit to represent the general affairs of business. Because of the preference of sectoral trade associations to take the lead on issues directly affecting them, they tend not to take positions on sectoral issues. However, such demarcation can become blurred. Cross-sectoral associations have taken up positions on sectoral business which are deemed to have an impact across business, particularly where they are encouraged to do so by sectoral interests. On the whole, however, the concerns of cross-sectoral business associations are those of the 'high politics' of European integration, often in areas where member states dominate the integration process through summitry, or where unanimity voting at the Council of Ministers still prevails.

'HIGH' AND 'LOW' POLITICS: BRITISH BUSINESS AND THE MANAGEMENT OF DIVERSITY

While undoubtedly 'grey areas' exist between what one might term 'high' and 'low' politics the broad categorizations retain their utility. It is clear that the arena of 'high politics' consists of multiple arenas with multiple players to which private interests have no monopolistic access. In 'low politics' arenas, as we shall see, interests can exert significant influence upon the outcomes of public policies.

Interests make their greatest contribution to 'low-politics' arenas, where the possession of powerful resources of expertise, information, and economic strength (some firms have more resources than member states) prove indispensable to public policy formulation and implementation. Business, on the whole, possesses more of these resources than do other types of interests. Typically, the possession or absence of these resources will determine the ability of an interest to achieve 'insider status', where near monopolistic influence can be exerted over public policies. At the European level, where the Commission is the key actor, such resources can play a significant role in influencing the character of public policy, because the relatively small and overloaded bureaucracy has become dependent upon their input. Agendas and drafts of directives can be shaped by information provided by a trade association, often in an institutionalized 'policy community', to which resource-poor 'outsiders' have little access.

A typical strategy is to politicize issues to bring them into the public domain away from 'insider' monopolistic influence where 'outsiders' can identify the need to exert influence. In such circumstances, issues have often been transformed into the arena of 'high politics' where business has no monopolistic access.

In 'high-politics' arenas, interests tend to operate more at the level of outputs than outcomes, where they can make a contribution to the shaping of debate and to the preferences of actors who participate, such as member states. As will be evident later, interest groups can also be the target of influence exerted by governments in such arenas.

Two areas where Britain's EU membership involves sensitive issues of high politics are those of 'social Europe', and monetary union, and here there are complex forces within, and between, the British business community and the UK government on the one hand, and the positions of different member states and their business communities on the other.

SOCIAL EUROPE

Times of economic recession do not favour labour interests, because the emphasis shifts from the quality of working conditions to employment creation and worker flexibility. Mass unemployment weakens the power of labour, and enhances the ability of capital to restructure labour markets, aimed at controlling production costs. Consequently, labour markets have been restructured across Europe since the shock of oil price rises in the mid-1970s sent economies into recession. The main labour market changes since the oil crisis have involved a decline in manufacturing with its partial replacement by service sector employment, and the reduction of full-time, permanent employment together with the rise of less secure and more flexible types of working patterns. The single market provided part of the answer to the reconstruction of European economies based on market principles. However, the reconstruction of markets has inevitably involved a reregulation of the principles of market exchange as well as deregulation. For instance, consistent with market principles, early positions of business were to restrict 'social Europe' to issues concerning barriers to the free movement of labour (and therefore competition), and to prevent binding social dialogue at the European level. However, supported by political action by labour and a Commission keen to expand its areas of competence, 'functional spillover' into labour market regulation to remove barriers has developed its own momentum. Indeed, since the Treaty of Maastricht, business interests have become institutionalized within social dialogue mechanisms, with their own legal basis. This expansion is now reinforced at the level of political ideas and rhetoric, where key speeches of Commission officials, including the President, emphasize the importance of extending the benefits of '1992' far beyond those accruing to business interests.

A further key dynamic in developing 'social Europe' arises from competing models and traditions of capitalism within the member states and the balance of interests in favour of 'social Europe' which has emerged. At one extreme the Anglo-American brand of capitalism stresses classic free market models, while in the 'northern' group of countries, embracing Germany, Austria, and the Nordic and the Benelux countries, there is a more interventionist 'social market' capitalism. Between these lie the 'Mediterranean' group of countries, comprising France, Italy, Greece, Portugal, and Spain (Rhodes 1995).

Labour markets are characterized by a high level of skills and a high degree of education, low levels of hierarchy within firms, consensual treatment of issues through participatory mode between workforce representatives and employers, and high pay in return for high productivity in the 'northern' group of countries. In the Anglo-American tradition, labour markets are less regulated and employment patterns more flexible, with a workforce characteristically lower in skills, with lower pay (ibid.). Employers in the northern group of countries therefore face higher production costs, which they are keen to 'export' to other member states through EU policies to ensure a 'level playing field' in the single market. Britain, on the other hand, firmly entrenched in the Anglo-American tradition, is keen to retain its low-cost production conditions as a strategy of competitive advantage, and therefore resists labour market regulation. This so-called 'social dumping' largely explains why Britain has attracted almost half of all inward investment to the EU. The British government caused controversy by placing advertisements in the German press extolling the benefits of Britain as a low-cost production centre for investment.

Significantly, the emphasis at the European level has now moved beyond labour market regulation to prevent distortions in the single market, towards the need for public spending and investment in the labour market. Equally, ideas of 'total quality management' in work organizations encourage practices such as 'investment in people', embraced by firms almost irrespective of national parentage. Clearly, these are somewhat inconsistent with 'social dumping'. In ways partly anticipated by neo-functionalist theory, 'social Europe' has therefore developed its own momentum, leaving Britain some way behind.

Driven by similar perceptions of benefits, British business has on the whole supported the position of the UK government to 'opt out' of social Europe. Nevertheless, some qualification of this attitude has been apparent. Twenty one per cent of firms in the UK recently surveyed by BCC/CBI disagreed with the opt-out (BCC/CBI 1995). Also, a handful of medium-sized and large firms of British parentage have acted unilaterally in implementing the provisions of the social charter. However, there is something of a division in the position of representatives of (mainly) large, and small businesses. The Forum of Private Business (FPB), representing the interests of small firms, is not opposed to the principles of the Social Chapter, and in some respects sees the culture of small businesses converging with its aims on the basis that the relationship between employer and employee is more personal. The BCC/CBI survey found that smaller firms were more favourable towards harmonization of industrial relations across Europe than large firms (BCC/CBI 1995). The FPB suggested in interviews conducted for the purposes of writing this chapter that many small businesses meet, if not surpass, the requirements of the Social Chapter, despite the fact that a significant proportion of their membership is exempt from the provisions. The IoD also takes the view that businesses are broadly in favour of the Social Chapter and its principles, but paradoxically are unanimously opposed to its *imposition* on UK businesses, due to the burdens and extra costs placed on, in particular, small and medium enterprises.

The BCC/CBI survey of member opinions indicated that 72 per cent of enterprises support the continued opt-out by the UK, including nearly half who 'strongly agreed' (BCC/CBI 1995). Consistent with the 'Anglo-American' model of capitalism, both the BCC and CBI see market solutions as the most effective way of delivering social progress, emphasizing the need for employment creation and mechanisms of creating further labour market flexibility (BCC 1995; CBI 1995a). BCC puts this most stridently, arguing that:

Improving working and living conditions by Community level intervention can only be achieved at the price of not achieving other objectives, notably global competitiveness, free and fair competition within the internal market

. . . . There are no further areas where the introduction of Union legislation impacting on the employment relationship would be useful. Indeed any further interventions are likely to be highly damaging, particularly SMEs. The lightest touch is preferable where Union legislation is deemed appropriate to overcome obstacles to the mobility of labour, or to facilitate the working of the internal market. (BCC 1995: 9)

The continuing development of 'social Europe' and the contrasting position of British business and the UK government to those of other players is perhaps best illustrated by the issue of industrial democracy. For some time, European business resisted measures aimed at the imposition of rules for worker participation in industrial decision-making. As 'social Europe' developed the Union of Industrial and Employers' Confederations of Europe became drawn into a social dialogue. Consequently, agreement seemed more likely between labour and business interests on a 'Works Council' Directive, requiring firms with more than 1,000 employees to create structures for dialogue and consultation with workers on significant decisions likely to affect their interests. UNICE was on the point of signing an agreement with the European Trade Union Confederation, ETUC, when a last-minute intervention by the CBI forced UNICE to withdraw. Significantly, the CBI's intervention was inspired by influence from the British government (Falkner 1995), illustrating how government/business influence can operate in both directions. In the event, the gridlock between the macroeconomic social partners, UNICE and ETUC, forced the intervention of the Commission, and following a cosmetic name change to the 'Directive on Information and Consultation', the Works Council Directive was agreed in 1994, with full implementation in September 1996. Ultimately, British intervention therefore proved unsuccessful.

Although the UK is not directly covered by the Works Council Directive because of its opt-out from the Social Chapter, UK multinationals have been in the forefront of establishing voluntary works councils ahead of EU implementation. Before this deadline, the UK came third in the number of voluntary agreements reached (*Financial Times*, 23 September 1996). The majority of these agreements (38 of 64) involved UK-owned multinationals, including firms such as Courtaulds, who have voluntarily agreed with the TGWU for twenty of the twenty-three members of the Council to be nominated directly by the unions (*Financial Times*, 20 September 1996). In such practical ways, a number of UK firms have demonstrated their 'Euro credentials' to be somewhat ahead of the UK government.

Of further interest is that there is now an 'understanding' within UNICE that whilst the CBI is likely to oppose measures to further 'social Europe', it should not veto UNICE action on which other members are agreed (Falkner 1995). This allows the CBI, at least, to be seen to be supporting the UK government position, although whether its commitment is as ideologically opposed to social Europe as its posturing may suggest is a matter for conjecture. CBI Director-General Adair Turner recently reflected that 'with many UK firms with continental operations social chapter terms already apply so we can't simply sit behind our opt out moat' (CBI 1996: 1). It appears that by participating in European structures spanning business interest groups and those of the European institutions the CBI has inevitably become socialized by its experiences, and the ideas, norms, and values of those around them.

MONETARY UNION

The complexity of the task of British business in seeking to manage European public affairs is also illustrated by the diversity of views towards monetary union. A 1994 Gallup poll indicated that 65 per cent of British businesses favoured monetary union, although this was the lowest level of support in the seven countries surveyed (Sandholtz 1993). The BCC/CBI survey indicated that more companies believed that a single currency would be of benefit rather than a disadvantage to UK business (BCC/CBI 1995). However, three broad positions were evident. The first, and largest, group were the most positive, a second view was more cautious, preferring to await further developments before deciding, while 11 per cent of respondents wanted to reject EMU now; these three 'camps' have each found a voice to represent their views.

The enthusiasts include among their ranks a number of members of the Association for the Monetary Union of Europe (AMUE), a European-level group formed to organize business support in favour of monetary union, of which UK businesses (including BAT industries, Barclays Bank, and ICI) account for approximately 10 per cent of membership. AMUE argues that '[t]he existence of different national currencies is not consistent with a single market', and that stability, growth, and employment would be enhanced by monetary union (AMUE 1995: 1). Partly because of divisions amongst its membership, a rather more qualified support for monetary union can be found in the CBI, which regards the Maastricht Treaty criteria for EMU as beneficial and suggests that the UK government ought to 'remain actively involved in the development and co-ordination of policy and plans for stage three of EMU' regardless of whether or not Britain ultimately intends to join (CBI 1995*c*). This support for EMU has been openly challenged by sections of the membership, with one member publicly accusing it of misrepresenting the views of a majority of British industrialists. In turn, however, this view has itself been publicly contradicted by players as significant as ICI and Unilever (Electronic Telegraph, 1995).

The 'wait and see' view is represented best by the BCC, which 'tries to be positive' on EMU and a single currency, but sees the lack of information, particularly regarding the likely impact on businesses, as problematic in enabling businesses to develop an informed opinion on EMU. Tackling the problem of awareness and information on EMU is regarded as a priority before further steps are taken. To this end the BCC has called for an independent UK commission on EMU to evaluate and advise on its likely consequences. It is argued that information provided by the Commission is not impartial, and therefore unlikely to furnish businesses with an objective analysis of the benefits and costs of monetary union.

Lack of awareness or knowledge about EMU among members also partly informs the position of the Forum of Private Business. Although a survey of members revealed a verdict generally against a common currency (48.8 per cent), a significant minority of the vote (22.2 per cent) were in the 'don't know' category. This result was further tempered by almost a third of businesses in favour of a common currency (28.9 per cent) (FPB 1995: 25–8).

The IoD perhaps best represents the views of the third group surveyed who wished to reject EMU now (BCC/CBI 1995) as it is opposed to EMU and a single currency. At a recent conference, 70 per cent of the 2,500 delegates present voted a resolution recording that the disadvantages of the single currency outweighed the advantages (Electronic Telegraph 1996: 1). In a 1995 report, the IoD argues that it does not believe EMU to be in the economic interests of the UK for the foreseeable future. This is partly because the UK, and the UK economy, are perceived by the organization to be significantly different from other potential members of EMU. It argues that not only would changes in monetary policy affect the UK differently, but the costs of EMU would be higher and the benefits lower for the UK than for other member states (IoD 1995). They analogize UK participation in EMU to the ERM problems of 1992, emphasizing that this time 'there would be no escape' (IoD 1995: 2).

These apparent divisions among British business interests are to some extent confirmed by surveys conducted by other organizations. Interviews conducted by the *Financial Times* in 1995 present a rather lukewarm attitude of elite industrialists towards the prospect of EMU by 1999, commenting that 'while most industrialists think that the UK will benefit from close economic and political ties with the rest of Europe, only a few believe that joining European economic and monetary union by 1999 should be a priority' (*Financial Times*, 17 February 1995). A MORI survey of finance directors drawn from 100 of the UK's biggest 500 companies indicated that 60 per cent believed a single currency would be good for the UK, and nearly half believed that the government was not doing well in its handling of the issue of a single currency on behalf of UK businesses (*Financial Times*, 17 February 1995). Such a response might well be expected amongst those from large companies, who are likely to have business interests throughout member states and who might be expected to support measures to lower transaction costs in trade. These firms have become increasingly politically active in the debates over Europe in an effort to make sure that the UK government did not cave in to its Euro-sceptic wing in the run-up to the 1997 general election. In 1996, the Chief Executive Offices (CEOs) of some of the largest UK multi-nationals wrote an open letter arguing that: 'as representatives of companies whose trade in Europe generates billions of dollars of export business and creates tens of thousands of jobs in this country, we believe that a self imposed exclusion from negotiations over EMU would be deeply damaging' (*Financial Times*, 5 September 1996).

CONCLUSION: MANAGING THE EUROPEAN INTERFACE

The CBI, in particular, has sought to 'manage' the UK government's participation in Europe for purposes of 'damage limitation' to business interests and to moderate its isolationist stance. The BCC/CBI survey indicated that almost three in five firms thought that the continuing debate about the UK's membership of the EU over the past year had been unhelpful to the government's ability to promote British interests in the EU, including one-fifth of firms who thought that it had been 'very unhelpful' (BCC/CBI 1995). British business, it seems, values EU membership somewhat more highly than the public positions of the present government seem to indicate.

CBI attempts to manage UK government has a number of finely balanced features. In recognition of the power of rhetoric and the depth of support among its members for Europe, it is careful not to criticize the EU. Yet, until very recently, it has also been careful to support the position of the government, particularly by bolstering the position of the Prime Minister in the face of turbulence from the 'Eurosceptic' wing of his party. Most recently (April 1996), the Prime Minister returned the compliment by using the occasion of a CBI dinner to attack those factions in his party agitating for exit from Europe, and to emphasize the benefits which Europe brings for business. Supporting this view, the Director-General of the CBI described the idea that Britain could be prosperous if detached from the EU as a 'Little Englander Fantasy' (Electronic Telegraph, 1996: 1). Similarly, in another speech former Foreign Secretary Douglas Hurd told his audience that:

British business people whom I have met in recent months are more and more concerned at the gap opening up in this country between the debate and the reality. They find that British interests are beginning to suffer because those with whom they wish to do business feel that as regards Europe we live in a world of fantasy. (Hurd 1996: 3)

Nevertheless, the 'Eurosceptic' wing of the Conservative Party has now forced the issue of British membership of the EU on to the political agenda, openly questioning its value. Increasingly alarmed, the CBI has launched initiatives which, whilst designed to re-present the benefits to Britain of EU membership, increasingly expose differences between its own 'Euro-enthusiasm', and the more cautious and divided position of the government as a whole. The CBI's 'Business in Europe' campaign, launched in June 1996, unfortunately coincided with the British government's campaign of non-cooperation at the Council of Ministers in response to the ban on the export of beef products. The CBI produced its highest-profile members for the launch, including the Chief Executives of British Airways, Unilever, British Petroleum, and British Telecom, who were inevitably drawn into criticism of the drift of rhetoric in the Conservative Party. Sir Colin Marshall, from British Airways, warned of 'an enormous amount at stake for British business if the damaging rhetoric continues . . . it is increasingly harmful to British business and industry interests in the EU' (BBC TV 1996). British Telecom's Sir Iain Vallance similarly warned that the rhetoric of the sceptics represented 'a great penalty to the wealth of the UK' (ibid.), while Unilever Chief Executive designate Niall Fitzgerald warned that withdrawal was a 'ludicrous idea . . . with dire economic consequences' (ibid.). For his part, CBI Director-General Adair Turner has complained of 'fact free rhetoric' (Electronic Telegraph, 1996). Consequently, the uneasy diplomacy of attempted CBI management of government policy towards Europe by quiet support may now be replaced by a more visible cleavage between the two. And business may have to find alternative strategies of damage limitation by further use of self-representation in Brussels.

One such strategy centres on the development of a number of informal networks amongst UK businesses in Brussels, of which the most important is the European Business Agenda (EBA). The EBA is an informal group of British companies including British Aerospace, British Gas, ICL, Guinness, Marks and Spencer, and Rolls-Royce, each of whom maintain offices in Brussels. Their aim was to produce brief, informative, semi-official position papers on various issues of European integration, with which to convey their opinions to the UK government and keep company executives updated. With the 1996 IGC largely under way, the EBA has adopted a new posture, looking more at industrial policy issues and the horizontal aspects of integration, such as research and development policy, energy, environment, and social policy. The EBA structure is described by its members as an 'autonomous collective', in that it has no formal secretariat and works on the principles of flexibility and expediency. Membership of EBA is kept deliberately small to enable flexibility and facilitate speed in reaching collective positions, although at the same time they seek to develop a membership in which each main sector of British industry is represented. Their chief concern is that their opinion is disseminated, exactly who in the group undertakes this task is less important. Thus, the necessary research is conducted by a lead member, formulating a position which is often agreed quickly, and a position paper, normally of no more than one page, is produced and disseminated to elites in the UK government and at the European level and to industry groups in Brussels such as the CBI, BCC, and sectoral associations.

This chapter has demonstrated that British business needs both to address the realities of domestic politics and to engage independently at the European level. As an actor in a number of high-politics fields, the flexible 'think-tank' role of EBA, with select powerful large-firm interests seeking to contribute by injecting ideas into 'high-politics' arenas with multiple players and multiple actors, is well suited to the challenges facing British business. Whilst the relationship between British business and the UK government is never likely to compare with that of the trade unions, where the principle route for labour interests is by participating directly in European level structures, business may become increasingly reliant on its own resources at the European-level, rather than upon what it perceives as the increasing idiosyncrasies of domestic channels. In such a scenario, British business is likely to become even more socialized and integrated into mainstream European values.

8

Civil Service Attitudes Towards the European Union

Jim Buller and Martin J. Smith

An assessment of civil service attitudes to the Europe Union (EU)[1] is both conceptually and empirically difficult. Conceptually, it is not clear whether a unified 'civil service attitude' exists or can be defined. Empirically, discovering civil service attitudes to the EU is more or less impossible, because constitutionally civil servants are neutral and therefore do not express political attitudes. Unlike a political party or a trade union, civil servants do not release policy documents indicating their view on European integration. Even if we accept that civil servants are not strictly neutral, it is certainly not clear that they have shared attitudes. Moreover, discovering a 'civil service view' on Europe would not indicate very much about Britain's relationship with the European Union. Whether civil servants are Eurofederalists or Eurosceptics varies from individual to individual, both within and between departments. Equally, personal attitudes will have little influence on government policy towards Europe. Finally, there is a further empirical problem: there are very strict rules about asking civil servants questions concerning their political beliefs and it is not clear that questions on their personal views on the EU would elicit a response. Therefore, this chapter will not examine EU attitudes *per se* but highlight the institutionally bounded interests that civil servants

---

The authors conducted interviews with senior officials between February and June 1996 in the Home Office, the Cabinet Office, the Foreign and Commonwealth Office, the Department of Trade and Industry, the Ministry of Agriculture Fisheries and Food, the Department of Social Security, and the Department of Environment.

[1] Although the European Union is shorthand and only in existence since 1992, we generally use EU throughout the article for convenience.

have developed in relation to the EU and how these interests may have affected their behaviour and the organization of departments.

There is no single civil service view of the European Union. That said, the EU does affect the behaviour and attitudes of civil servants and it has had a significant affect on the structure of departments and Whitehall in general. However, to understand the impact of the EU on Whitehall, we have to be aware that attitudes of civil servants vary according to departments, history, policies, and time. In other words, an institutional public choice approach provides a useful explanation for the variation in departmental attitudes towards the EU. From an institutional public choice perspective the preferences of actors are determined by 'social structures, institutions and social roles' (Ward 1996: 292). The attitudes of civil servants are not endogenous but will be shaped by the institutional interests of their departments and the nature of the department's long-term relationship with the EU.

For some departments, for example, Agriculture, the EU generally provides new opportunities. For others, such as the Treasury, it provides constraints. In addition, departments have a very different history of relationships with Brussels, for some, the EU has been integral to their work since 1972, whilst for others a European role has only really developed post-Maastricht. The attitudes of departments also vary, to an extent, according to the policy. Some policies are much more effectively developed at a European level whilst others can be better developed and implemented at the national or local level.

Finally, despite the criticisms of the constitutional view, civil servants are very sensitive to the wishes and views of their ministers. From an institutional rational choice perspective civil servants have an interest in respecting the policy preferences of ministers. As Dunleavy suggests for public expenditure increases, the advocacy costs of Euro-enthusiasm to a Eurosceptical minister would be very high (Dunleavy 1991) and even pro-EU civil servants are unlikely to bear the costs of a conflict with ministers that may affect their influence or even their careers. Civil servants can, therefore, maximize their utility by supporting the policies of the minister rather than suggesting alternatives. Consequently, the position taken by a department on Europe will vary according to the view of the minister.

There are a range of exogenous variables that affect the interests of civil servants and the nature and relationship of these variables will depend on the department. Consequently, any attempt to assess the impact of Europe on Whitehall needs to be disaggregated. The views of departments vary greatly, with we will suggest two variables having the greatest impact: the preferences of the ministers and the institutional interests of departments. From a public choice perspective we can see that for some departments membership of the EU provides greater opportunities and increased autonomy. These departments have a clear interest in integration and tend to be more pro-European. For other departments, EU membership means a loss of functions and a reduction in their autonomy. Consequently, they tend to be more sceptical.

Nevertheless, despite these departmental differences, there are signs of some general changes in Whitehall. First, all departments now have some sort of European capacity and there is a growing convergence of organizational arrangements in relation to the EU. Second, membership of the EU has had some influence on the role and general behaviour of civil servants. It increases the extent to which relatively junior Officials are involved in the negotiation of policy matters. This can increase their freedom and may give them a more political role. Third, Britain's membership of the EU has resulted in the development of a complex coordinating procedure which is an important institutional development within Whitehall.

TRADITIONAL VIEWS OF THE CIVIL SERVICE AND EUROPEAN UNION

In the very limited extant material on Whitehall and the European Union two stereotypical portraits of civil servants are depicted. The first is a 'political view'. From this position, according to Tony Benn, Brussels is a 'mandarin's paradise' (Young and Sloman 1982: 75). In his view:

Every item of EEC legislation automatically acquires the status of an Act of Parliament but is first negotiated by Officials, often leaving ministers with a mere power to approve or disapprove the package as a whole. As a result, the infection of Common Market bureaucracy has spread back into the heart of Whitehall from the source of the virus in Brussels. The permanent secretaries who masterminded the preparatory work for all these activities through the Cabinet Office and the Foreign Office have now got a legitimated excuse to by-pass and override departmental ministers in the interests of co-ordination and the need to be good Europeans. (Benn 1981: 61–2)

This perspective is also supported to an extent by Thatcher. She saw the Foreign and Commonwealth Office as being excessively pro-European as a means for ensuring its continued status. For example, Thatcher believed the Foreign Office misled her concerning the integrationist consequences of signing the Single European Act (Thatcher 1993: 473; Lawson 1992: 894). This view is supported by an ex-Foreign Office Official who suggested that the Foreign and Commonwealth Office (FCO) had misled Thatcher over the SEA. He maintained that this was defensible, because it suited Britain's 'higher' national interests, the continuing development of the European Union. He even suggested that transferring 'sovereignty' away from the UK Parliament was legitimate, because it meant that power was only being shifted to a European (supranational) institution in which he had equal confidence.

To a certain degree, people like Thatcher and Benn saw the European Community as a mechanism for allowing civil servants to reimpose policies which they had lost at the domestic level (Benn 1979). This is, in a sense, an adaptation of the traditional public choice view that bureaucrats are chiefly concerned with maximizing their individual utility, something best achieved in a European context because it increases the freedom of officials from their political masters and gives them a greater role in policy-making.

The second view is an extension of the 'awkward partner' thesis. George pays little attention in his discussion of Britain's relationship with the European Community, to the role of civil servants and indeed points to the need for more research. However, he does make the point that: 'Adjusting to the EC ways was difficult for both British politicians and officials' (1994: 257). He also suggests that British officials often appeared awkward in that they were not adept, in the way French officials were, 'at wrapping the pursuit of their national interests in a *communautaire* vocabulary' (George 1994: 258). Moreover, he sees the administrative and political elite as being 'suspicious of what were seen as the centralizing tendency of the Commission' (George 1993: 182).

Britain frequently, as do other nations, enters EU negotiations with the goal of protecting the national interest. This often appears as awkwardness because there is little doubt that coordination of the British position is extremely good. There are generally fewer cracks in the British 'common line' than amongst other countries, and so British officials present a more unified front in negotiation. Second, officials are aware of the political constraints on them when they are negotiating and this makes them much less flexible on the ground. If they are representing sceptical ministers they have little choice but to try not to concede too much ground. Hence, the style of British officials can give their more consensual and political continental colleagues an impression of scepticism (Edwards 1992: 74; Stack 1983: 130). These caricatures of official attitudes towards the EU see civil servants as either excessively pro-European or maintaining Britain's tradition of awkwardness. As we shall show, such positions are an oversimplification.

WHITEHALL AND EUROPEAN UNION: DEVELOPING COORDINATION

It is important to note two things when considering the background to Whitehall's relations with the EU. First, some departments have a much longer history of involvement with the EU. Second, Britain's membership has led to the establishment of a complex coordinating machinery which has been very effective in socializing departments into the EU.

In the relationship between Whitehall and Europe there are two countervailing tendencies which are indicative of the British core executive: on the one hand the strong centripetal forces of departments with their own separate histories and interests which result in particular relationships with Europe; on the other, strong centralizing tendencies emanating from the Cabinet Office and the FCO which attempt to control and standardize responses to Brussels.

Unlike other member states, each department created its own division for dealing with EEC matters. The FCO created two new European Integration divisions to receive and redistribute all material from UKREP. At the time of entry, the Heath government rejected the need for a Minister for Europe, along the lines of the French, instead being content to parcel out European work to the relevant Whitehall departments. Two reasons have been suggested for this arrangement. First, this method made entry into the EEC less politically obvious. Given the divisions in both main parties over Europe, even at this time, it suited both leaders to avoid a European Ministry which would be an easy target for Eurosceptics. Second, and more practically, spreading the work of the EEC throughout Whitehall was the best way of making use of a short supply of expertise on the subject (Stack 1983: 130–1).

Thus adaptation to the EU and coordination of European policy has been more ad hoc in Britain than in some other countries; as a result of the Single European Act and the Maastricht Treaty an increasing number of departments have become involved in EU business. When Britain originally joined the EEC membership had implications for only a handful of departments: in the case of the FCO it was thought by many to have experienced a new lease of life from Community membership after the shock of the decline of Empire. Another department immediately affected was MAFF which was dealing with the most comprehensive European policy, the CAP. Finally, the DTI was soon dealing with the implication for British industry of the developing common market and the Community's trade policy *vis-à-vis* third countries (Edwards 1992: 78–85).

Today every department is affected by the plethora of decisions taken at the community level and this imposes new burdens of work on ministers and their civil servants. Often directives passed by Brussels do not correspond precisely with existing British law. This leads to the formulation of new legislation, which has to be passed at Westminster, and this can have the affect of reopening policy issues at a domestic level which governments have previously tried to close (Bender 1991; Toonan 1991: 109)

A number of academics have begun to question whether a useful distinction can still be made between 'foreign' and 'domestic' policy, faced with this Europeanization of public policy (Clarke 1988). This process received a large boost after the signing of the Single European Act (SEA), which provided for the completion of the Single Market by 1992. Henceforth, a whole raft of supply side economic measures were to be decided by qualified majority voting in the Council of Ministers. The impact has been to Europeanize domestic policy-making (Bender 1991). As would be expected, departments only recently affected by EU membership have found adaptation much more difficult than departments involved since 1973. Departments that have only recently become involved still lack knowledge of how the EU works, which makes them more dependent on the FCO, or the Cabinet Office. There is also some resentment in departments like the Home Office and Department of Social Security (DSS) of EU interference in certain policy areas.

Nevertheless, increasing directives from Europe have elicited the need to invest more in coordination of the national decision-making machinery. In Britain this has occurred with limited formal institutional change at the centre. However, EU membership has also seen the rise of an informal, yet powerful, elite comprising Number 10, the FCO, the Cabinet Office, and UKREP. Burch and Holliday (1996) point to the existence of a European network with the task of managing EU policy formation centring on the Overseas and Defence Committee (OPD(E)) chaired by the Foreign Secretary; the relevant official committee; and the European Secretariat in the Cabinet Office. 'Together these are the elements which form the core of the European network' (Burch and Holiday 1996: 88). The role of the European Secretariat is to coordinate the responses of Whitehall to the EU. The FCO also has a coordinating function. Whilst the coordinating role of the FCO is important for all departments, other departments are also aware that unlike the Cabinet Office it has its own departmental interests and are perhaps more wary of its advice.

On the whole departments appear happy with the process of coordination at the centre. An official in the Treasury described it as 'excellent' and a DTI official remarked that 'although to the outsider the structure looks very complicated, and to some extent duplicatory . . . actually it works quite well because we all know one another . . . and so a lot of it is done very informally'. There seems to be little overlap between the FCO and the European Secretariat despite the division of functions between them. The departments find FCO and Cabinet Office knowledge of the EU useful and there is a constant process of consultation between the departments and the coordinating machinery. Key policy papers have to go through the FCO and the Cabinet Office and then on to UKREP. The Cabinet Office coordinates within Whitehall but the FCO coordinates instructions to the British ambassador at UKREP. A weekly meeting involving the FCO, the Cabinet Office, the ambassador, and the relevant departments irons out problems and any unresolved issues are passed to the Cabinet Committee.

As departments have become more adept and better resourced in their dealings with Europe, they have relied much less on Cabinet Office or FCO support. As a result the role of the coordinating bodies has become less important and has also changed. To some extent the FCO believes that it still controls contact with Brussels through its contacts with UKREP: 'any input that a UK Government department wants to make into the system in Brussels goes through the UK permanent representative in Brussels. They are the people who talk to the Commission, talk to other member states and so on.'

The reality, however, is that as EU business increases the FCO and the Cabinet Office are losing control. Individual departments are increasingly conducting business with the Commission and other member states directly. Clearly departments with a lot of EU contact like the DTI and MAFF are competent at conducting their own negotiations. A DoE official said that, except for major issues of legislation:

the majority of our links are bilateral . . . There is a continuous process of consultation and communication on a bilateral basis. . . . We also have a lot of direct bilateral contact with Officials in DG 11 in the Commission who are dealing with the areas that we are concerned with. We also have a lot of bilateral contact with our opposite numbers in the Environment Ministries in other member states.

Therefore, the preferences of officials in relation to Europe has been influenced by the process of integration. The FCO and Cabinet Office have adapted well to the need to coordinate European policy. Individual departments are aware of the need to build coalitions.

INSTITUTIONAL INTERESTS

History has a profound affect on departmental attitudes towards the EU. But perhaps more important are the institutional interests of departments. For some departments, legislation coming out of Brussels provides an opportunity for increasing their role and autonomy whilst for others it is a constraint on their activities. According to a senior Cabinet Office official:

Departments tend to have a view of Europe which at least in part reflects the nature of the impact of Europe on their work. MAFF, because the impact of Europe has made the department more important and determines its policy, finds itself very closely involved. Whereas the Treasury, because it is such a bloody nuisance for them, tends to find itself rather irritated.

For three of the departments we examined, prolonged exposure to European integration has provided new opportunities and enhanced their functions. Consequently, they tend to be positive in their approach. In the case of the DTI and Ministry of Agriculture, the EU has given the departments an important *raison d'être* without which they may well have disappeared.

The Ministry of Agriculture is a small department in terms of budget, economic importance, political weight, and size. Despite the logic of Thatcherism to end the subsidization of agriculture and to abolish the department, it has outlived larger departments such as Employment and Energy. To a large extent EU membership has saved the Ministry of Agriculture and probably increased its autonomy (Smith 1993). There is no national agricultural policy and much of the time of many MAFF officials is spent in Brussels. Officials within MAFF, despite their acknowledgement of CAP's problems, are generally pro-European. The impact of the European agricultural policy has been to save their department and, at time of economic retrenchment, to ensure that farmers' subsidies are protected. Membership of the EU has meant that agricultural expenditure is not subject to Treasury control and whilst the Council of Agricultural Ministers remains pro-farmer, it is unlikely that MAFF expenditures can be radically reduced and the department has, to some extent, resisted Treasury calls for the reform of CAP. Despite several rounds of reform, farmers still receive large subsidies and CAP continues to take 50 per cent of the EU budget (Grant 1995), maintaining a crucial role for MAFF.

In line with the public choice view of bureaucracy the EU has increased both the institutional and individual utilities of MAFF officials. A Cabinet Office official points out with EC membership:

MAFF suddenly found itself conducting its own foreign policy. MAFF officials at a rather junior level suddenly found they were going off to Brussels to negotiate. Not only that, they were flying all over the world to negotiate but to negotiate in a way that the Foreign Office couldn't control. So suddenly there was a small element of foreign policy which was run by MAFF instead of the Foreign Office. Unsurprisingly, MAFF officials really rather liked that. I think that naturally enough they really rather enjoy negotiation. They find it fun and the Brussels game is a big game, its a fun game. Officials at a far more junior level than before found themselves speaking on behalf of Britain playing this game for all they were worth, and that partly goes to explain why MAFF has always been more pro-European.

The DTI has faced similar questions to MAFF over its existence. As in agriculture, the logic of Thatcherism is to abolish the department, and with privatization, and the end of many industrial subsidies, questions are often raised over its existence (Purnell 1995). Therefore, the DTI sees significant benefits in EU membership: 'the DTI has always had positive objectives in Europe. We have had some defensive ones too but there have always been things that we have wanted to achieve, and those things on the whole have been less controversial in party political terms.'

The DTI has had three important reasons for seeing the EU as beneficial. First, directives from Brussels provide the DTI with a significant amount of work. Issues relating to the single European market, regulation, monopolies and mergers, technology, trade and industrial subsidies are key aspects of EU policy dealt with by the DTI. Fortunately whilst the state has been rolled back at the national level, it has been extended at the EU level and thus provided new functions for the department.

Second, a strong theme throughout the history of the DTI is support for free trade. Trade issues are best resolved at the multinational level and therefore the DTI is one of the few departments that actually believes in the need for a strong Commission. As a DTI official commented:

I think that the department has consistently been in favour of: a Europe that is open to the outside world; a Europe that creates an effective internal market that is tough on state aids, on monopoly practices; has effective competition policy; and looks at the regional dimension; that spends money wisely . . . We have also become one of the departments that has been arguing for deregulation in Europe, or at least better regulation . . . All of which leads us in institutional terms to favour on the whole a strong Commission which is capable of policing the single market, policing state aid and which is capable of devising and seeing through an effective liberal trade policy . . .

The logic of this position has led the DTI to accept the need for QMV despite the implied loss of national sovereignty.

Third, unlike other departments, EU policies have complemented DTI domestic policy goals. The view in the DTI is: 'in the areas that are core to the DTI, trade policy and Single Market policy, we are closer to the Commission probably than any other member state.' To a certain extent the EU has provided convenient cover for difficult policies. For example, the retrenchment of the steel industry was conducted within the context of the European steel industry and this allowed the DTI and the government as a whole to deflect some of the criticism of the policy (Buller 1996). This is not to say that the DTI is a Eurofederalist department. Their position on the latest IGC negotiations seems to be that they are fairly happy with the status quo.

The Department of Environment (DoE) increasingly finds much of its work deeply enmeshed at the EU level. In the past twenty years the Council of Ministers has agreed over 300 items of legislation affecting the environment. One official commented: 'the extent to which one can consider what is done in the UK in terms of controlling pollution, as being separate from European legislation, the distinction is almost non-existent.' This provides opportunities and constraints for the DoE. On the one hand, the EU enables the DoE to press environmental legislation on other departments, in particular MAFF and the DTI which, if decided at the domestic level, may be opposed. On the other hand, nearly all environmental legislation is now *made* at the EU level and this greatly restricts what the DoE can do on its own in this area. There is an explicit awareness in the DoE, expressed in an internal report, that Europe limits what the department can do:

Building alliances will make it more likely that decisions taken in Brussels are nearer to our policy objectives. But we must not delude ourselves about what is deliverable even by a truly professional approach to Europe. No one member can determine the Community's agenda, the pace of discussion or the final outcome. What it can do, however, is make sure that its own views are understood by other EC actors . . .

The general feeling in the DoE seems to favour EU integration as a means of strengthening environmental legislation. Nevertheless, officials are very aware of the political context. Because of the domestic cost of implementing environmental directives, one official commented:

In many ways we are more sceptical than we might wish to be if we were masters of our own house. The stance that we take up generally on European policy, but also on individual issues, is not something that we dream up in isolation in our ivory towers. In fact, the theory of collective Cabinet responsibility turns out to work, and this is something we are very conscious of. We do have in Whitehall a very strong commitment to obtaining cross-government clearance for stances we take up in individual policy areas.

The EU is important for the Foreign Office, because it is effectively the lead department on European policy and as Britain's world role has declined the FCO has managed to maintain its status as a central negotiator in key European issues. An official highlighted how, 'Britain's involvement in Europe is central to its future as an international power . . . and I think we may be particularly conscious in the Foreign Office that the UK's future on the international stage is very much bound up with its being a major player in Europe'. Edwards (1992: 78) confirms this view:

In terms of European Political Co-operation, the FCO has received a new lease of life. To the relief of many within the Office, here was an area that concerned the FCO above all, for procedurally it involved few other departments since it was all largely a matter of declarations rather than expenditure, and, since it was intergovernmental in character, it aroused little hostility . . .

More than any other department there is a perception of a pro-EU line within the FCO. Moreover, it is not just confined to the more radical/extreme sectors of political opinion in Britain. Owen is particularly interesting on this point. In fact, despite being pro-European in general, he is rather scathing of the Foreign Office 'approach' or 'style' to Europe, and his viewpoint is startlingly close to Thatcher's (Owen 1991).

However, this view of the FCO as excessively pro-European may be an exaggeration. An FCO official made the important point that the interpretation of the FCO as excessively pro-European

comes from the fact that it is the Foreign Office which is the channel to the UK permanent representative in Brussels . . . and we are normally the messengers, if you like, who are bringing the news that this line may not be negotiable after all because we can't get the support for it . . . So there is that kind of perception that is kind of shoot the messenger . . .

The FCO does have institutional interests in EU integration. It helps to maintain its status as a lead department and membership provides it with an important coordinating role. It is also evident that the FCO sees Britain's political future as being within the EU (as do most other departments) and there is a greater flexibility concerning the notion of sovereignty within the FCO than amongst certain ministers.

Perhaps the most important issue in terms of the FCO is its policy style. It accepts the EU as a reality and so the strategic approach is to work within to try to change policies, rules, and institutions to suit British interests. The European Union will not grind to a halt if we leave, and developing policy will still have important consequences for Britain, whether we take part or stay out. In the past, this has meant reluctance to have a 'row' even if Britain's interests appear threatened by a particular policy development.

Departments which have only recently become involved in Europe tend to be more sceptical about its involvement in domestic policy. A Cabinet Office official suggested:

I think it is certainly true that departments like the DSS or the Department of Health or the Department of National Heritage, all of which over the last few years have found European policies intruding on their areas, are still largely operating on the basis of a discreet and hermetically sealed group of people who deal with Europe. And they see it as an imposition and a difficulty. At the same time, the rest of the department, which goes on creating domestic policy, thinks that the European aspect is a distraction.

For the DSS the EU is a burden rather than an opportunity. The department continually finds the EU is adding both legislative and expenditure burdens as a result of the Commission's attempts to harmonize social policy, despite Britain's opt-out from the Social Chapter. They have a team of lawyers continually examining and contesting EU regulations. For the Home Office the relationship is more ambivalent. In certain policy areas such as drugs the EU level is seen as useful for organizing and cooperating on policy. On others such as immigration the relationship has been more problematic. In some senses the Home Office is the least integrated of the departments, coming very late to Europe. It is also apparent talking to Home Office officials that the third pillar, being intergovernmental, operates very differently from business conducted within the European Community and that to a large extent the Home Office is still concerned with limiting EU competence, maintaining sovereignty, and protecting perceived national interests. The Home Office does not see it as in its interest to lose control of immigration, law and order, or criminal justice issues, especially as these have such domestic political importance.

But such scepticism doesn't exist only in newly integrated departments. The Treasury has always been involved in European policy. As a Treasury official admitted: 'There are no bits of Treasury work now that don't have some kind of European Dimension.' Nevertheless, the relationship with the EU is sometimes difficult. Treasury officials find the EU frustrating because it reduces their autonomy, economic policy is no longer purely a domestic concern: 'There are more attempts by Europe to try and dictate the way that financial and monetary policy is run' and whilst the Treasury accepts the convergence criteria it does have to submit to EU pressures. As Thain and Wright (1996: 550) indicate, the implications of free movement of capital and labour are 'a convergence of regulations and payments in social security and income maintenance' which will further constrain Treasury control. Questioning one official about these issues, a trace of Treasury superiority remained: 'I don't think that membership of the European Union has changed the Treasury much. I think its more the other way around, in the sense that the UK thinks that it can try and persuade the Europeans that its approach to economic policy is the sensible one.'

In the area of public expenditure the EU is even more of a problem for Treasury officials. In a range of policy areas the EU can force expenditure that the Treasury cannot control and would prefer not to exist. This has become increasingly apparent in the area of regional spending where the EU has provided funds to Britain on the grounds that there would be 'additionality' (subsidies which are additional to, not a replacement of, existing expenditure). Not surprisingly, the Treasury has continually sought ways of circumventing the additionality requirement (Bache 1996).

The Treasury's instinct is to say no to any new legislation and this scepticism continues at the EU level. A Treasury official suggested: 'I suppose the Treasury is very suspicious and doesn't think that it can trust anybody.' Indeed, even with a pro-European Chancellor like Clarke, the Treasury tried to slow up integration measures that resulted in increased costs.

To sum up: the attitude of departments and the way they relate to Europe varies greatly. Civil servants do not have a set of endogenously determined preferences. Instead their preferences are largely institutionally determined. For some departments Europe creates new opportunities and may increase autonomy in relation to the Cabinet or the Treasury. For others it clearly indicates a loss of control. In such cases the tendency is to attempt to slow further integration.

DEPARTMENTAL COORDINATION

The impact of Europe on attitudes within Whitehall is varied; in particular it has affected the way in which departments are organized. There are common changes, but the way in which departments view relations with the EU has also affected their internal coordination. In the post-Maastricht era there seems a concerted effort to integrate Europe much more into the everyday operations of departments. Yet different departments organize in very different ways. The Treasury provides a good example of how intradepartmental coordination has changed:

Five years ago, all the relations with Europe were handled by the Europe Division in the International area. Today every team that deals with a particular policy domestically also deals with it at an international and European level. For example, the team that dealt with MAFF expenditure also deals with CAP. (Treasury official)

So rather than there being EC specialists, all officials within the Treasury have some EC competence. There is also a small EU Coordination and Strategy team, ensuring a unified departmental line is maintained and dealing with issues where a domestic section lacks departmental expertise. It also plays the coordinating role at the external level and represents the department in Cabinet Office meetings. Nevertheless, there is still an impression that Europe is not, as yet, that important or central to its work. A Cabinet Office official suggested: 'There is a culture within the Treasury, there is a smallish cadre of people who have made their careers dealing with EU matters ... And perhaps the vast majority of Treasury Officials do see European issues as something not to be touched with a barge pole.'

Even in the FCO, centrally involved in the EU since the beginning, there has been a change in the way that EU business is integrated. Developments such as the collapse of Eastern Europe, greater European Political Cooperation, and a common security policy 'mean that there is virtually nobody in any corner of the Foreign Office not sometimes having to go off to attend a working group in Brussels ... There is generally a far greater consciousness of the European dimension of business all through the office.'

In terms of formal organization the FCO has a EU command structure with three departments: EU Department External for external economic policy of the EU; EU Department Internal which covers EMU, the IGC and all institutional questions and shadows the work of domestic departments; and the Common Foreign and Security Policy division briefing the political director and all the second pillar work.

Likewise, the DTI, also closely involved in European policy, has always had a European division. Now, however, 'we have concluded that the only way you can now run EU policy in reality is by letting the individual experts get on with it' and so whilst there is some central coordination, on a range of policy areas, such as telecoms or consumer protection, the department does not coordinate. The current role of the European Division is to try to keep an overview of what is going on in the department in relation to Europe and to provide advice on the working procedures of the EU, and in some senses to act as a European secretariat for the department. Much of the contact with the EU is now bilateral with officials within the department consulting with people in the EU and the governments of other member states.

In this sphere the DoE has been the most proactive. In areas where there is a high European content, contact is bilateral rather than through a coordinating body. The department undertook a review of its handling of European business. One of the problems for the DoE is that whilst responsibilities, such as water, are almost completely European, others like Housing and Local Government have little contact with the EU. Therefore, there has not been an attempt to force all divisions into adopting similar approaches to the EU. Rather a high-level European Strategy Group brings together grade two officials from different policy areas every three to six months to review the department's European strategy. In addition, there is a European Division within the Environmental Protection Group for dealing with day-to-day European issues and providing expertise for the whole of the department on Europe.

Clearly, in recent years the majority of departments have made significant organizational changes in order to adapt to the requirements of the EU. In most cases they have attempted to integrate EU business throughout the department rather than concentrate it within a European coordination body as was the case. However, in some departments, notably the Home Office and the DoE, where large sections have little EU relevance, the European Division takes on a much more central role. There are significant differences in the way that departments deal with the EU. The DTI and DoE seem to have come to terms with the importance of the EU and see the relevance of intimate and regular contacts, others like the FCO and Treasury still tend to see the EU as external and more of an aspect of foreign rather than domestic policy. For the DoE there is evidence that EU engagement obtains more rigorous environmental regulation than would be the case in a purely domestic context. For departments like MAFF, the DTI, and DoE, Europe increases their scope and they have adapted well to developing transgovernmental links. Those departments developing much greater integration within the EU raise the question of whether this is leading to the adoption of an EU-style bureaucratic culture within the UK.

THE 'EUROPEANIZATION' OF BRITISH DECISION-MAKING: WHITEHALL MODEL UNDER PRESSURE?

As the British policy process has become 'Europeanized', there is evidence suggesting that the different outlooks and practices of continental decision-making have affected Whitehall's ethos, and decision-making culture. Indeed, according to Lodge, there is a growing 'bureaucratic interpenetration' of civil servants at the EU level (Burnham and Maor 1995: 189). Increasingly, civil servants from member states are working for short periods within Whitehall, but as one official pointed out these are of very limited duration (two to three months) and there are resource and language constraints. There are however a number of exchange programmes to facilitate greater interaction between bureaucrats.

Christoph (1993) suggests a number of ways in which EU membership may have altered the roles of British civil servants: a greater acceptance of bureaucratic individualism and creativity; less tolerance of the demands of hierarchy in Whitehall; and a franker acknowledgement of the presence of political factors in administrative activity. Bureaucratic individualism and creativity originate from two sources. First, as more and more policy is decided in Brussels civil servants not only brief ministers before the flight to Brussels, but also take part in extensive negotiations with their opposite numbers before final decisions are taken by ministers. Second, within these negotiations, the style of decision-making will be quite different from that experienced by British civil servants in London. At the EU level, civil servants will necessarily have to bargain and construct alliances with other European officials around a negotiation position. Reviewing how it should reorganize its policy-making process, an internal paper in the DoE argues: 'While direct experience will undoubtedly build on knowledge and skills acquired "in the classroom", the context and manner of EC business is so different from domestic administration that the foundations for handling EC work need to be laid in a conscious and concentrated way.'

When British officials deal with their opposite numbers at the European level, it is important to remember that these will often be 'political' appointments, unlike the constitutional position in the UK. One civil servant was willing to acknowledge that exposure to this process of negotiating and bargaining had changed the approach of civil servants to decision-making in significant ways:

I suppose inevitably, one is drawn into a political world. If you are going to negotiate with these people and share their ideas, and communicate on the part of the government, I don't mean that you go in and give them a political line, but inevitably you have to operate a little bit on a political level. I don't believe this means that we are politicized, this doesn't mean we end up saying that we are representing the Conservative Party. It remains the case that we are representing the government of the day. But I think it is true that we have to handle political issues more than traditionally was the case. (Interview with Cabinet Office official)

As already noted, the Treasury remains less integrated into the Community because of its institutional position. That said, one official closely involved in coordinating the department's policy towards the EU commented on changes to the decision-making procedure in similar fashion:

. . . you have to have some degree of knowledge of the way the EU institutions work. And that's a bit of a shock. Most new jobs that you go to, you have to get some knowledge about a particular policy area, for example, social security policy. You have to find out something about it, and from my experience, you sort of pick it up. Whereas on the European side, from my experience, you don't just pick that up. You have to have some kind of training. And the Civil Service College run a number of courses. So you may go off for an afternoon and have a session on the Treaty, and pillars, and all this mysterious stuff. The office is now waking up to the fact that it needs to promote these kinds of European skills if we're going to cope. (Treasury official)

Christoph (1993) also suggests that British civil servants are becoming less tolerant of the demands of hierarchy in Whitehall as a result of the impact of the EU on the domestic political process. Interviews provided little direct evidence of this change, but a number of officials admitted that as more and more policy was being negotiated in Brussels, it was becoming increasingly difficult for the

Centre to monitor, let alone control, the detail of policy. Two other factors added to this picture of junior and middle-ranking officials in European divisions enjoying unprecedented autonomy from the rest of Whitehall. First, it was suggested that a number of civil servants were endeavouring to make a career out of specializing in Union business: the EU would provide their 'career anchor'. Second, officials made the point that EU policy-making is a continuous process, and knowledge about the historical development of policy could be a source of power when it came to interdepartmental battles over present and future policy.

Nevertheless, the impact of exposure to EU working methods is still relatively limited, although there is every reason to think that it may grow providing the UK remains a member of the EU. In particular, two factors continue to militate against increasing bureaucratic individualism, creativity, and autonomy. First, despite the critiques from the left and the right that civil servants are a power unto themselves and often pursue policies regardless of the desires of ministers, there is strong evidence to suggest that ministers *can* make a significant impact on any departmental view. Civil servants are very conscious of constitutional conventions and ministerial preferences clearly limit their actions when they negotiate in Brussels. As a result the attitude of a department towards the EU does vary according to who is minister. One civil servant was very explicit about the impact of ministers:

When Mr Portillo was Secretary of State in the Department of Employment, his officials took a stunningly Eurosceptical line because that's what he wanted them to do. And Home Office officials take a very Eurosceptical line now because that is what Mr Howard wants them to do and Treasury officials take a much more Europhile line because that is what Mr Clarke wants them to do.

To some extent the support of Kenneth Clarke for the EU places Treasury officials, who have long been cautious about Europe, in a difficult position: 'You have to judge fairly carefully, very often what the Chancellor is likely to think, and how he is going to play it.' However, it is also the case that departmental interests can make ministers look at Europe in a different light and in that sense they too are affected by institutional interests: 'If you look at an issue like qualified majority voting, for example, the experience of the Minister of Agriculture shows on most agricultural issues QMV works in favour of the UK's position, because we have been able to get through decisions against the resistance of one or two protectionist member states.'

The DTI have had ministers with sharply contrasting views on Europe, ranging from Ridley to Heseltine, who have changed the emphasis of policy towards Europe, but on the whole there has been some degree of consistency. So ministers do influence how officials deal with Europe, but their positions also reflect institutional interests towards Europe. Despite strong ideological preferences, their positions in office are not only endogenously determined.

CONCLUSIONS

From our work, there was no evidence of a single civil service attitude towards the EU. In so far as it was possible to generalize, attitudes of civil servants varied according to the institutional interests of the department, and its historical relations with the EU. That said, membership of the EU and the increasing process of European integration have wrought general and common changes on the behaviour of civil servants. On the one hand, it was noted that there was a growing convergence in the way that various departments organized their relations with the EU. On the other hand, there was some evidence that as the British policy-making process has become more 'Europeanized' different methods and attitudes towards decision-making at the Union level have rubbed off on British officials.

However, two factors appear to militate against these trends. Civil servants continue to insist that politicians remain in ultimate control over policy towards the EU. There seems little scope for individual bureaucratic discretion if one combines this with the fact that the British negotiating machinery has the reputation for being one of the 'tightest outfits' in the EU.

9

The British Press and European Integration: 1948 to 1996

George Wilkes and Dominic Wring

Between 1948 and 1975, the British press moved from a vaguely 'pro-Community' consensus to a pronounced and nearly unanimous Euro-enthusiasm. Gradually this gave way to widespread Euroscepticism in large sections of the press in the 1990s.

The initial pro-Community stance of the press was not simply due to the influence of an economic or political elite on editorial policy, through media magnates or politicians. Nor do the international contacts of the media explain the professedly independent approach of the pro-Community press. Journalists and editors in much of the pro-Community media betrayed an underlying uncertainty over the benefits of committing the UK to European institutions and policies, beneath an increasingly strident campaign in favour of EC membership. 'Pro-Communityism' during this period often related as much to a desire for domestic political change as it did to a favourable outlook on developments in the rest of Western Europe. By taking a stand in favour of entry into Europe, the press was cutting a profile for itself in domestic politics. This meant that, not only did the focus of editors on domestic debate frequently relegate events elsewhere to a minor position in coverage of the issue, but also that the British media was often blind to what was really happening across the Channel.

WESTERN UNION AND THE CREATION OF THE EUROPEAN MOVEMENT, 1948

The creation of the European Movement in 1948 and the first speeches in favour of Western European unity of Ernest Bevin,

Labour's Foreign Secretary, prompted the first press debate over the merits of European cooperation. With the notable exceptions of Beaverbrook's *Daily Express*, devoted to an Empire-oriented foreign policy, and the trade union-owned *Daily Herald*, chiefly concerned with the Labour government's economic freedom to act, most national newspapers and weekly magazines favoured the UK giving a lead in uniting Western Europe in the face of the Soviet threat.

Agreement stopped there. The *Observer*, edited by a federalist, David Astor, supported economic, political, and military integration in Europe, largely in view of the potential threat of a German *revanche* (25 April and 2, 23 May 1948). The paper's coverage of the founding congress of the European Movement at The Hague stressed the federalist influence among British Labour delegates there and declared Winston Churchill's speech in support of a European Assembly his greatest ever (9 May 1948). The *News Chronicle*, owned by a leading pro-Community activist, Lord Layton, was the only other publication which solidly supported the Hague initiative. Coverage in the centre-left *Manchester Guardian* was far less substantial, reflecting the editors' dislike for ambitious and 'divisive' federalist schemes and for the party political point-scoring which had accompanied Labour and Conservative proposals (5, 8, 10 May 1948). The *Financial Times* largely ignored the political aspects of the European issue and gave scant attention to the economic aspects of the Western Union and Hague Congress proposals (8, 11 May 1948). *The Times*, though consistently anti-federalist, was otherwise unpredictable. Its editorials on 3 and 4 May praised Bevin for uniting parliamentarians behind a 'pragmatic' approach, 'organic, practical and developing always as needs require,' but were critical of Labour's 'isolationist' ban on its MPs attending the Hague Congress. Thereafter, its scorn for federalists was turned against supporters of the Congress, attacking preparations for the Congress as unpractical, though backing its declaration on human rights; Labour were now criticized for being both too federalist and too dogmatic to cooperate with non-socialists. A leader on 8 May welcomed the fact that Churchill's approach to a European assembly was 'vague', while coverage of Congress proceedings in the days which followed focused on criticism of its federalist elements.

However, the leading weekly journals began to treat the European issue regularly and in more depth than the dailies, paying less attention to the domestic politics which surrounded the Hague Congress or

Western Union initiatives. Leaders in the *New Statesman* (1, 8, 15, and 29 May 1948) attacked the supranationalist plans of the *Observer*, stressing the need for British-led European unity in the face of US and Soviet domination; arguing that economic unity, mixing trade liberalization with economic planning, appeared more hopeful than political unity across the Roman Catholic-Socialist divide. *The Economist*, critical of federalism as utopian and cautious about European cooperation reversing American involvement in Europe, urged Bevin to be specific about what sacrifices of sovereignty he would make (8 May 1948). The Hague Congress, according to an *Economist* editorial on 15 May, was 'unrepresentative', and had failed to address the main 'practical' questions: Germany's place in Europe and interstate cooperation. It nevertheless noted with interest that an assembly might become a 'European opposition'.

Though it is difficult to know what effect press support for European unification had on the UK government, a Foreign Office Cabinet paper in November did take note of 'pressure' from 'sections of public opinion in this country' to make the proposals for 'Western Union' more concrete, and used this as a partial justification for increasing European cooperation (Public Records Office 1948).

THE SCHUMAN DECLARATION, MAY 1950

Editorial reactions to the French initiative of 1950 to create a European Coal and Steel Community (ECSC) suggest that British journalists were now more open to a continental initiative than they had been two years earlier. The *Herald* and *Express* remained implacably opposed to closer ties to the Continent, but most of the press welcomed the Schuman initiative, in spite of the difficulties which it presented for the UK. The *Manchester Guardian* noted that the Schuman Plan had 'exhilarating possibilities', suggesting that there were enough grounds for the UK to look 'fully and frankly' at membership despite the differences which marked it off from its continental neighbours (11 May 1950); *The Times* and the *Daily Telegraph* reached a similar conclusion. The *Financial Times* gave it little attention, but emphatically approved the decision to start integration without the Americans and British (11 May 1950). The *Observer*, giving the initiative even less coverage, urged UK membership of the European organization as a step towards an Atlantic Union (14 May

1950). *The Economist*, favouring UK participation in order to bolster its ability to plan its own economy, maintained that the plan would 'stand or fall' on its effects on links with the USA, warning that Adenauer and other Europeans harboured 'neutralist' designs for the new Western European organization (20 May 1950). The *New Statesman*, declaring that Labour should lead a neutralist 'Third Force' Europe, balanced the risks of a 'reactionary' Western Union, dominated by cartels, with hopes for an independent Western Europe, bolstered by 'socialist safeguards' (13 May 1950). The Schuman Plan, it believed, would dissipate pressure for a solution to the 'German problem' which left states sovereign and kept the possibility of German rearmament open. Coverage in the *New Statesman* was clearly influenced by Maurice Edelman, a Labour delegate to the Council of Europe Consultative Assembly; mirroring his positive judgement of Schuman's initiative, it asserted that Britain could not afford to reject the plan (20 May 1950). Its position reversed once it became clear that Britain would not join. There was a broad correlation between the shift of opinion against the Schuman Plan in parliamentary debate and in the press (Moon 1985: 107–15); both seem likely to have been influenced by the pre-election political atmosphere.

THE BIRTH OF THE EUROPEAN ECONOMIC COMMUNITY, 1955–1959

The media took a considerable time to realize the significance of Britain's exclusion from the European Economic Community (EEC). Not until the collapse of the free trade area negotiations in 1958 did the bulk of the press begin to question the wisdom of the UK government's European policy.

Broadsheet newspapers such as *The Times* and *Telegraph* played down the significance of the Messina conference in early June 1955, and the popular press ignored it entirely (Moon 1985: 152–3). This reaction was in line with the consensus among diplomats and politicians from the Six and the USA, believing a more supranationalist direction for Europe to have been thwarted, supposedly symbolized by the resignation of Jean Monnet, President of the ECSC. Later that month, a visit from the Dutch Foreign Minister, Beyen, received mixed responses from the broadsheets: the *Telegraph* (22 June

1955) stressed the importance of Britain's role in the recently modified Western European Union; the *Financial Times* (22 June 1955) noted that the apparent improvement in the Six's attitude to the UK was due to the knowledge that Britain had more to give than it would receive in terms of the 'most important' aspect, the proposed European atomic energy agency, or 'Euratom'. A handful of radio broadcasts were also dedicated to British relations with the Six at this time.

In February 1956, *The Economist* took an isolated stand in favour of Euratom (11 February 1956). The signing of the EEC and Euratom treaties on 25 March 1957 although not covered in depth in the British press, prompted editorials in the broadsheets, and the *News Chronicle* also printed a supplement for the occasion (26 March 1957). Newspaper coverage of the development of the UK's counter-initiatives from this time was just as weak. A *New York Times* article on a possible British political initiative to the Six was missed in the British press, and they entirely passed over subsequent diplomatic developments in the winter of 1956–7. Broadsheet, radio, and television coverage of the free trade area plan increased gradually over 1956–7,[1] following the government's developing public position and giving little attention to growing backbench support for closer links with the Six.

By 1957 the tendency of the print media was to favour a European free trade area. The free trade area negotiations of 1957–8 and the establishment of the European Free Trade Association in 1959–60 provoked a greater level of news coverage on television and in the press. In the quality newspapers the issue still provoked infrequent comment, while the tabloids with fewer European correspondents relied greatly on the more specialist publications for background comment. One such specialist journal, *The Economist*, had been increasingly critical of the British government's approach to the negotiations, and though their collapse in late 1958 left *The Times* simply indignant at 'France the Wrecker' (18 November 1958), a few journalists suggested that the UK should consider entering the EEC.[2]

---

[1] For example, Independent Television News and Panorama began to devote more attention to relations with the Six in 1957 (see ITN archives; and BBC Written Archives).

[2] *The Economist, Guardian,* and *Observer* began to discuss joining the EEC, while economist and journalist Alan Day made the earliest broadcast appeals for entry on BBC radio, Dec. 1958 (Camps 1964: 287).

THE FIRST 'GREAT DEBATE' OVER ENTERING
THE EEC, 1960–1963

The British press launched its first serious debate over membership of the EEC in 1960. Until spring 1961, the increasingly pro-entry press was the main forum for public debate of the pros and cons of membership. Once the application was under way television became a major medium for public debate over the issue, the coverage of news and discussion programmes being biased more towards entry than against it. By the autumn of 1962, the press was no longer the largely pro-entry influence it had been at the time of the decision to open negotiations, and the government turned to television to persuade the public of the wisdom of entering the EEC (Wilkes, forthcoming).

The first publications to support entry in 1960 were those of the political centre ground which had already discussed the option in late 1958. Though their advocacy of the merits of entry remained qualified,[3] they were less cautious about the need for change than pro-Conservative publications. Beaverbrook's papers, prompted by a government leak, began to attack the pro-entry case in mid-1960. By the summer of 1961, almost all of the press had taken sides, and the *Mirror*, its equally pro-entry sister paper the *Herald* (no longer linked to the trade unions), and the *Express* had launched 'campaigns' on the issue, stepping up the number of leader articles on Europe and regularly featuring polemical pieces, clearly distinguished from news items.[4] The main news and discussion programmes on television, including *Panorama*, *Tonight*, and *Gallery*, only began regular coverage of the issue late in the spring of 1961. Political balance in broadcasting was carefully monitored by the political parties, but not by pro-or anti-entry campaigning groups, and at this stage coverage was often biased towards the case for entry by the lack of news items

---

[3] Those in favour of entry in 1960 included *The Economist, Observer, Mail, Spectator, Encounter,* and *Time & Tide*. The *Guardian* maintained a positive outlook towards joining the EEC from January 1960, while insisting there was no hurry to decide. Editorials in the *Financial Times, The Times,* and the *Telegraph* also began to consider the merits of entry at this time.

[4] The continued balance of news items in the *Express* did contrast with the slant given to their headlines. Also in favour by June 1961: the *Financial Times, The Times, Telegraph, Guardian, Mirror, Herald, Scotsman, Statist, Sunday Times*. Opposed: the Express newspapers (*Daily and Sunday Express, Evening Standard*), *City Press, Daily Worker, Reynolds News, Sunday Citizen, New Statesman, Tribune, New Left Review*.

clearly unfavourable to an application, and the relatively small number of journalists and politicians publicly opposed to an application.

To some extent, most pro-entry publications still took their cue from the government as it began its ambivalent shift towards membership of the EEC in 1960. In 1961, contacts between the Prime Minister, Harold Macmillan, the minister responsible for relations with the EEC, Edward Heath, and the editors of Cecil King's papers, the Mirror and Herald, may have given encouragement to both parties in the pursuit of a clearer pro-entry position (Macmillan 1973: 14; Edelman 1965: 165). Also influenced by relations with pro-entry politicians were the decisions of much of the press to strike a pro-entry line, along with the launching of the *Mirror* and *Herald* 'campaigns'. The pro-entry lobbies in the parties and the press had similar approaches: entry into Europe meant the revitalization of the UK economy. Significantly supporters of entry in both the press and parliament based their approach on shared sources of information on the issue, perhaps most influentially of all *The Economist* articles by Christopher Layton (Edwards 1993: 923–4).

The role of the pro-entry press in the government's approach to negotiations for entry into the EEC has often been exaggerated. When the press were most solidly supportive, in mid-1961, the government was most cautious; when the press became less convinced, the government became more publicly enthusiastic. Increasingly, the Conservative government and party turned to television interviews and ministerial broadcasts in an attempt to attract popular support for its European policy, and plans were being developed for a more sustained public campaign in the event of a successful conclusion to negotiations. Macmillan made his first ministerial broadcast on the issue on 24 January 1962, revealing the importance which he attached to it (ministerial broadcasts were not normally used for single issues), and on 20 September he made a broadcast which was so unequivocally supportive of entry that the Labour leader, Hugh Gaitskell, felt forced to contest it in similarly strong terms (BBC 21 September 1962). In contrast with his diffident approach to informing parliament, Heath made a priority of giving television interviews during the negotiations. As the government became beset by political misfortune in mid-1962, the pro-entry bias of much of the Conservative press did not seem to be translating into loyal grass-roots support for the government. Macmillan made only the slightest attempt to 'woo' Beaverbrook, as he put it, knowing the personal attention Beaverbrook gave to anti-European coverage of the issue in the Express newspapers (Macmillan 1973: 33).[5]

Gaitskell's relationship with the press in the summer of 1962 was more direct than Macmillan's. For instance, Alistair Hetherington, editor of the *Guardian* consciously followed Gaitskell, rejecting the attempts of a number of Conservative ministers to persuade him to continue to support the application (Hetherington Papers). Having come down clearly against Macmillan's application Gaitskell discussed the issue with Beaverbrook, though with little evident result (Beaverbrook Papers; Donnelly Papers).

In the summer of 1962, during the Commonwealth Prime Ministers' Conference and the party conferences, the Common Market application was the most frequently covered issue in press and broadcasting news. The early dominance of support for entry across the press and broadcasting spectrum had now waned, as objections to the terms agreed at Brussels appeared in the *Observer* and *The Times* as well as the *Guardian* (see leaders October–November 1962 *passim*). The *Mirror* and *Herald*, by contrast, remained forthright in their support for entry even after de Gaulle's veto in January 1963 and the breakdown of negotiations, hailed by the *Express* with the headline 'Glory Glory Hallelujah!' (30 January 1963). In January this was followed avidly by the 'serious' media, though the issue was already fading in the popular press. Soon afterwards the bulk of the media dropped the subject as they became absorbed in the implications of Gaitskell's death and the ensuing Labour leadership struggle.

THE LABOUR GOVERNMENT'S APPLICATION

Though Wilson's government also made an EEC membership application, it maintained an uneasy relationship with the pro-entry Labour press throughout. The increasingly federalist *Guardian* and the *Mirror* had returned to pressing for entry while others, like the successor to the *Herald*, the *Sun*, tempered their support for joining the EEC with advocacy for Wilson's attempts at 'bridge-building' between the EEC and EFTA. In 1966, the generally pro-Community press opposed the

---

[5] Beaverbrook's personal interference in his papers' Common Market coverage is suggested by his correspondence with Peter Walker (Beaverbrook Papers) and from the testimony of Clive Jenkins (1990: 130).

tendency of the party leaders to play the European issue down in their election campaigning (Butler and Kitzinger 1976: 214); the *Guardian* and *Financial Times* were so optimistic as to insist that the French now actually wanted the UK to join the EEC (17 March 1966). Against them, the *Daily Express*, despite Lord Beaverbrook's death, almost alone continued to hold out a 'golden vision' of a greater Commonwealth association (28 October 1967). Public opinion moved in favour of entry over 1964–6, though the role played by the pro-Community bias of the press in this is unclear (Butler and Stokes 1969: 176–7 and 225–7). Wilson continued to skirmish with the *Mirror* and the other enthusiastic pro-entry publications, which for their part doubted the sincerity of his conversion to the pro-entry case. Privately he claimed to have been influenced towards the pro-entry case by an article in *The Economist* in 1966, though one close colleague, George Wigg, believed Wilson was more concerned with avoiding a Cabinet crisis than with the merits of entry into the EEC (Wigg 1972: 339; Kitzinger 1973: 226 and 280).

ENTRY INTO THE EUROPEAN COMMUNITIES, 1970–1973

Media coverage of the debate over entering the EEC reached a new level of intensity in 1971 when it became clear that British membership was within reach. Again the debate was skewed: anti-Marketeers believed the increasing media bias in favour of the EEC was created by pressure from pro-Europeans and by the interests of certain newspaper proprietors. Uwe Kitzinger, a pro-Marketeer, has written of a natural tendency for journalists to support 'reasoned', 'internationalist' argument against sentimental 'nationalism' and 'simplistic' fears (Kitzinger 1973: 70–2 and 337 ff.). Both arguments have some validity, though the majority of journalists supported entry without pressure from outside, and their decisions were focused more on domestic politics than on developments within the EC itself.

Changes in the ownership of a number of publications underline the point that pro-Community bias was usually not simply a matter of directives sent down to journalists from above. For instance, there was no relaxation of the passion with which the *Daily Mirror* supported entry after it passed from King to Reed International, nor had the *Sun* become less pro-European. However, editorial policy in the *Express* did continue to be influenced more by its new proprietor, Sir Max

Aitken, than most publications. The *Express* remained the main anti-European publication until the Commons voted for entry in October 1971, threatening to fight against a 'Yes' vote. But shortly afterwards Aitken wrote that the *Express* would accept the will of parliament, a decision which meant that from now on the *Express* would fight for British interests within rather than against the EC (*Express*, 30 October 1971; Kitzinger 1973: 345). The *Spectator* swung against an application in the autumn of 1970 (1 August and 1 October 1970) under the influence both of its proprietor, Harry Creighton, and its editor, George Gale. Reacting to the signature of the Treaty of Accession in 1972, Gale declared the *Spectator* would reverse its policy again and become federalist; he left before the referendum campaign of 1975, however, and both the *Spectator* and his own programming on London Broadcasting Corporation (LBC) remained vigorously opposed to EEC membership (Kitzinger 1973: 342).

The influence of politicians on the national dailies was less obvious than it had been in 1960–3. The leading anti-Community weeklies, however, were clearly linked (through Richard Crossman of the *New Statesman*, Patrick Cosgrave of the *Spectator*, and via the Tribune group) to backbench politics, and the sympathy of *The Economist* for Labour's Marketeers may well have been increased by the personal contacts provided by John Harris (Kitzinger 1973: 337–9).

Despite the attempts of broadcasters and of much of the press to achieve a balance in their reporting, the pro-Community lobby gained some advantage through its organized approach to media liaison, based on the 'media breakfasts' directed by the Conservatives' former Director of Publicity, Geoffrey Tucker. Against this, anti-Marketeers paid little attention to media liaison. This made reporting of the pro-Community lobby easier, and the media breakfasts also prompted Independent Television News (ITN) (with a larger audience than any newspaper) to include regular information bulletins on various aspects of Britain's application (Kitzinger 1973: 196 ff. and 237; Hollingsworth 1986: 46). However, not all broadcasting coverage favoured the entry case: the rules stipulating that 'balance' be calculated strictly according to political tendency rather than size of support also had the effect of exaggerating the importance of the political extremes (Kitzinger 1973: 70–2).

The 'pro-Community' bias of most of the press, both during the parliamentary debate of 1971 and the referendum debate of 1975, was partly tempered by the continued freedom given to the few firmly anti-Market journalists by many of the pro-Community newspapers (notably *The Times*, *Financial Times*, and *Telegraph*), and by their inclusion of occasional articles commissioned from anti-Marketeers, though in 1975 there were cases in which zealous editors on *The Times* and the *Scotsman* were accused of subverting both practices (Kitzinger 1973: 337–9; Butler and Kitzinger 1976: 78; Hollingsworth 1986: 46–9). Finally, the overwhelming domestic focus of the debate was as pronounced as it had been in 1960–3, that is, biased towards the 'pro-Community' case (Kitzinger 1973: 336).

THE 1975 REFERENDUM

In 1975, controversy over pro-Community bias in the press reached a climax. Not only was there a near-total dominance of editorial coverage for the pro-Community case, but news coverage also followed the pro-Community strategy in emphasizing personality over policy differences. To anti-Marketeers, the newspapers' clear pro-Community bias seemed to explain the shift of public opinion polls from opposition to entry in 1974 and to the widespread acquiescence signalled by the 'Yes' vote in the referendum; though there are a number of other factors which might help to explain the shift (Hollingsworth 1986: 50; Butler and Kitzinger 1976: 176). Television broadcasting authorities, on the other hand, had largely quelled doubts about the balance of their output over the European issue, providing a large proportion of voters with a more reliable source of information from which to make their judgement.

A pro-Community bias dominated much news coverage on the issue in the press. Throughout the period of campaigning preceding the referendum, the 'pro-Community' press focused on the personalities of the few leading anti-Marketeers. The focus on personality had always affected coverage of the anti-Community camp more than the pro-Community camp, since a relatively small number of politicians dominated the anti-Community campaign, most of whom were prominent on the far left and right wings of their parties (Butler and Kitzinger 1976: 194). Nevertheless, the focus on personality now went further than it had previously, various publications alleging that the purpose of the referendum had been to prevent Tony Benn from dividing the Labour Party. Assailed by the *Mirror* as the 'Minister of Fear' for his gloomy prediction of the effect EEC membership would have, Benn was also portrayed by Conservative dailies as a dictatorial leftist, or, as the *Evening News* colourfully put it, 'a vampire, a fanatic and a bully' (Hollingsworth 1986: 47–50).

Editorial coverage of policy questions in the pro-Community press show that they were not simply camouflaging the case for entry in domestic politics, as anti-Marketeers suggested. Bemoaning the focus of the domestic political debate on jobs and food prices, broadsheets and tabloids alike insisted that EC membership was above all a political ideal, which most publications had supported for over a decade (Butler and Kitzinger 1976: 214, 218, and 229 ff.). The press were generally critical of the government's decision to hold a referendum. So too were the rest of the pro-Community lobby, though—as Colin Seymour-Ure has noted—the press had its own reasons for opposing a referendum, naturally defensive of its political role as interpreter of popular opinion, and believing the European issue was too old and too complex for renewed public campaigning to be able to treat it satisfactorily (Butler and Kitzinger 1976: 214).

Broadcasters too approached the referendum aware that they had to tread a fine line between boring audiences with too much coverage, on the one hand, and providing too little information on the other (Butler and Kitzinger 1976: 190). The government White Paper laying ground rules for the referendum established a consultative mechanism for ensuring balanced broadcasting coverage which increased the freedom of broadcasting authorities to determine their approach. As a result, programming could balance the two sides of the debate with less need to balance the participation of partisans and parties in each item, and the result was generally approved by both pro- and anti-Marketeers (Butler and Kitzinger 1976: 190–213).

INTO THE 1980S: THE DEBATES OVER INTEGRATION

Prior to 1983 the declared scepticism of the Labour Party reflected a wider public debate on European integration centred on the issue of whether Britain ought to remain in the EEC. The press, overwhelmingly supportive of the Conservatives, tended to reinforce Prime Minister Thatcher's belief in the economic benefits of membership. Whilst pro-government journalists like George Gale advocated withdrawal, they tended to be undermined by more mundane newspaper criticisms of EEC policy on UK budget contributions, agricultural subsidies, and fishing agreements. If anything the complexity of the subject and perceived public disinterest combined to keep the issue off the top of the agenda, as did the coverage given to what were deemed to be more salient and understandable political topics like the power of trades unions, Labour left-wingers, and the Soviet threat.

The passage of the Single European Act in 1986 opened a new era of cooperation between Community partners. Following the largely untroubled passage of the Act in each member state, integrationist thinkers came to the fore of public debate. President of the European Commission and the former French Socialist minister Jacques Delors articulated a vision of closer union and mutual cooperation. Others, particularly Margaret Thatcher, were less impressed. In her famous sceptical speech at Bruges in September 1988 Thatcher attacked the federalist position by arguing that the Community should be nothing more than a partnership of trading states. The Conservative press, which backed the Prime Minister in other matters, tended to agree. Significantly they were joined by the Labour-supporting *Daily Mirror* which sympathetically reported 'Thatcher scorns identikit Europe' (21 September 1988). However, as the debate began to intensify during the late 1980s into something altogether more important, it was interesting that the Prime Minister saw it necessary to question whether Brussels-based correspondents were in danger of going 'native' (Morgan 1995).

Ironically it was an attack by populist tabloid the *Sun* which brought Jacques Delors and his vision of Europe to greater public attention in Britain. Three weeks prior to the resignation of Thatcher, a move itself exacerbated by serious Conservative divisions over EC policy, the paper attacked Delors for being 'the most boring bureaucrat in Brussels' (*Sun*, 30 October 1990). Nevertheless within a couple of days the President was deemed sufficiently interesting to merit a front-page story, which opened with the memorable headline 'Up Yours Delors!' and continued, 'The Sun today calls on its patriotic family of readers to tell the feelthy French to FROG OFF!', before ending by asking the public to collectively shout across the English Channel: 'At midday tomorrow Sun readers are urged to tell the French fool where to stuff his ECU' and in the same edition more detailed analysis attacked the French farmers' burning of British livestock, 'dodgy food' exports, and even Napoleon Bonaparte (*Sun*, 1 November 1990). Less tastefully, the *Sun* also questioned the country's record during the Second World War. As Gertrude

Hardt-Mautner points out this, the most infamous attack by a London-based newspaper on an EC politician, is emblematic of a tendency on the part of the press to merge isolationist British pride with a fear that European integration threatens this in prejudiced reports attacking continental neighbours (Hardt-Mautner 1995). Nor is this tendency solely the domain of the popular tabloids, as a reporter on the *Daily Telegraph* showed when commenting on how a breakthrough in the building of the Channel Tunnel was enabling British people to smell 'the first whiffs of garlic' (31 October 1990).

Following the resignation of Margaret Thatcher from government in November 1990, the press, not to mention Conservative leadership, have appeared less predictable in their European policy. Warning of the problems inherent in the Maastricht Treaty, the *Daily Telegraph* was typical of much print media commentary when it urged John Major and his government to exercise leadership by 'strapping the visionaries into their seats . . . to check the extremists and put the EC on a sane and realistic path for the future' (9 December 1991). The press's initial, grudging acceptance of the complex Maastricht settlement was partially revised in the autumn of 1992, following the debacle over Britain's forced withdrawal from the European Exchange Rate Mechanism. This event, popularly termed 'Black Wednesday', heightened sensitivities to the integration question and provided obvious support to the accusation that, as the leading tabloid put it: 'The European dream is in tatters' (*Sun*, 21 September 1992). The following day an editorial in the same title declared it did not want to see a 'United States of Europe . . . run from Brussels' deciding policies on tax, immigration, and the economy with recourse to a Central Bank (*Sun*, 22 September 1992). A survey of ten readers, together with the inevitable phone-in poll that followed, backed the paper's call for the government to 'Tear up the Treaty'. Reflecting print media divisions over party political matters, the press was not uniform in its response to the ERM crisis, and it was the *Daily Mirror* which defended the Community by arguing it had created 'ever closer unity in Europe' and been a force for stability and bulwark against war.

'EUROMYTHOLOGY'

Apart from the serious concerns that further European integration might cost jobs and cede sovereignty, one tabloid journalist admitted his professions' frame of reference was also governed by a view of an EC perceived to be 'interfering more and more in trivia' (Morgan 1995). Most obviously this perspective has manifested itself in a series of so-called 'Euromyth' reports. These arise because, as one correspondent put it, the 'British are over ready to build on a little information'. Coupled with the large amount of material available from various sources within the Community there has been obvious scope for misunderstandings and inaccuracies. As the *Sun* put it in one renowned 'Euromyth': 'Now They've Really Gone Bananas: Euro bosses ban "too bendy" ones and set up minimum shop size of 5 and a half inches' (21 September 1994). Features of this kind, together with a mass of other press reports about the EC's intention to outlaw anything from British prawn cocktail crisps to the pound, were judged sufficiently harmful to merit a formal rebuttal by the government in the form of two Foreign Office booklets.

The FCO pamphlets *The European Community: Facts and Fairytales* (Foreign and Commonwealth Office 1993) and *Facts and Fairytales Revisited* (Foreign and Commonwealth Office 1995) featured analysis of what were termed 'euromyths', 'euroscares', and 'eurolunacies'. Interestingly the latter category, unlike the other two, did not support the sentiment that EU decisions and directives were always based on sound logic and common sense. By contrast the more avowedly pro-Union pamphlets issued by the Commission itself: *Do you believe all you read in the newspapers?* (European Commission 1994) and *Do you STILL believe all you read in the newspapers?* (European Commission 1995), were unanimous in attacking what they saw as unfair reporting in the British press. Perhaps surprisingly their list of offending titles included normally sympathetic journals the *Guardian* and the *Independent* alongside usual suspects like the *Sun* and *Daily Star*. It would be wrong, however, to portray all press criticism of the EU as essentially trivial or superficial in nature and content. In 1994, for instance, the *Guardian* challenged the Commission to make itself more account-able by allowing greater public access to documentary accounts of its procedures (Tumber 1995).

According to one Brussels-based journalist, the 'nationalistic' coverage apparent in much of the London-based media derives from the fact that 'EU news still comes from British government sources' (Morgan 1995). This is perhaps strange, given the existence of Foreign Office booklets aimed at countering press misrepresentations of

Community matters. Arguably this reflects the complex, ongoing debate over integration. Consequently whilst Downing Street has been keen to protect Britain's trading partnership it is also conscious of asserting the national identity and independence of the country.

Given recent moves toward greater political and economic integration amongst Britain's Community partners it is perhaps inevitable that the Westminster government, comfortable with the non-federal status quo, has emitted mixed messages which vary according to given policies or circumstances. Thus, where conflicts between London and Brussels have arisen, the Eurosceptical press has unsurprisingly opted to follow the lead and promote the views of the former. This bias is further compounded by an organizational culture evident in highly centralized states like France and Britain where journalists can regularly rely on one or two authoritative ministerial or civil service sources.

The fact that the media can help to inform public opinion and ultimately the different member states' policies on integration has been recognized within Brussels. In particular the ongoing hostility of the British press and, perhaps more importantly, the initial rejection of Maastricht in the first Danish referendum on the Treaty encouraged the Commission to reconsider how it might best promote the Union. Consequently reports from marketing and other publicity specialists have been the subject of recent discussions (Tumber 1995). Accordingly EU officials are now taking greater care to service and monitor the print media which, in a country with public service broadcasting like Britain, are often the source of the most flamboyant agenda-setting stories (Morgan 1995). This fact, together with the residual hostility of much print media, was amply demonstrated during 1996 in a controversy over a hitherto minor public concern to do with the safety of British beef.

THE 'BEEF WAR' OF 1996

Ironically in its 1990 'Up Yours Delors!' attack on the Commission President, the *Sun* cited the decision of a French ban on imports of British beef as one of the factors motivating the paper's strong editorial content. Few at the time would have predicted that by mid-1996 this issue would be at the centre of media debates over government policy on Europe. The catalyst behind this development lay in a Department of Health statement issued by Secretary of State Stephen Dorrell in response to the appearance of a leaked memo in the *Daily Mirror* towards the end of March. Having made public their concern over the safety of British beef the government 'appeared to give credibility to the idea that there might be a link between BSE, the so-called 'mad cow disease', and the human equivalent CJD. The move triggered a crisis of confidence in British beef, culminating in a controversial decision by European Union member states to ban all imports of British beef and its derivatives. As the *British Medical Journal* (30 March 1996) reported, the scientific complexities, public concerns, and questions surrounding the wisdom of government agricultural and deregulation policies arising from the case were soon sidelined in a media-driven debate about European integration.

The *Sun* chose St George's Day to offer its lengthiest response to the beef ban in the form of a front-page editorial asking readers to act as 'EU THE JURY' (23 April 1996). The item attacked the Union as a 'beast . . . which aims to devour our national identity' and 'a very real dragon which threatens every single one of us throughout the United Kingdom'. Unusually for the *Sun* the editorial continued inside on a full page complete with an illustration of a dragon which had also appeared on the front cover. Declaring 'a thousand years of civilisation is being tossed away', the paper even cited Orwell's literary classic *1984* in declaring: 'We want to see free trade between friendly nations, a genuine Common Market, not an Orwellian superstate which blindly tries to make Germans like Britons, or Spaniards live like Irishmen.' Interestingly the piece made sympathetic mention of the Referendum Party led by businessman and MEP Sir James Goldsmith. Like Goldsmith's newly formed organization, the paper and over 95 per cent of the 23,000 callers to a special *Sun* phone poll agreed that the government should organize a referendum on the desirability of further European integration.

Predictably the officially sanctioned 'Europe Day' triggered a hostile response from the *Sun* (9 May 1996). By comparison with the editorial of 23 April, argument was substituted with abuse in a feature, entitled 'WE ATE EU', which went on to attack corruption, sleaze, and the notion that British government buildings ought to fly the Union flag. These points were further reinforced by television critic Garry Bushell in his attack on European federalism: 'Stuff your Union, Jacques'. Soundbites of assorted Eurosceptic MPs, all Conservative, were also placed throughout the edition under the caption 'Why I Hate

EU.' However it should be noted that the editorials in the *Sun* stopped considerably short of the call made by Lord Woodrow Wyatt in another News International title *The Times* for a complete British withdrawal from Europe (7 May 1996). Rather, like other sceptical leaders in the *Telegraph*, *Express*, and *Mail*, the papers' commentaries tended to concentrate on the perceived loss of sovereignty rather than the issue of membership itself.

Arguably more of a revelation than editorials in the *Sun* were the equally passionate opinions articulated by the *Daily Mirror*. Declaring 'Britain needs EU', the paper developed its argument: 'If we ever cut ourselves loose from our partners across the Channel, we would become an isolated irrelevant island' (28 May 1996). In reality the actual policy position of the paper, while more favourable to the idea of a European single currency, differed from that of the *Sun* in tone rather than substance. Indeed, professed *Mirror* enthusiasm for the European ideal did not prevent it from making what editor Piers Morgan later admitted was an error of judgement when his paper published the headline 'Achtung Surrender!' on hearing the England football team's Euro 96 semi-final opponents would be Germany (*Daily Mirror*, 25 June 1996).

The debate over the media response to the beef ban created some odd alliances. Whilst Chancellor and enthusiastic European Kenneth Clarke must have welcomed the pro-EU coverage in the Labour-supporting *Daily Mirror*, he was clearly less well disposed to those newspapers critical of the Union. Pointedly Clarke made explicit his view of the owners of what were once loyal Conservative titles when he admitted: 'Quite a lot of the press is owned by anti-European people and they go to great lengths to try and arouse prejudice in their readers to match that of their own political opinions' (BBC Radio 4, 31 May 1996). It is likely that the Chancellor was venting his frustration at two well-known non-European sceptics with extensive media interests: the Australian turned American citizen Rupert Murdoch and Conrad Black, Canadian-born owner of the *Daily Telegraph*.

Predictably Jacques Santer, President of the European Commission, went further than Kenneth Clarke in expressing his concern about the 'anti-European propaganda, and even xenophobic propaganda, in the British press' (BBC Radio 4, 31 May 1996). Similar sentiments informed the observations of a London-based German journalist Ulrich Schilling: '*The Sun*, the *Mail* and *Express* are not harmless leaflets: they are read by 20 million people, and they may not all understand the special brand of humour which seasons *Sun* headlines' (*Guardian*, 3 June 1996). The combined activities of the press and Referendum Party were enough to prompt pro-Union MPs such as Edwina Currie and Peter Mandelson to consider a response which took the form of a public relations' offensive coordinated by the European Movement's director of communications David Vigar (*Guardian*, 1 June 1996).

Following their varied attacks on the decision of European member states to ban imports of British beef the print media focus eventually moved to assess the performance and role of the domestic government. Particular attention was given to John Major. Following on from the broadly hostile comments made in normally loyal Conservative newspapers about the Prime Minister during the 1995 Conservative leadership campaign, the *Sun* once again questioned the premier's judgement when it suggested he might be 'raising the white flag' in his dealings with Community partners (23 April 1996). Major did eventually organize a government response to the beef ban which took the form of a general policy of non-cooperation with the EU. If this move upset member states, it did manage temporarily to appease many of the more sceptical papers, including the *Daily Mail*, which declared 'Major Goes to War at Last', and the *Daily Star*, whose headline announced 'Eff EU lot blasts Major'. For its part the *Sun* was fulsome in its praise for the strategy: 'Britain said No to Europe yesterday—12 times . . . Major must be strong. There must be no wavering. The people are behind him all the way on this one' (29 May 1996).

From the beginning of the policy of non-cooperation, certain news-papers were less than praiseworthy about what they perceived to be an inadequate and potentially counter-productive government strategy for getting the beef ban lifted. Predictably analysis of this kind centred on the liberal papers like the *Guardian*, the *Independent*, and *Daily Mirror*. Interestingly this line of argument was supported by the traditionally pro-Conservative *Evening Standard* and its editor Max Hastings. Within a month media critics of the government's 'beef war' appeared to be vindicated when papers such as the *Sun*, *Daily Telegraph*, *Daily Mail*, and *Daily Express* expressed dissatis-faction with subsequent changes in government policy which one of them eventually denounced as a 'cave in' (*Observer*, 23 June 1996).

The impatience and ill-will towards Major resurfaced again in the

Sun following the resignation of junior minister David Heathcoat-Amory on the European issue. Declaring him a 'hero', an editorial supported the hitherto little-known Conservative MP's opposition to the single European currency by demanding 'Time you Major mind up' (*Sun*, 23 July 1996). Accusing the Prime Minister of 'dithering and fudging', the newspaper made plain the depth of its displeasure: 'Major's policy of appeasing Europe, staging phoney wars that inevitably lead to surrender, is exposed as a sham.' As former News International employee and *Sunday Times* editor Andrew Neil has since admitted, the opinions of the *Sun* tend to represent those of proprietor Rupert Murdoch more accurately than any of the other British newspapers he owns. Put more simply, Murdoch is a Eurosceptic with a disrespect for John Major and a more positive regard for Labour leader Tony Blair. The European issue may have damaged more than just Conservative Party unity: it might also be in the process of breaking up what was once commonly termed the 'Tory press'.

CONCLUSIONS

The reversal of the trend towards Euro-enthusiasm in the British press developed gradually over the 1980s, affecting first the right-wing tabloids and then the Conservative broadsheets. This was not an automatic corollary of the shift to Thatcherite economics or trade policy as *The Times*, *Telegraph*, and *The Economist*, for instance, having taken up the crusade against 'state interventionism' continued to support the EEC on economic and increasingly on monetary grounds. Nor was it simply a product of a 'populist' media reaction to the apparent growth in the gulf between the main parties and the electorate, a factor which previously appeared to bolster the pro-EEC shift among the centrist press. It was certainly not an automatic reaction to having discovered upon entry what the Community was like.

Behind the growing press attacks on the Community there lay a combination of all of these factors. Dramatic changes in Conservative and Labour positions over the UK's role in Europe in the mid-1980s meant the right-wing press would now gain a domestic political premium from attacking the Community. The renewal of confidence among European federalists in the mid-1980s also gave the press more of a target to aim against. Added to this was the problem of the print media as a 'national' gatekeeper: 'The main problems for the EU is that, as Euro-scepticism grows, it is having to compete for publicity with national governments of Member States in a game still officiated by national media and particularly the national press. At the moment it is still the EU which is receiving most of the yellow cards' (Tumber 1995). Finally, the 1980s heralded a revolution in the production, ownership, and marketing of the British press. Competition, which had driven the press of the 1960s and 1970s into an increasingly enthusiastic 'pro-Community' campaign fed the appetite of broadsheets and tabloids for sensational 'scoops' and anti-European populism in the 1990s.

10

Britain Viewed from Europe

Peter Brown Pappamikail

> Your politics reminds me of your bath taps: In British hotels I am
> always struck that you have two separate taps: you have a choice
> of either scalding hot or freezing cold water. But you can never
> get a convenient mix of the two. (Shimon Peres)

It is the intention of this chapter to look at Britain's relationship with
Europe through the eyes of some of those at the sharp end of European integration, namely Brussels-based politicians and officials.[1]
British politicians may feel flattered that continental politicians pay
them the attention they feel is their due. Recently, regretfully, this

---

This essay is dedicated to the memory of Derek Enright, former MP, MEP, and
diplomat, who 'kept the faith' during the dark years of Labour Europhobia.

[1] A note on methodology: the contributions included here are the results of a mixture
of traditional face-to-face interviews and participant observation. Attributed quotations
are taken from the interviews or based on my own extensive notes taken on a continual
basis over the past six years. Interview dates:

The Lord Plumb, 17 Apr. 1996
David Martin, 18 Apr. 1996
Enrique Barón, 12 Dec. 1995
Rt. Hon. Neil Kinnock, 14 Mar. 1996
Jean-Pierre Cot, 10 Apr. 1996
Ian White, 7 Feb. 1996
Christos Papoutsis, 10 Apr. 1996
Wilfried Martens, 5 Feb. 1996
Wayne David, 11 Jan. 1996
Elmar Brok, 9 Apr. 1996

I have kept unattributed material to a minimum, resorting only when there is a specific
and original point to be made. One common methodological problem encountered in
this type of study can be that of 'over-rapport'. I hope to have avoided that and have
followed much-used academic references in guiding my research (see, in particular,
McCall and Simmons 1969 and Susan Ostrander's article on studying elites, 1993). I am
grateful to Marilisa Xenagiannakopoulou and Niceia Pappamikail for help with some
translations. Responsibility for the accuracy of these, and my own, remains entirely
mine.

attention is mainly a mixture of disbelief and sadness that a nation that had such a positive image in the minds of other Europeans could now have such an uncomfortable relationship with the Continent. All national parties share difficulties in their relationships with their MEPs, 'frequent contacts are not a guarantee of identity of views. MEPs and MPs will inevitably have different perspectives and, on occasion, will respectively accuse each other of "having gone native" or being "parochial" '(Corbett et al. 1995: 91). Although the phenomenon of gradually identifying with the wider European group is not restricted to the British, it does seem to have greater importance in British domestic political discourse, particularly when the EU is seen as external to that polity, rather than as an integral part of it.

BRITISH LABOUR AND EUROPE

While continental European socialists welcomed the arrival of such an important sister party into the EEC in 1973, Labour itself was playing hard to get. The party should have automatically become a member of the then embryonic Community-wide socialist transnational organization, the Confederation of the Socialist Parties of the European Community, the Confed.[2] But, although entitled to join and despite reforms to the organization's structure, Labour refused to participate as a full member party, contenting itself with informal participation in some working groups, even after the 1975 referendum.

In 1978, when socialists met in Brussels to put together the framework for an 'electoral platform' for the first ever direct elections to a multinational Parliament, Prime Minister Callaghan, who had fought hard in Westminster to enact the legislation for elections to the European Parliament, against the opposition of most of his party, was the only socialist leader absent. Labour fought consistently against any common programme. It was only after being shamed into action by the Liberal and Christian Democrat families producing common texts, that a minimal message to the electorate was finally and grudgingly agreed for the election campaign (Hix 1995).

Those first elections held only a month after Thatcher's first victory

---

[2] The name itself was a source of some initial tension: although the organization's name in French, German, and Spanish translates literally into English as 'Union', the *official* English translation was 'Confederation'.

in 1979 returned a delegation of sixty Conservative members along with seventeen for Labour. Labour now joined together with socialist members from all other member states in the most ideologically coherent political group. Yet, as one member recalls: 'while socialists across Europe together celebrated the new democratically elected parliament, the Labour delegation, with a few honourable exceptions, kept us at arms length.'

Meanwhile, the domestic situation was beginning to change. Kinnock had argued that the 1983 general election campaign was the last one in which Labour would fight on an anti-EEC platform: 'I made it clear that the party policy would have to change. . . . It was very clear that the integration of economies by then meant that unilateral action was not going to be enough. . . . It was coming home to me, as it was coming home to Trade Unionists, that unless we were calling from the inside, we weren't calling.'

In the European Parliament, Labour's attitudes were changing, partly due to the experience of working together with socialists from across Europe and exposure to European institutions (Westlake 1994; Corbett et al. 1995). Lord Plumb, a Conservative MEP since the first direct elections and former President of the parliament, commented: 'I can think in particular of Barbara Castle, who in her early days was anti-European . . . but was a good European by the time she had finished here.'

The Labour contingent in the parliament, the British Labour Group (BLG), contained a core of pro-Europeans. David Martin, Labour MEP and a Vice-President of the parliament, stresses that this Europhile group 'had a double set of problems: they were in a minority in the BLG, which was being run by the hard Left . . . but were also marginalized from the Party at home and got no support at all from the Party during that period'. Although the BLG was still deeply divided, the situation improved for the Europhile MEPs after the 1984 elections. Martin, the first avowedly pro-European leader of the BLG, was elected on a knife-edge vote in 1987 after a concerted effort by the BLG Europhiles, ousting the anti-Market incumbent, Alf Lomas. Martin commented, 'Neil [Kinnock] had been Labour Leader for a year and . . . initially didn't pay too much attention to what was going on at the European level . . . he didn't get involved until we'd actually made the change, but once I became BLG Leader, I couldn't fault him or the Party for their assistance.' The victory was short lived, however, and Martin subsequently lost to another anti-Marketeer, Barry

Seal. The BLG thus went into the 1989 elections with a leader committed to British withdrawal. Consequently, the Labour delegation were not yet considered a reliable partner by fellow socialists.

The 1989 European elections were to prove decisive for Labour's standing in Europe Labour moved 'from indifference to engagement' (Martin), as seen in its attitude towards the drafting of the European manifesto. The Confederation had nominated a young federalist Spaniard, Enrique Barón, to chair the manifesto working group:

> After that experience, I think I could have got a job as a peace negotiator in the Lebanon. . . . The British, with their idea that 'Your word is your bond', would argue over every single detail of the text whereas most of us were happy with the main intellectual thrust. . . . I don't think this was capriciousness, however, they really were taking it all very seriously. . . . At the end of it all, there were still some reservations, but the progress that Labour demonstrated was extraordinary. Kinnock and his team deserve the credit for this.

In early 1989 national party leaders, concerned to give some political coordination to the work of their parliamentary wing in the European Parliament, discussed the idea of a 'package deal' with each of the main parties who claimed a slice of the leadership cake in the parliament. For the first time Labour was in on such a deal: 'We were nearly the biggest national delegation within the Group in 1984–89, but nobody even thought about offering Labour one of the senior positions in the Group or the parliament' (Martin). Kinnock won an important argument in favour of Julian Priestley, a British staff member in parliament, becoming the Group's Secretary-General.

Despite Labour's defeat in the 1992 election, Kinnock's services were quickly sought to head the Confederation. Kinnock himself turned down the opportunity, putting a 'first obligation' to the national party rather than risking: 'a bloody great row over the integrationist character of the Confed. You could put it down to post-electoral stress syndrome. Glenys [Kinnock] was bewildered by my decision not to accept nomination for the Confed. presidency. As she said at the time: "You know you're not Labour leader now, but you don't understand it yet: you're taking the responsibility as if you still were!" '

Nonetheless, Kinnock had a profound impact on the Confed. The organization took a leap forward in this period, not least because Labour dropped its opposition to key developments that were to evolve into the newly christened Party of European Socialists (PES), a title itself inconceivable even a year earlier. Jean-Pierre

Cot, leader of the socialists in the European Parliament from 1989 to 1994 and former French Minister, recalls that: 'The decision to change the old Confed into the PES, and to adopt a common logo and identity with the [Socialist] Group in the European Parliament was largely due to the change in attitude of the British Labour Party and of Kinnock himself.'

The 1994 European Parliament elections returned the biggest ever single national party contingent with sixty-two British Labour MEPs. This put Labour at the top of the pecking order within the European socialist family. Although some sister parties were initially disgruntled by what they saw as Labour's over-representation, owing much to the first-past-the-post electoral system, the mathematics could not be ignored. Labour now accounted for nearly a third of the fifteen-party Socialist Group in the parliament.

This inevitably shaped the debates within the Group. At the 1994 Party Leaders' Conference in Corfu, Europe's socialist leadership set about agreeing, as they had in 1989, a 'package deal'. Of the clutch of political posts to be filled, both within and beyond the parliamentary group, Labour leader John Smith had argued, in the months before his death, for the leadership of the Group itself to come to Pauline Green a Labour MEP, a line followed through by the Labour delegation in Corfu.

Ian White, a new MEP in 1989 and among those that had expressed reservations about the elitist nature of the deal, was somewhat mollified by 1994: 'Although the parliamentary group formally elected Pauline, the "deal" was put together by the national party leaders. I believe that, had it been an open election, she would have won in any case, hands down, on competence alone. But the endorsement by the party leaders was also a signal to all that Labour could now be relied upon in Europe.' Martin agrees: 'I think the decision was indicative that we've moved towards the mainstream of the Socialist Group. Our behaviour in the 1989–94 parliament made people realize that we could be trusted as partners.'

Pauline Green went to great lengths to consult and cajole socialist ministers across Europe on behalf of the whole Group. In her dealings with senior national party figures, it could be difficult to separate her Group role from the fact that she is a senior British Labour politician. One socialist minister commented: 'She is seen partly as an ambassador for the forthcoming Blair government in London.'

However, Labour's new found prominence in Europe has not been risk-free, because the centre of gravity within the Socialist Group has been distinctly more Eurofederalist than the Labour leadership could feel comfortable with (*The Times* and *Financial Times*, 7 February 1995). Ms Green had to be seen by her Brussels colleagues as being above diktat from London, at the same time as steering the Group to 'temper' its demands in a way that would not antagonize the constructive relationship established with Blair (*Sunday Telegraph*, 12 February 1995). Evidence of the delicate nature of this balancing act is offered by Cot: 'Before, you had a pro-European and an anti-European wing within the British group of MEPs, now the delegation is united, but on a very cautious position.'

In Blackpool in 1994, at the party's annual conference, Blair launched his high-risk initiative to reform and modernize the party's constitution. One of the first moves by his office, only hours after his conference speech, was to agree to look through the rule books and programmes of Labour's sister parties in Europe, an indication that Blair would welcome inspiration from them as much as he would from internal party debates. Thus, not only the tone set by the speech, but his whole approach, put Labour's cooperation in Europe on a new plane. This diplomatic signal was not lost on European parties long frustrated by Labour's reluctance and antagonism.

MEPs have rarely been seen as an important part of Labour's hierarchy. However, as one individual commented: 'Holding on to office particularly in the current legislature where [some members] are politically marginal both within the Labour delegation and the Socialist Group as a whole, has given them a space for potential mischief.' An advertisement placed in the *Guardian* (10 January 1995) by thirty-two Labour MEPs criticizing the proposed reforms to the party's constitution was timed to coincide with a keynote speech in Brussels on Europe by the Labour leader. This single act alerted the national party to the role that their colleagues in Brussels could play, destructively as well as constructively.

Recognizing this Blair appointed Larry Whitty the party's former General Secretary, as a European Coordinator, precisely with the remit to keep the links between Brussels and London strong. Blair also undertook a high-profile series of bilateral meetings with government and socialist leaders across Europe, selling his vision of Europe and reminding other EU governments that even if the Conservatives were at the conference table at the beginning of the 1996 Intergovernmental Conference called to revise the EU treaties, 'we will be the ones doing the signing' (*Independent*, 3 March 1996).

As a result of such changes and the deepening Euroscepticism of the Major government, there is optimism on the European mainland that a Labour government would mark a new phase for Europe. Greek member of the European Commission and former International Secretary of PASOK, Christos Papoutsis believes that 'A Labour Government really could work positively. Its European declarations seem to be much nearer the mainstream of what is going on at the European level.'

Wilfried Martens, leader of the Christian Democrat group in the European Parliament and former Belgian premier is more sceptical: 'everyone tells me that [Blair's] Europeanism is only tactical,' but admits 'it would be historic were it to be true.' However, few believe that a Labour government would be able to keep all of its commitments about Europe. Papoutsis reiterates this point:

I will not be surprised if Tony Blair, who is a committed European, and everybody believes that, . . . might adopt a very strong stand on several issues of great importance for his country. This is understandable and no more than any other country would do. It would be in the context of being part of the mainstream and without putting into question the basics of the European Union.

THE BRITISH CONSERVATIVES AND EUROPE

For the conservatives in Europe, the period from the first direct elections in 1979 up to the late 1980s represented the antithesis of Labour's position. The Conservative MEPs, then as now, were largely pro-European with a sprinkling of 'Eurofederalists'. Derek Prag, a senior Conservative MEP, was one of the authors of the 1984 European Parliament report on the future of the European Union that represented the high water mark of the parliament's federalist ambitions. The sixty Conservative MEPs of the 1979 cohort formed, and inevitably dominated, a Conservative group in the parliament, the European Democrats, joined by Danish and, for a few years, Spanish Conservatives, enjoying a comfortable and generally constructive relationship with the larger centre-right grouping of Christian Democrats, the parliamentary wing of the European People's Party (EPP).

The Conservative government, on the other hand, had a less comfortable time. 'The British government has always seemed fundamentally in favour of the intergovernmental, rather than supranational, approach, in Europe', argues Wilfried Martens. 'We always had a very tense relationship with them. I ask myself, do they really have a notion of a communitarian Europe?' Mrs Thatcher's approach in the mid-1980s was characterized, as one former Finance Minister put it, by 'an obsession with money, the budget rebate, and a European free market'. Thatcher's appointee at the European Commission, Lord Cockfield, had already drafted his White Paper on the Internal Market early in 1985 and proposed the abolition of all controls to the four freedoms of movement—of goods, capital, services, and people—a package initially opposed by Thatcher. Martens explains:

For me, the great surprise was over the Single Market. At the European Council in June 1985, Craxi—who was President-in-Office, Andreotti was Foreign Minister—proposed an Intergovernmental Conference on the single market. Thatcher was opposed, so he proposed to move to a vote. Thatcher exclaimed 'but you can't!', and so Andreotti took the Treaty and showed her that they could convene the IGC on a majority vote, which we went ahead and did. A few months later she was in favour of the Single Market! . . . So in a matter of months she changes opinion, conviction, and became a partisan for the market. But the Single Market is in the Community domain. She didn't see it as anything more than intergovernmental.

Conservative MEPs seemed to understand the ramifications much more clearly. Conservative MEP Ben Patterson argued in November 1986, that 'the case for allowing people to invest their money where they want is both economic and political. . . . The case for the Internal Market is not just one of economic freedom, it is also one of political freedom.'

This period was marked by a quest for a continental identity. Conservative MEPs had difficulty in placing themselves and their party on the European political map. Fellow Conservatives, in the British sense, only existed in Denmark and the Christian Democrat group was too progressive on social policy and European integration for the national party's liking. Conservatives MEPs seemed divided, as one put it, 'between those that were prepared to find out and give what the Government wants, and those who were prepared to find out and give what the Christian Democrats want'. More pressure occurred when the Spanish Conservatives deserted their Group to join the Christian Democrats, and the Conservatives themselves started their *rapprochement*, joining the EPP group in parliament, albeit as 'allied members', in 1992 (Corbett et al. 1995: 74–91).

With the 1984, 1989, and 1994 elections all marking periods of

mid-term unpopularity of the government at home, combined with the
vagaries of the British electoral system, Conservative representation
in the European Parliament has steadily declined, from the high
mark of sixty to just eighteen. From the third legislature (1989–94)
onwards, internal tensions had begun to show more publicly. The two
IGCs on EMU and Political Union in the spring of 1991 were moving
into a crucial period and government ministers were telling their
European colleagues that they were 'steadfastly opposed' to bolstering European social legislation (*Financial Times*, 22 May 1995), an
attitude that led to Britain's Social Chapter 'opt-out' at Maastricht.
Meanwhile, Conservative MEPs were arguing in parliament that
social policy 'is not an optional extra. You cannot bolt it on afterwards. It is integral to the way we operate in this Community' (Lord
O'Hagan, MEP, VRPEP, 15 May 1985).

After Maastricht, the British government claimed that it had
stopped the 'conveyor belt' leading inevitably towards a federal
Europe, even having the 'F' word deleted from the new treaty. But,
again, the MEPs gave a different signal: 'First, we in the European
Democratic Group do not much mind whether one refers to a federal
vocation or a union of a federal type, we know what we mean that the
Community should act in fields where it can better attain its objectives
than can the members states acting separately. We know that we are
moving towards European union, a European Community which will
be deeper and in due course wider, too' (Derek Prag, MEP, VRPEP, 9
October 1991).

In the run-up to the fourth direct elections to the European Parliament in 1994, the Christian Democrats increased the pressure. Pre-
senting the European People's Party manifesto to the press, Wilfried
Martens had made clear that British Conservatives neither discussed
nor approved it. He explained further that 'good collaboration'
existed, particularly since the 1992 agreement with the Conservative
MEPs giving them 'allied' status in the Group. He warned however
that, aside from the Maastricht opt-outs, the Conservatives would be
expected to accept the rest of the manifesto's objectives if that collaboration was to continue (*Agence Europe*, 26 February 1994).

In the same period, the British government was heading towards
another clash with its Christian Democrat government partners.
First, in considering the succession to Jacques Delors as President
of the European Commission, there seemed to be a consensus that
after a period led by a socialist from a large member state, there

should be a period led by a Christian Democrat from a smaller one. The Belgian Prime Minister, Jean-Luc Dehaene, was blocked by Major on the grounds of his 'ultra-federalist' ideas. Ironically, the man appointed, Jacques Santer, came from the same political mould, a detail only remarked upon after the hubbub had died down and Major had 'won' the media-hyped showdown staged largely for domestic political purposes.

Second, in examining the implications of enlargement to the Scandinavian countries and Austria, Major managed to create a crisis out of a minor readjustment of the voting threshold needed to attain the qualified majority needed in many Council votes (Corbett et al. 1995: 5).

In Britain, the Eurosceptics were becoming increasingly vociferous. The decision of eight Conservative MPs to break party discipline in November 1994, avowedly on a 'question of principle' (opposing a largely technical and financial bill in order to 'uphold the sovereignty of Parliament'), was perceived by European partners as a 'little local difficulty' for John Major. The increasingly strident Eurosceptics, however, supported by Employment Secretary Michael Portillo, set new levels with attacks on the European Court of Justice, and dishonest foreigners. The domestic troubles of Major's party were starting to spill over to the Continent, as Major's partners saw his government's strategy towards Europe being dictated by this domestic faction (*The Times*, 16 January 1995 and *Independent*, 2 February 1995). Many Conservative MEPs were keen to distance themselves from such beliefs, although Lord Plumb shrugs off their relevance: 'I've never lost sleep over it. I think my continental friends know me well enough to know that certainly isn't my view and I've never hesitated to say so.' Nevertheless, it undermined the MEPs attempts to maintain that they reflect the views of their national party. As Cot argues, 'The Conservative Group here is completely out of line, not only with the party's line on Europe, *if* it has a line on Europe, but also with the divisions within the Conservative Party itself.'

Evidence that Conservatives in the European Parliament were starting to bend to the pressure from London came early in 1995, when some Conservative MEPs in Brussels mounted an unsuccessful challenge to their chairman, Tom Spencer, for following the federalist road with the Christian Democrats. Their concern was the potential embarrassment such an association could have for the party, and government, back in Britain. Even more disturbing, the EPP had nominated a popular, young, and combative German federalist, Elmar Brok, as one of the two representatives of the European Parliament on the Group set up to prepare the 1996 IGC.[3]

Like Labour MEPs before 1984, Conservatives have only a 'semi-detached' relationship with their parliamentary political group. Plumb suggested that, although some Conservative MEPs felt that they would 'fit better alongside the Gaullists' rather than being part of the Christian Democrat Group, 'this would only be a minority view'. British Conservatives felt, and were seen as, certainly until recently, outside the traditional European Christian Democrat mould. More recently, and particularly following the accession of Sweden and Finland, a clear Conservative profile is developing within the EPP family.

When parliament had to consider its position regarding the 1996 IGC, pressure was brought to bear on the Conservative MEPs by the party at home. Despite receiving a letter from Foreign Secretary Douglas Hurd asking them to vote against the report, Plumb simply ignored the 'order' and advised abstention (*Sunday Telegraph*, 16 June 1995).

The Conservative Party has painted itself into a corner with its 'Jekyll and Hyde' approach to Europe: whilst in their everyday dealings with the EU government ministries and ministers seem generally realistic about what Brussels does and should do, this is rarely broadcast for domestic consumption. Privately, in his discussions with Conservative MEPs in Brussels, John Major seemed to admit that the most effective and suitable way to achieve some key government objectives in Europe—combating fraud in the EU, greater police cooperation against drug trafficking and terrorism—would involve greater powers for the European Commission. But, to admit this publicly, let alone argue for it forcefully, would be to precipitate open civil war in his party. This 'policy *vs.* tactics' dilemma has worried many in Brussels.

The crisis over 'mad cow disease' exemplified the dangerous game being played of scapegoating Brussels. Gijs de Vries, Dutch MEP and leader of the Liberals in the European Parliament remarked: 'The British conservative government is very successfully turning the

---

[3] The so-called 'Reflection Group', under the chairmanship of Spanish European Affairs Minister Carlos Westerdorp, was set up by the European Council meeting in June 1994 in Corfu.

issues from an issue about its incompetence into an issue of European conspiracy against the United Kingdom.' All EU governments at one time or another seek to deflect criticism of their policies or tactics onto Brussels, but none allows such tactics to call into question the fundamentals of the EU, in the way that Britain has under the Conservatives.

WINNER TAKES ALL: BRITISH PROBLEMS AND CHARACTERISTICS

Viewed from Europe, Britain's political and civic culture appears permeated with the convictions of a damaging adversarial bipolar culture. To accept that there is a middle way, a possibility of com-promise, of coalition, is anathema. Wayne David, an MEP since 1989 and leader of the British Labour MEPs in the European Parliament, comments: 'confrontation is a style of politics, a weapon of politics used to achieve objectives. British politics is black and white, them and us, totally wrong or totally right and that encourages a confronta-tional style that also fits into the electoral system.'

It may also be at the heart of Britain's parliamentary-based understanding of 'sovereignty'. Whilst most continentals accept sovereignty as being multi-layered, local, regional, national, *and* European, the British often view it as something indivisible, either you have it or you don't: 'The winner takes all! It's unimaginable in Belgium . . . I remember when I was touring the capitals as President-in-Office of the Council in 1987, I met with Mrs Thatcher and had the opportunity of explaining how my government—being a multiparty coalition—relied on compromise to function. Her reply, bluntly and simply, was "You've got the wrong system" '(Martens).

Sir Leon Brittan, European Commission Vice-President, believes the British debate over Europe is artificially polarized: 'Our European partners look aghast at a nation driving itself to distraction over its place in Europe . . . [They] perceive us to be perpetually vexed over the question of *whether* Europe is good for Britain at all, rather than seeking to discover *how* we could best promote our national interests by advancing a positive agenda' (*House Magazine*, 20 February 1995). This is exemplified with Goldsmith's proposed referendum question: 'Who governs Britain, Westminster or Brussels?' (*The Times*, 24 April 1996). As Brittan says, 'It is tempting under the current parliamentary arithmetic to stoke up alarmist visions of encroaching federalism and then pledge to fight them off in order to appear victorious in advance of battle' (ibid.).

Unlike mainland Europe, where one can speak of a 'national interest' being forged from the shared views of a wide spectrum of political ideologies, 'Britain's European policy positions have been adopted by the Government of the day in the light of its own prevalent preferences' (Wallace 1995: 50). If one looks at countries with a tradition of coalition government, one sees a broader view of national interest, with consequences also for their understanding of sharing sovereignty. However, as one Italian MEP points out: 'They [the Conservative government] know their EU stuff better than anyone, that's what sickens me most about the two-faced debate in Britain, they are scared of telling the public what they themselves know, that they need to cooperate with others and that national sovereignty died years ago' (author's translation). In 1985, Conservative MEP William Newton-Dunn stated that 'The logical goal of an "ever closer union" between the peoples of Europe is the creation of a federal European system,' and in answering the question as to whether Britain would lose its sovereignty in a federal Europe, he replied 'Yes, but we have lost most of it already' (Newton-Dunn 1985: 81–2).

Paddy Ashdown has pointed to the dangers such appeals to British national sovereignty contain when linked to anti-German sentiments: 'One of the worst aspects of Britain's current political debate is that it has become acceptable in Conservative circles to talk about Germany and the Germans in the same tone which English politicians reserved for the Jews eighty years ago and for the Irish a century ago' (speech to the Royal Institute of International Affairs in March 1996). These sentiments have been echoed by fellow Liberal, Gijs de Vries:

The key challenge for the Continent is how to find a proper role for Germany. Rather than see this process as a threat, I would have expected British politicians to shape British policy according to the opportunities it wishes to create for itself. . . . I'm alarmed at the crass xenophobia which seems to have become *bon ton* in parts of the Conservative Party and indeed in parts of the British media. How does one think any foreigner responds to accusations such as Mr Michael Portillo's that anyone who has his A levels in the UK has worked for them and anyone who has them on the Continent has been bribing? . . . A country which is sure of its place in the world doesn't need to shout at its partners. It doesn't need to insult them in order to feel better.

German Christian Democrat MEP Elmar Brok also takes the mass media to task:

I must say that this part of the press in Britain is the most irresponsible in Europe. It is not just to do with EU affairs, it uses xenophobia as a way to sell papers. What they write about people from other countries, not just in politics, even the sports correspondents, the British are always the best, the 'clean', and the others are always the bad guys. This reminds of the time before the First World War, classical nationalism . . . I think we should have learnt our lessons . . . what I worry, however, is that from the political side, I hear nothing about it. . . . When I think of some things that have been written recently, here is a point reached where politicians have to stand up and say 'Stop it, It's just not true'. Instead we hear, privately, 'Oh, it's just our press', or even 'its an Australian with an American passport that is responsible', but why not stand up and say something?

Such attitudes clearly do not help when it comes to building alliances and relationships with continental Europeans.

David Martin argues that the electoral system also helps to explain the British preoccupation with the seemingly parochial: 'We often raise questions like local factory closures or a problem of pollution . . . Continentals wonder what this has to do with Europe.' The attachment to a local constituency means 'dealing with politics at a lower level'. Delors commented that, although only counting for a tenth of the parliament, half of the correspondence he received from MEPs was from British members. As Martin states: 'His assessment was that we were more in touch with the people, we had to respond to real issues. I think this makes us less theoretical and I think there is sometimes merit in that.' As a mainland European politician, Cot is less impressed: 'I think it is a bit of a hoax. The British parliamentary system is not any better or any worse than others in terms of repre-sentation. I don't feel that they really have a more systematic relation-ship with their parliamentary constituency than other MEPs. . . . So I think that this is a story that the Brits like to tell and like to take advantage of but I'm not fooled by that one!'

CONCLUSIONS

Helen Wallace (1995) argues that for Britain to be at the heart of Europe would require Europe to be in the hearts of the British. There is little evidence that this is happening in Major's supposed comment that the EU hierarchy was behaving like a 'bunch of shits' over the BSE crisis (*Sunday Express*, 21 April 1996). The Union is often seen in British political discourse as an 'external' imposition. As Gijs de Vries comments:

There is a tendency in the UK to speak to the British people as if the United Kingdom is negotiating *with* Brussels, rather than negotiating *in* Brussels. There tends to be an 'us against them' lager mentality, which one also hears in British Labour speeches. It has even crept in to some of what the Liberal Party is saying, simply because the British conservative press exerts so much influence in the country. The people are being fed a constant diet, a drip feeding of acid, lies, and insults.

The European Union is seen as being outside the British body politic, rather than a key part of it. This approach inevitably lends weight to the idea of 'foreign' intrusion. In other states, particularly those with a federal system, where different centres of political authority coexist, the additional EU 'layer' is more easily understood and accepted. Viewed from the European mainland this hostile attitude to the EU project appears to run through the whole of British political society.

Plumb points out that British politicians 'still have an island mentality. We've never been fought over and we've never been in a situation where we've been really dominated by anybody else, not in their history, not in their ancestors' history, and I think it does have a bearing.' This is by no means a new argument, but is clearly felt among many to be a factor. This isolation from continental history has other consequences. Richard Corbett, a former senior adviser to socialist MEPs and now an MEP himself, claims that 'the nationalist right on the mainland of Europe was completely discredited after the War because of its association with Fascism, in a way that never happened in Britain.' From this perspective such ideas have thus been able to gain respectability in mainstream British political debate in a manner unimaginable on the mainland. In addition, the 'Maastricht Treaty', or more precisely the debates around its ratification, brought to the fore the relationship between the European Union and its component nation states. It 'unveiled concerns about loss of national identity and on the meaning of nation and statehood that had not been part of political discourse in western Europe for many decades' (MacShane 1995: 23).

Jean-Marie Guéhenno has convincingly argued that territory, as the cornerstone of two fundamental notions of modern history, nationhood and law (and upon which modern politics is founded), has been undermined by the advance of technology and communications. For him, the events of 1989, following the fall of the Berlin Wall, drew a line under 'that which was institutionalized thanks to 1789. It closes the book on the age of nation states' (Guéhenno 1993, this author's translation). The era of unitary territorial governance has gone in the eyes of many continental Europeans. What remains, sadly undernourished, and oft neglected, but a potential rallying standard for political parties, is democratic governance. To many on the Continent and their friends in Britain, this means embracing federalism in the more generally accepted mainland European sense of the term.

Conclusion

David Baker and David Seawright

The contributions to this volume show that Europe still remains an issue which has the capacity to engender ambivalence and division within British political institutions. They also illustrate the complexity of the European issue for British political elites and the potential dangers the issue has for British policy-making. The ambivalent stances on Europe taken by the many elites in this volume highlight the minefield of the European agenda that any British government has to navigate. The very fact that no government has learned properly to square the circle on Europe suggests to us that this will remain a crucial area of study and necessary research for the forseeable future.

Since the chapters in this book were written the 1997 general election has taken place and a Labour government with a 179-seat overall majority under Tony Blair has replaced John Major's ailing Conservative administration. This would ordinarily be seen as an important development in British politics. But after eighteen years of continuous Conservative government it is nothing short of sensational. In many policy areas questions were being asked as to how 'New Labour' would react and great expectations were placed on the election of a Blair administration to end the widely perceived British intransigence over Europe, not least by the heads of government in continental Europe and despite the fact that during the election campaign it became increasingly difficult to tell the two parties apart on Europe.

These dramatic changes throw up a whole series of new research agendas on Britain in Europe linked to Labour in power and the Conservatives in opposition, as well as the new relationships generated with other political and administrative elites.

For instance Peter Brown Pappamikail's findings on the critical attitudes of European officials and politicians under the previous administrations may now need to be revised to take account of a softening of such attitudes towards Britain. In this context further research will be necessary to ascertain whether New Labour's 'charm offensive' will prove to have been a matter of electoral style rather than real substance. Certainly, within weeks of taking office, Britain's European partners had begun to realize that a Labour government would not be unequivocally pro-integrationist. In the run-up to the June 1997 Amsterdam summit Labour's unwillingness to sign up for common justice, immigration, and boarder controls caused great disappointment amongst their European partners. The Dutch Minister for European Affairs, Michiel Patijn, said: 'The new Labour government still seems to be afraid to move out of Mrs. Thatcher's shadow'; while the German EU minister Werner Hoyer stated: 'The improvement in the climate with Britain is translating into something which has no substance' (*Guardian*, 30 May 1997). This has implications for the British civil service in departments like the Foreign Office which may have anticipated that the advent of a Labour government would lead to a period of more cordial relations with their European counterparts. However, as Buller and Smith point out, the constitutional neutrality of the British civil service means that such sentiments, if indeed they do exist, are not easily researchable.

With the work of Wilkes and Wring, we need to know if the advent of a new Labour government will generate a noticeable difference in the coverage of Europe by the British press. It is too early to say in any detail what the attitudes of the British press will be towards Europe under Labour. However, as yet there is little sign of a radical change. By the end of week three of the election campaign, according to a *Guardian*/Loughborough University study, Europe had climbed to number two on the list of campaign topics after the election itself, with 15 per cent of the total coverage (*Guardian*, 21 April 1997). During the campaign both major parties frequently repeated their patriotic credentials through the British media (Blair's bulldog and Major's Churchillian chats with the electorate) and indulged in a great deal of fudging of the European issue. The patriotic theme was picked up by the *Mail*, setting the tone with its front-page leader on 'The Battle of Britain'. The campaign also saw the *Sun* aligning itself with Labour for the first time, although without any comparable change on their stance on Europe. The *Sun* 'came out' for Tony Blair on 18 March 1997, after stressing Tony Blair and New Labour's Eurosceptic credentials. This was at a time, however, when Labour's traditional supporters in the print media were eulogizing New Labour's positively Euro-enthusiastic approach (*Mirror* and *Guardian*, 18 March–1 May 1997, *passim*).

With regard to the issue of Labour in power, in our chapter we found that the PLP had indeed moved some considerable way along the road of pro-European integration, particularly from the high water mark of anti-European sentiment reached in 1983. With constituency changes and some of the older parliamentarians standing down, the PLP that we surveyed now only accounts for 56 per cent of the present parliamentary party. Do we really have a massive 44 per cent of the PLP reinforcing an ethos of Euro-enthusiasm? Our post-1983 cohort analysis does infer such a level of Euro-enthusiasm. One finds further evidence of this trend reflected in the adoption of, and subsequent election of, Oona King to the Bethnal Green and Bow seat. Peter Shore, the indefatigable Labour sceptic, had been the occupant of this constituency since 1964. In contrast, his successor, Ms King, enters parliament with a history of assistance to the MEPs Glyn Ford and Glenys Kinnock.

Equally, the New Labour landslide swept into power a large number of unknown and ordinarily excluded Labour candidates, creating an unknown factor in the parliamentary equation. Not only does our own research suggest that the old Labour Party was moving in a pro-European direction, but a study in June 1996 of candidates inheriting safe Labour seats and those contesting Labour target seats which asked the question 'If other European countries establish a Single Currency, should a Labour government join it?', elicited a positive response of 64 per cent (*Guardian*, 9 June 1996).

The fundamental research question relating to this phenomenon is what are the prospects of such a Euro-enthusiastic trend continuing within the new PLP against the background of a Labour administration already showing signs of distinctly circumspect attitudes towards European integration?

There is no doubt that Labour appeared as a party 'positively bubbling with enthusiasm' for Europe in the *immediate* aftermath of the 1997 election. But, could this enthusiasm, bubbling on the backbenches, be a recipe for potential conflict between a pragmatic Prime Minister Blair, an enthusiastic Chancellor Gordon Brown, and a more 'cautious' Foreign Secretary Robin Cook? Mr Blair has never offered unqualified enthusiasm for Europe: his comments are always tempered with important caveats, so that party opinion is never seen to get too far ahead of public opinion. Blair's attitudes towards Europe were best expressed by Martin Kettle:

The second essential theme of Blair's approach to Europe is that it is not expressed in terms of institutional change. He has no time for the rhetoric of 'building Europe' beloved of the older generation of present day European Leaders. He is hostile to the delusion of 'ever closer union' enshrined in the treaties and represented by the bureaucracy of the nascent European state. And as he said again yesterday at Noordwigk he does not believe that the peoples of Europe are very interested in that either.

Instead Blair clearly regards European cooperation as primarily a means to practical and popular ends. Where the Heath generation 'believed' in Europe as, at least in part, an affirmation of the cooperative alternative to warfare between nations, the Blair generation takes cooperation much more as a given, but is sceptical about the constant emphasis on institutional change that has marked European relations over the past two decades. In contrast to Heath, Blair 'believes' in Europe as a means rather than an end.

In this, he is surely at one with the general mood in Britain which is pro-European in principle and well disposed towards practical results which prove the benefits of co-operation, but which is sceptical about windy rhetoric and hostile towards over-regulatory grand designs financed at taxpayers' expense. That explains why, for instance, Blair is not at all hung up about the principle of qualified majority voting, while at the same time he is deeply hostile to mindless institution building. (*Guardian*, 24 May 1997)

This approach could spell danger for a populist Labour government, cautious about moving too far ahead of such public opinion, in light of Labour backbench Euro-enthusiasm. For instance, shortly before his election Mr Blair emphasized in an 'exclusive' to the *Sun* (17 March 1997) that German-style social security costs would not be imported into Britain. But if a majority of backbenchers, enthused with such collectivist values, decided that such social legislation was a central pillar of further European integration, they may not easily accept party discipline on the issue for the sake of 'market flexibility'. It must, therefore, have been deeply disconcerting for many Labour backbenchers to wake up to headlines in the popular Sunday press of 25 May 1997, which spoke of 'Blair in Secret Talks with Thatcher' and to discover that it was relations with world leaders which topped their agenda.

The issues surrounding the Conservative Party since 1 May 1997 are centred on the devastating defeat in the election, which not only deprived of office what had seemingly become the 'natural party of government', but reopened the running sore of divisions over Europe within the party. John Major's decision to opt for a rapid leadership election was followed by a scramble between several leading contenders who tended to define themselves in relation to their Europhilia or Euroscepticism.

Worse still, the Europhiles blamed the Eurosceptics' obsession with British sovereignty for the extent of the defeat, while the sceptics blamed it on the decision to enter the ERM and the subsequent ignominious withdrawal. As Professor Philip Norton has pointed out, of great significance was the fact that the election cut a swathe through *both* the pro- and anti-European factions, with sceptics such as Michael Portillo, Norman Lamont, Nicholas Budgen, and Tony Marlow losing their seats, alongside Europhiles such as David Hunt, Edwina Currie, and David Mellor: 'They took them out in equal proportions', he said. Norton's research also reveals that more than half of the new intake hold pro and anti views on Europe so passionately that they are willing to see the party split on the issue. At the same time, Professor Paul Whiteley insists that the Tory Party's rank and file are 'fiercely Eurosceptic' (*Guardian*, 3 May 1997), but significantly, at the moment they have no say in the election of a new leader. In this scenario what Ludlam inferred in his chapter may come to pass; Europhiles like Kenneth Clarke leaving to set up a 'fourth party'.

Future research on the Liberal Democrats and the Nationalists at Westminster will have to take into account their relative strength in the new parliament and the devolved Scottish and Welsh legislatures proposed by Labour and their associated referendums. Ironically, just at the time the Liberals doubled their parliamentary representation to 46, Labour obtained 419 seats and an absolute majority of 179. This means that the 'balance of power' scenario looks highly unlikely over Europe, unless a future Labour administration was considerably at odds with its pro-European backbenches. In the case of the Nationalist parties, a 'Yes' vote in the referendums on devolved government, and the implications of Welsh and Scottish legislatures, if combined with the Lothians Labour MEP David Martin's proposed 'Europe of the Regions', has the potential to undermine the nationalist message in Wales and Scotland, since one school of thought views such changes as weakening calls for complete national independence.

In terms of the research by Rosamond, and Greenwood and

Stancich, it is important to focus on the few areas of policy on Europe where Labour differs markedly from the Conservatives. During the election campaign both main parties had much in common on the broad issues of substance and differed principally on matters of style. Both offered a referendum over Britain's entry into a single currency should it be necessary. Both stated that they would retain 'intergovernmental' policy-making on Common Foreign and Security policy and on asylum, frontiers, and police cooperation. Both professed a belief in enlargement of the EU but, while the Conservatives welcomed the 'variable geometry' (opt-outs for some nations) that this might bring, Labour rejected such 'flexibility', preferring all member states to move forward together, although not necessarily at the pace dictated by the German Christian Democrats. Both parties wished to see more power accruing to the larger states in the Council of Ministers at the expense of the smaller ones. However, the Conservatives were against extending the powers of the European Parliament, while Labour favoured giving it equal 'co-decision' powers with the Council of Ministers on all policies settled by majority voting. Both parties also sought to extend the single market and reform the CAP.

Matters of real substance on which the parties disagreed included the judicial powers of the EU institutions, with some influential Conservatives seeking to limit the powers of the European Court of Justice. On the other hand, Labour are content to leave this aspect of administration at the European level and are seeking to incorporate the European Convention of Human Rights into British law. The biggest division, however, is over the Social Chapter provisions of the Maastricht Treaty which Labour will sign, admittedly with certain reservations over EU rules on Works Councils; while most Conservatives firmly reject all aspects of this legislation as placing unacceptable extra burdens on industry and reducing Britain's competitiveness in global markets.

The immediate concern of the new Blair government was the Amsterdam IGC, intended to revise the Maastricht Treaty and scheduled for June 1997, but delayed by the British election. At the IGC the heads of government will face the prospect of a new draft treaty and will have to discuss difficult issues which they will face in the near future, such as majority voting on common defence policy; harmonization of immigration and asylum procedures; the abolition of frontier controls; 'flexibility' provisions to allow 'variable geometry' to operate; enlargement of the Union and the associated issues of the 'over-representation' of the smaller countries, and increasing budgetary costs for countries like Britain.

Potentially the most divisive European issues the incoming British Labour government faces are those of fish quotas; the Beef ban; 'flexibility'; and *above all* questions surrounding the ERM and the single currency. On fish quotas Labour is seeking to secure a ban on 'quota hopping', thus undermining the selling of fishing rights, which will meet stiff opposition from the Spaniards unless a compromise can be reached. On the ban on exports of British beef to Europe, Labour have already announced their intention to impose a unilateral ban on imports of European beef, which they now consider to be a health risk. On 'flexibility' Labour is against too much allowance of a 'two-speed' Europe and will have to decide whether 'flexibility' should involve moving ahead on issues by a majority vote, excluding those not participating in certain policies. Given the present strength of feeling in Europe on these issues Labour may well have to compromise.

With regard to the vexed question of the single currency, perhaps the biggest irony is that the Labour government will take over the presidency of the EU on 1 January 1998 and will, therefore, have to preside over the decision on who is to join the single currency. Labour is unlikely to take Britain into the first wave of membership in 1999, should it occur, and is committed to a referendum thereafter. However, the French Socialists' election victory in June 1997 and the difficulties experienced by the two leading continental nations, France and Germany, in reducing their budget deficits to the Maastricht convergence criteria of 3 per cent of GDP, may assist Labour's own reticence on this issue. Equally, amongst others Denmark, Sweden, Italy, and Greece, for various reasons, look most unlikely to join in 1999. But this may only postpone the real decisions for Britain if, in three or four years' time *Euro* notes begin to circulate and others contemplate joining the system, since 'in' or 'out' the single currency would have a dramatic effect on the British economy.

These issues and events then will provide the broad context within which research into Britain's relationship with Europe will have to take place over the next decade. In particular, if a referendum on the single currency takes place it would provide a fertile ground for psephologists to delve once again into the psyche of the British electorate on such issues. The campaign itself may well force individual members of the elites to reveal their hands, so opening up further research opportunities into British institutional divisions.

REFERENCES

ABEL, K. (1954), *Free Trade Challenge*, London. Action Centre for Europe (1995), *Mission Statement*, Whittle-le-Woods.

ANDEWEG, R. (1995), 'The Reshaping of National Party Systems', *West European Politics*, 3: 58–78.

ASHFORD, N. (1980), 'The European Economic Community' in Z. Layton-Henry, (ed.) *Conservative Party Politics*, London.

—— (1992),'The Political Parties', in S. George (ed.), *Britain and the European Community*, Oxford.

Association for the Monetary Union of Europe (AMUE) (1995), *Monetary Instability Threatens the Single Market*, Paris.

BACHE, I. (1996), 'EU Regional Policy: Has the UK Government Succeeded in Playing the Gatekeeper Role over the Domestic Impact of the Regional Development Fund?', unpublished Ph.D., University of Sheffield.

BAKER D., GAMBLE, A., and LUDLAM, S. (1993a), 'Whips or Scorpions? The Maastricht Vote and the Conservative Party', *Parliamentary Affairs*, 46/2: 37–60.

—— —— —— (1993b), '1846 . . . 1906 . . . 1996? Conservative Splits and European Integration', *Political Quarterly*, 64/4: 420–34.

—— —— —— (1994a), 'The Parliamentary Siege of Maastricht: Conservative Divisions and British Ratification of the Treaty on European Union', *Parliamentary Affairs*, 47/1.

—— —— —— (1994b), 'Mapping Conservative Fault Lines: Problems of Typology', in P. Dunleavy and G. Stayner (eds.), *Contemporary Political Studies 1994*, Exeter.

—— FOUNTAIN, I., GAMBLE, A., and LUDLAM, S. (1995), 'The Blue Map of Europe: Conservative Backbencher Attitudes to European Integration', *Political Quarterly*, 66/2.

—— —— —— —— (1996),'The Blue Map of Europe: Conservative Parliamentarians and European Integration', C. Rallings, D. M. Farrell, D. Denver, and D. Broughton, *British Elections and Parties Yearbook 1995*, London.

—— GAMBLE, A., LUDLAM, S., and SEAWRIGHT, D. (1998),'Backbenchers with Attitude: A Seismic Study of the Conservative Party and Dissent on Europe', in S. Bowler, D. M. Farrell, and R. S. Katz (eds.), *Party Cohesion, Party Discipline and the Organization of Parliaments*, Ohio.

BAKER, K. (1993), *The Turbulent Years: My Life in Politics*, London.

BALL, M. (1996), *The Conservative Conference and Euro-sceptical Motions 1992–95*, London.

BALSOM, D., and MADGWICK, P. (1978) Wales, European Integration and Devolution', in M. Kolinsky (ed.), *Divided Loyalties: British Regional Assertion and European Integration*, Manchester.

BBC Television (1996), *Newsnight*, 5 June.

BBC Written Archives Centre, Caversham.

BCC/CBI (1995), *Report*, London.

Beaverbrook Papers, House of Lords Library.

BENDER, B. (1991),'Governmental Processes: Whitehall, Central Government and 1992', *Public Policy & Administration*, 6: 13–20.

BENN, T. (1979), *Arguments for Socialism*, London.

—— (1981), *Arguments for Democracy*, London.

—— (1989), *Against the Tide: Diaries 1973–76*, London.

BENNIE, L., CURTICE, J., and RUDIG, W. (1995), 'Liberal, Social Democrat or Liberal Democrat? Political Identity and Centre Party Politics', in D. Broughton, D. Farrell, D. Denver, and C. Railings (eds.), *British Elections and Parties Yearbook 1994*, London.

—— —— —— (1996), 'Party Members', in D. MacIver (ed.), *The Liberal Democrats*, London.

BERCUSSON, B. (1992), 'Maastricht: A Fundamental Change to European Labour Law', *Industrial Relations Journal*, 23.

BERNSTEIN, G. L. (1986), *Liberalism and Liberal Politics*, London.

BERRINGTON, H. B. (1973), *Backbench Opinion in the House of Commons 1945–55*, Oxford.

BEYME, K. VON, (1985), *Political Parties in Western Democracies*, Aldershot.

BHASKAR, R. (1979), *The Possibility of Naturalism*, Brighton.

BRADLEY, I. (1981), *Breaking the Mould? The Birth of the Social Democratic Party*, Oxford.

—— (1985), *The Strange Rebirth of Liberal Britain*, London.

BRAND, J., MITCHELL, J., and SURRIDGE, P. (1994*a*), 'Social Constituency and Ideological Profile: Scottish Nationalism in the 1990s', *Political Studies*, 42.

—— —— —— (1994*b*) 'Will Scotland Come to the Aid of the Party?', in A. Heath, R. Jowell, and J. Curtice (eds.), *Labour's Last Chance? The 1992 Election and Beyond*, Aldershot.

British Chamber of Commerce (BCC) (1995), *Business and Citizens of Europe*, London.

BRIVATI, B., and JONES, H. (eds.) (1993), *From Reconstruction to Integration: Britain and Europe Since 1945*, Leicester.

BROWN PAPPAMIKAIL, P. (1995), 'Europe's Modern Prince', paper to the conference Party Politics in the Year 2000, Manchester.

BULLER, J. (1996), 'Thatcher and the Single European Act', unpublished Ph.D., University of Sheffield.

—— (1995), 'Britain as an Awkward Partner: Reassessing Britain's Relationship with the EU', *Politics*, 15: 1.

Bullock, A., and Shock, M. (eds.) (1956), *The Liberal Tradition from Fox to Keynes*, London.

Bulpitt, J. (1986), 'The Discipline of the New Democracy: Mrs Thatcher's Domestic Statecraft', *Political Studies*, 34/1

—— (1992), 'Conservative Leaders and the 'Euro-Ratchet': Five Doses of Scepticism', *Political Quarterly*, 63: 3.

Burch, M., and Holliday, I. (1996), *The British Cabinet System*, Hemel Hempstead.

Burgess, M. (1995), The British Tradition of Leadership, London.

Burkitt, B., Baimbridge, M., and Whyman, P. (1996), *There is an Alternative: Britain and its Relationship with Europe*, London.

Burnham, J., and Maor, M. (1995), 'Converging Administrative Systems: Recruitment and Training in EU Member States', *Journal of European Public Policy*, 2: 185–204.

Burnham, P. (1996), 'The Internationalisation of the State: A New Agenda for Researching the Regulation of Labour', paper presented to the ESRC Labour Studies Seminar.

Butler, D., and Kitzinger, U. (1976), *The 1975 Referendum*, London.

—— and Rose, R. (1960), *The British General Election 1959*, London.

—— and Stokes, D. (1969), *Political Change in Britain: Forces Shaping Electoral Choice*, Harmondsworth.

Butt Philip, A. (1983), 'The Liberals and Europe', in V. Bogdanor (ed.), *Liberal Party Politics*, Oxford.

—— (1992), 'British Pressure Groups and the European Community', in S. George (ed.), *Britain and the European Community: The Politics of Semi Detachment'*, Oxford, 149–71.

—— (1993), 'Europeans First and Last: British Liberals and the European Community', *Political Quarterly*, 64: 147–61.

Camps, M. (1964), *Britain and the European Community, 1955–63*, Princeton.

Cash, W. (1992), *Europe: The Crunch*, London.

—— (1996), *The Blue Paper: A Response to the Government's White Paper*, London.

CBI (1995a), *A Europe that Works*, London.

—— (1995b), *The CBI's Brussels Office*, Brussels.

—— (1995c), *European Policy*, London, June.

—— (1996), 'A Business Driven Approach to Europe', *CBI WorldWide Web*, pages, 15 Apr.

Cerny, P. (1990), *The Changing Architecture of Politics: Structure, Agency and the Future of the State*, London.

Channel 4 (1995), *The Last Europeans*, 26 Nov., 10 Dec.

Child, D. (1970), *The Essentials of Factor Analysis*, London.

CHRISTOPH, J. B. (1993), 'The Effects of Britons in Brussels: The European Community and the Culture of Whitehall', *Governance*, 6: 518–37.

CLARKE, K. (1993), 'The Lovable Pooch at Number 11. Kenneth Clarke interviewed by Andrew Hicks', *Crossbow*, Oct.

CLARKE, M. (1988), 'The Policy Making Process', in M. Smith et al (eds.), *British Foreign Policy: Tradition, Change and Transformation*, London.

COATES, K. (ed.) (1986), *Joint Action for Jobs; A New Internationalism*, Nottingham.

Conservative Party (1994), *A Strong Britain in a Strong Europe: The Conservative Manifesto for Europe 1994*, London.

COOK, C. (1993), *A Short History of the Liberal Party, 1945–92*, London.

CORBETT R., JACOBS, F., and SHACKLETON, M. (1995), *The European Parliament*, 3rd edn., London.

COUPLAND, R. (1954), *Welsh and Scottish Nationalism*, London.

COWLES, M. G. (1995), 'The European Round Table of Industrialists: The Strategic Player in European Affairs', in J. Greenwood, (ed.) *European Casebook on Business Alliances*, Hemel Hempstead.

CRAIG, F. W. S. (1974), *British Parlimentary Election Results, 1885–1918*, London.

CRAM, L. (1994), 'The European Commission as a Multi-organization: Social Policy and IT Policy in the EU', *Journal of European Public Policy*, 1: 2.

CREWE, I., and SEARING, D. (1988), 'Ideological Change in the British Conservative Party', *American Political Science Review*, 82: 2.

CRIDDLE, B. (1978), 'Scotland, the EEC and Devolution' in Martin Kolinsky (ed.), *Divided Loyalties: British Regional Assertion and European Integration*, Manchester.

CROUCH, C., and MARQUAND, D. (eds.) (1989), *The New Centralism: Britain out of Step in Europe?* Oxford.

CURTICE, J. (1988), 'Great Britain: Social Liberalism Reborn?', in E. Kirchner (ed.), *Liberal Parties in Western Europe*, Cambridge.

—— and PAYNE, C. (1991), 'Local Elections as National Referendums', *Electoral Studies*, 10: 3–17.

—— and STEED, M. (1995), 'An Analysis of the Results', in D. Butler and M. Westlake (eds.), *British Politics and European Elections: 1994*, London.

DAHRENDOR, F. R. (1972), 'A New Goal for Europe', in M. Hodges (ed.), *European Integration*, London.

DAVIDSON, I. (1996), 'UK Attitude Problem', *Financial Times*, 26 June.

DAVIES, Q. (1996), *The United Kingdom and Europe: A Conservative View*, London.

DENMAN, SIR R. (1995), 'Missed Chances: Britain and Europe in the Twentieth Century', *Political Quarterly*, 1; 36–45.

Desmond Donnelly Papers, National Library of Wales.

Dolez, B. (1991), 'Euro-girondins et gallo-jacobins', *Revue politique et parlementaire*, 953.

Dorfman, G. (1977), 'From the Inside Looking out; The Trades Union Congress and the EEC', *Journal of Common Market Studies*, 15.

Dott, G. (1956), 'Towards a Better Europe', *Scots Independent*, Glasgow.

Douglas, R. (1971), *History of the Liberal Party; 1895–1970*, London.

Dunleavy, P. (1991), *Democracy, Bureaucracy and Public Choice*, Hemel Hempstead.

Duvall, R., Wendt, A., and Muppidi, H. (1996), 'Institutions and Collective Representation in International Theory: The Global Capital Regime and the Construction of Capitalist State Identities', paper presented to the Minnesota-Stanford-Wisconsin MacArthur Consortium on Globalization and Global Governance, Minneapolis, March.

Dyson, K. (1991), 'Preparing for the Single Market: A New Agenda for Government/Industry Relations', *Political Quarterly*, 62/3 (July–Sept.), 338–50.

Eberlie, R. (1993), 'The Confederation of British Industry and Policy Making in the European Community', in S. Mazey and J. Richardson (eds.), *Lobbying in the European Community*, Oxford.

Edelman, M. (1965), *The Mirror: A Political History*, London.

Edwards, G. (1992), 'Central Government', in S. George (ed.), *Britain in the European Community: The Politics of Semi-Detachment*, Oxford.

Edwards, R. D. (1993), *The Pursuit of Reason: The Economist, 1843–1993*, London.

Electronic Telegraph (1995), 'CBI Backs Monetary Union', *Electronic Telegraph*, 21 June 1995, City News, p. 1.

—— (1996), 'Business Leaders Split on Europe', *Electronic Telegraph*, 374, 1 May 1996, p. 1.

European Commission (1993), *Growth, Competitiveness and Employment: The Challenges and Ways Forward into the 21st century*, Brussels. (http://www.cec.lu/en/record/white/c93700)

—— (1994), *Do you Believe all you Read in the Newspapers?*, London.

—— (1995), *Do you STILL Believe all you Read in the Newspapers?*, London.

European Foundation (1994), *The Bournemouth Speeches: Bill Cash MP, Sir James Goldsmith MEP, Rt Hon Lord Tebbit*, London.

European Movement (1996), *Europe 2000: Positive Proposals for the Reform of the European Union*, London.

European Research Group (1995), *A Europe of Nations: Conclusions of the European Research Group*, London.

Evans, G. (1995), 'The State of the Union: Attitudes towards Europe', in R. Jowell (ed.) (1995), *British Social Attitudes; The 12th Report*, Aldershot.

Falkner, G. (1995), 'Social Europe in the 1990s: After All an Era of Corporatism?', paper prepared for presentation to the Fourth Biennial International

Conference of the European Community Studies Association, Charleston, South Carolina, 11–14 May 1995.

FINER, S., BERRINGTON, H. B., and BARTHOLOMEW, D. J. (1961), *Backbench Opinion in the House of Commons, 1955–59*, Oxford.

Foreign and Commonwealth Office (FCO) (1993), *The European Community: Facts and Fairytales*, London.

—— (1995), *Facts and Fairytales Revisited*, London.

Forum of Private Business (FPB) (1995), *38th Quarterly Survey of Small Firms*, Knutsford.

FRIEDBERG, A. (1988), *The Weary Titan: Britain and the Experience of Relative Decline*, Princeton.

GAMBLE, A. (1994), *Britain in Decline: Economic Policy, Political Strategy and the British State*, London.

—— (1995), 'Economic Recession and Political Disenchantment', *West European Politics*, 18/3: 158–74.

—— and PAYNE, A. (eds.) (1996), *Regionalism and Economic Order*, London.

GELLNER, E. (1983), *Nations and Nationalism*, Oxford.

GEORGE, S. (1985), *Policy and Politics in the European Community*, Oxford.

—— (1990, 1994), *An Awkward Partner: Britain in the European Community*, Oxford.

—— (ed.) (1992), *Britain and the European Community*, Oxford.

—— (1993), 'The Awkward Partner: An Overview', in B. Brivati and H. Jones (eds.), *From Reconstruction to Integration: Britain and Europe Since 1945*, Leicester.

—— (1995), 'A Reply to Buller', *Politics*, 15/1.

—— (1996), 'The Approach of the British Government to the 1966 Intergovernmental Conference of the European Union', *Journal of European Public Policy*, 3/1 (Mar.).

—— and LUDLAM, S. (1994), 'The Euro-election Manifestos', *Parliamentary Brief*, June.

—— and SOWEMIMO, M. (1996), 'Conservative Foreign Policy towards the European Union', in S. Ludlam and M. J. Smith (eds.) *Contemporary British Conservatism*, Basingstoke.

GIDDENS, A. (1984), *The Constitution of Society*, Cambridge.

GILMOUR, I. (1993), *Dancing with Dogma: Britain under Thatcherism*, London.

GLADSTONE, W. E. (1879), *Gleanings of Past Years, 4*, London.

GOODHART, P. (1976), *Full-hearted Consent: The Story of the Referendum Campaign, and the Campaign for the Referendum*, London.

GORMAN, T. (1993), *The Bastards: Dirty Tricks and the Challenge to Europe*, London.

GMB (1990), *Getting Ready for the European Social Charter*, Esher.

GRANT, W. (1990), 'Organized Interests and the European Community', paper prepared for presentation to the VIth International Colloquium of the Feltrinelli Foundation, Cortona, 29–31 May.

—— (1995), 'The Limits of Common Agricultural Policy Reform and the Option of Denationalization', *Journal of European Public Policy*, 2: 1–18.

GREENWOOD, S. (1996), *Britain and European Integration Since the Second World War*, Manchester.

GUÉHENNO, J. (1993), *La Fin de la démocratie, Paris*, Flammarion.

HAAS, E. (1968), *The Uniting of Europe*, Stanford, Calif.

HARDT-MAUTNER, G. (1995), 'How does one Become a Good European' The British Press and European Integration', *Discourse & Society*, 6: 177–205.

HEATH, A., JOWELL, R., CURTICE, J., and TAYLOR, B. (1995), 'The 1994 European and Local Elections: Abstention, Protest and Conversion', paper presented at the Annual Conference of the Political Studies Association, Apr.

—— —— TAYLOR, B., and THOMPSON, K. (1997), 'Euroscepticism and the Referendum Party', paper to the Election, Parties and Opinions Polls Conference, University of Essex, 26–8 Sept.

Hetherington Papers, London School of Economics Library.

HILL, S. (ed.) (1996), *Visions of Europe: Summing up the Political Choices*, London.

HIX, S. (1995), in P. Brown Pappamikail (ed.), *A History of the Party of European Socialists*, PES Research Series, Brussels.

—— (1996), 'The Transnational Party Federations', in John Gaffney (ed.), *Political Parties and the European Union*, London.

HOLLAND, S. (ed.) (1983), *Out of Crisis: A Project for European Recovery*, Nottingham.

HOLLINGSWORTH, M. (1986), *The Press and Political Dissent: A Question of Censorship*, London.

HOLMES, M. (ed.) (1996), *The Eurosceptical Reader*, London.

HOWE, G. (1990), 'Sovereignty and Interdependence: Britain's Place in the World', *International Affairs*, 66/4.

—— (1994), *Conflict of Loyalty*, Basingstoke.

HURD, D. (1996), Speech to the Scottish Council of the European Movement, 26 Apr.

HUTTON, W. (1996), 'Here comes the Euro', *Observer*, 22 Sept., p. 24.

ICM (1994), Results of a Poll conducted after the European Elections, London.

Institute of Directors (IoD) (1995), *A Single European Currency*, London.

ITN Archives, London.

JENKINS, C. (1990), *All against the Collar: Struggles of a White Collar Union Leader*, London.

JENKINS, R. (1991), *Life at the Centre*, London.

JUDGE, D. (1988), 'Incomplete Sovereignty: The British House of Commons and the Internal Market', *Parliamentary Affairs*, 57/3.

JUDGE, D. (1995), 'The Failure of National Parliaments?', *West European Politics*, 3: 80–100.

KELLAS, J. (1991), *The Politics of Nationalism and Ethnicity*, London.

KITZINGER, U. (1973), *Diplomacy and Persuasion*, London.

Labour Euro-Safeguards Campaign (1995), 'Labour's Bid Decision', *Newsletter*, No. 1, Summer, 72 Albert Street, London.

Labour Party (1995), 'The Future of the European Union: Report on Labour's position in preparation for the Intergovernmental Conference', *Conference 1995*, John Smith House.

LADRECH, R., and BROWN PAPPAMIKAIL, P. (1995), 'Towards a European Party System?', *Démocratie et construction européenne*, Brussels.

LAMONT, N. (1993), 'The Day I Almost Quit', *The Times*, 16 Sept.

—— (1995), *Sovereign Britain*, London.

LANGE, P. (1992), 'The Politics of the Social Dimension', in A. Sbragia (ed.), *Euro-Politics: Institutions and Policymaking in the 'New' European Community*, Washington, DC.

LAWSON, N. (1992, 1993), *The View from No. 11: Memoirs of a Tory Radical*, London.

LEWIS, S. (1926) *Principles of Nationalism*, Carnarven.

—— (1938) *Canlynarthur*, Abersytwyth

Liberal Party Organisation, *Annual Report and Accounts 1980*, London.

—— *Annual Report and Accounts 1985*, London.

LINDBERG, L. (1963), *The Political Dynamics of European Economic Integration*, Stanford, Calif.

LUDLAM, S. (1995), 'Britain and the European Union', in P. Catterall (ed.), *Contemporary Britain: An Annual Review 1995*, London, Institute of Contemporary British History.

—— (1996), 'The Spectre Haunting Conservatism: Europe and Backbench Rebellion' in S. Ludlam and M. J. Smith, *Contemporary British Conservatism*, Basingstoke.

—— and SMITH, M. J. (1996), *Contemporary British Conservatism*, Basingstoke.

LYNCH, P. (1995), 'From Red to Green: The Political Strategy of Plaid Cymru in the 1980s and 1990s', *Regional and Federal Studies*, 5/2: 197–210.

—— (forthcoming), *From Versailles to Maastricht: Minority Nationalism and European Integration in the Twentieth Century*, Cardiff.

MCALLISTER, L. (1995), 'Community in Ideology: The Political Philosophy of Plaid Cymru', Ph.D. thesis, University of Wales.

MCCALL, G., and SIMMONS, J. L. (eds.) (1969), *Issues in Participant Observation*, New York.

MCGLYNN, S. (1996), 'Britain and Europe: A Medieval Comparison', *Politics*, 16/3.

McLaughlin, A. (1992), 'Underfed Euro Feds?', paper prepared for presentation to the Annual Meeting of the Political Studies Association, Belfast, Apr. 7–9.

Macmillan, H. (1973), *At the End of the Day 1961–1963*, London.

MacShane, D. (1995), 'Europe's Next Challenge to European politics', *Political Quarterly*, 66: 1, 23–35.

Major, J. (1993), 'Raise Your Eyes, There is a Land Beyond', *The Economist*, 25 Sept.

—— (1994a), *Europe: A Future that Works*, William and Mary Lecture given by the Prime Minister, the Rt. Hon. John Major MP at the University, Leiden, 7 Sept. 1994, London.

—— (1994b), *Variable Geometry: Speech at Ellesmere Port, 31 May 1994*, London.

—— (1995), *The Cannes European Summit 26–27 June 1995. Statement by the Prime Minister, the Rt. Hon. John Major MP, Wednesday 28 June 1995*, London.

—— (1996), *The Future of Europe: Speech by the Prime Minister, the Rt. Hon. John Major MP, Goldsmiths' Hall, London, Wednesday, 19 June 1996*, London.

Marquand, D. (ed.) (1982), *Parliament and Social Democracy*, London.

Marsh, D. (1992), *The New Politics of British Trade Unionism: Union Power and the Thatcher Legacy*, Basingstoke.

Matthew, H. C. G. (1973), *The Liberal Imperialists: The Ideas and Politics of a post-Gladstonian Elite*, Oxford.

May, J. D. (1973), 'Opinion Structure of Political Parties: The Special Law of Curvilinear Disparity', *Political Studies*, 21: 135–51.

Meadowcroft, M. (1980), *Liberal Values for a New Decade*, London.

Meyer, A. (1991), *A Federal Europe: Why Not?*, London.

Middlemas, K. (1995), *Orchestrating Europe: The Informal Politics of the European Union 1973–1995*, London.

Miller, K., and Steele, M. (1993), 'Employment Legislation: Thatcher and After', *Industrial Relations Journal*, 24/3.

Milward, A. (1992, 1994), *The European Rescue of the Nation-State*, London.

—— (1996), 'Approaching Reality: Euromoney and the Left', *New Left Review*, 216: 55–65.

—— and Brennan, G. (1996), *Britain's Place in the World: A Historical Enquiry into Import Controls 1945–1960*, London.

Minogue, K. (1990), 'Is Sovereignty a Big Bad Wolf?', in *Is Sovereignty a Big Bad Wolf?*, London.

Mitchell, J. (1990), 'Factions, Tendencies and Consensus in the SNP', *Scottish Government Yearbook, 1990*, Edinburgh.

—— (1995), 'Lobbying Brussels: The Case of Scotland Europa', *European Urban and Regional Studies*, 2/4: 287–98.

—— (1996), *Strategies for Self-Government*, Edinburgh.

MONKS, J. (1995), *Speech to Unions '95 Conference*, 18 Nov., London.

MOON, J. (1985), *European Integration in British Politics, 1950–63*, Aldershot.

MORGAN, D. (1995), 'British Media and European Union News', *European Journal of Communication*, 10: 321–43.

NAIRN, T. (1973), *The Left against Europe*, Harmondsworth.

National Library of Scotland (NLS), Scots Secretariat files.

NEWTON-DUNN, B. (1985), *Greater in Europe*, London.

NORTON, P. (1975), *Dissension in the House of Commons 1945–1974*, London.

—— (1978), *Conservative Dissidents: Dissent within the Parliamentary Conservative Party 1970–74*, London.

—— (1980), *Dissension in the House of Commons 1974–1979*, Oxford.

NORUSIS, M. J. (1993), *SPSS for Windows: Professional Statistics*, Chicago.

No Turning Back Group (1994), *A Conservative Europe: 1994 and Beyond*, London.

OSTRANDER, S. A. (1993), 'Access, Rapport, and Interviews in Three Studies of Élites', *Journal of Contemporary Ethnography*, 22/1: 7–27.

OWEN, D. (1991), *Time to Declare*, London.

PATTIE, C., and JOHNSTON, R. (1996), 'The Conservative Party and the Electorate' in Ludlam and Smith 1996.

Plaid Cymru (1983), Resolution 11, 'European Common Market' Plaid Cymru National Conference, 1983.

Public Records Office (1948), CAB 128/22, CM(48)68, 4 Nov. 1948.

PURDY, D., and DEVINE, P. (1994), 'Social Policy', in M. Artis and N. Lee (eds.), *The Economics of the European Union: Policy and Analysis*, Oxford.

PURNELL, S. (1995), 'An Empire Falls Back', *Financial Times*, 16 Oct.

RABINOWITZ, G., and MACDONALD, S. E. (1989), 'A Directional Theory of Issue Voting', *American Political Science Review*, 83: 93–121.

RALLINGS, C., FARRELL, D., DENVER, D., and BROUGHTON, D. (1996), *British Elections and Parties Yearbook 1995*, London.

REIF, K. (1984), 'National Electoral Cycles and European Elections 1979 and 1984', *Electoral Studies*, 3: 244–55.

RHODES, M. (1995), 'A Regulatory Conundrum: Industrial Relations and the Social Dimension', paper prepared for presentation to the Fourth Biennial International Conference of the European Communities Studies Association, Charleston, South Carolina, 11–14 May.

RIDLEY N. (1992), *My Style of Government: The Thatcher Years*, London.

ROBINS, L. J. (1979), *The Reluctant Party: Labour and the EEC, 1961–75*, Ormskirk.

ROSAMOND, B. (1992), 'Beyond Nation State Socialism? British Trade Unionism and European Integration in the Thatcher Years, 1979–1990', Ph.D. thesis, University of Sheffield.

—— (1993a), 'The British Left and the New Politics of European Integration', paper presented to the annual conference of the Political Studies Association, University of Leicester.

—— (1993*b*), 'National Labour Organisations and European Integration: British Trade Unions and "1992"', *Political Studies*, 41/3.

—— (1996), 'Whatever Happened to the "Enemy Within"? Contemporary Conservatism and Trade Unionism', in Ludlam and Smith 1996.

ROSE, R. (1982), *Understanding the United Kingdom: The Territorial Dimension in Government*, London.

ROSS, G. (1995), *Jacques Delors and European Integration*, Cambridge.

RUGGIE, J. (1993), 'Territoriality and Beyond: Problematising Modernity in International Relations', *International Organisation*, 47/1: 139–74.

SABATIER, P. (1988), 'An Advocacy Framework of Policy Change and the Role of Policy-Oriented Learning Therein', *Policy Sciences*, 21: 128–68.

SANDHOLTZ, W. (1993), 'Choosing Union: Monetary Policy and Maastricht', *World Politics*, 47/1: 95–128.

SARGENT, J. A. (1987), 'The Organisation of Business Interests for European Community Representation' in W. Grant, with J. Sargent, *Business and Politics in Britain*, London, 213–38.

SEARLE, G. R. (1995), *Country Before Party: Coalition and the Idea of National Government in Modern Britain: 1885–1987*, London.

SEMMEL, B. (1960), *Imperialism and Social Reform*, London.

SIDORSKY, D. (ed.) (1970), *The Liberal Tradition in European Thought*, New York.

SILLARS, J. (1986), *Scotland: The Case for Optimism*, Edinburgh.

SMITH, M. J. (1993), *Pressure, Power and Policy*, Hemel Hempstead.

SOLEDAD, G. (ed.) (1993), *European Identity and the Search for Legitimacy*, London.

SOREL, G. (1960), *Reflections on Violence*, London.

SPENCE, D. (1992), 'The Role of British Civil Servants in European Lobbying: The British Case', in S. Mazey and J. Richardson (eds.), *Lobbying in the European Community*, Oxford.

SPICER, M. (1992), *A Treaty Too Far: A New Policy for Europe*, London.

STACK, F. (1983), 'The Imperatives of Participation', in F. Gregory (ed.), *The Dilemmas of Government*, London.

STEPHENS, P. (1996), 'Britain's Bitter Blast from the Past', *Financial Times*, 25 May 1996.

STEPHENSON, J. (1993), *Third Party Politics Since 1945: Liberals, Alliance and Liberal Democrats*, Hemel Hempstead.

STEWART, D. (1994), *A Scot at Westminster*, Sydney, Nova Scotia.

STIRLING, J. (1991), 'This Great Europe of Ours: Trade Unions and 1992', *Capital & Class*.

STOW, B (1991), 'UK Co-ordination of EC Policy', paper presented at the conference on Europe 2000 at the Netherlands Management Studies Centre, Noordwijk, 28 Nov.

TAYLOR, G. (1993), *Changing Faces: A History of the Guardian, 1956–88*, London.

TAYLOR, I. (1993), *The Positive Europe*, London.

TAYLOR, R. (1994a), *The Future of the Trade Unions*, London.

—— (1994b), 'A Union Rallying Cry Echoes in Europe', *Financial Times*, 13 Dec.

TEAGUE, P. (1984), 'Labour and Europe: The Response of British Trade Unions to Membership of the European Community', Ph.D. thesis, University of London.

—— (1989b), 'The British TUC and the European Community', *Millennium: Journal of International Studies*, 18.

THAIN, C., and WRIGHT, M. (1996), *Whitehall and the Treasury*, Oxford.

THATCHER, M. (1993), *The Downing Street Years*, London.

—— (1995), *The Path to Power*, London.

TOONAN, A. J. (1991), 'Europe of the Administrations: The Challenges of '92', *Public Administration Review*, 52/2: 108–15.

TUC (1957), *Report of the Proceedings of the 89th Annual Trades Union Congress*, London.

—— (1961), *Report of the Proceedings of the 93rd Annual Trades Union Congress*, London.

—— (1971), *Report of the Proceedings of the 103rd Annual Trades Union Congress*, London.

—— (1972), *Report of the Proceedings of the 104th Annual Trades Union Congress*, London.

—— (1980), *Report of the Proceedings of the 112th Annual Trades Union Congress*, London.

—— (1984), *Report of the Proceedings of the 116th Annual Trades Union Congress*, London.

—— (1988a), *Report of the Proceedings of the 120th Annual Trades Union Congress*, London.

—— (1988b), *Maximising the Benefits: Minimising the Costs*, London.

—— (1989), *Europe 1992: Progress Report on Trade Union Objectives*, London.

—— (1990), *Managing the Economy towards 2000*, London.

—— (1991), *Unions and Europe in the 1990s: Trade Unions and the European Community—a TUC Perspective*, London.

—— (1996a), *Economic and Monetary Union*, press release, 2 Feb. (http://www.tuc.org.uk/press/release/emu.htm.)

—— (1996b), *Social Chapter: Impact on Business*, speech by John Monks to the Fabian Society, 2 Apr. (http://www.tuc.org.uk/press/release/fabeusp.htm.)

TUMBER, H. (1995), 'Marketing Management: The EU and News Management', *Media, Culture & Society*, 17: 511–19.

VIPOND, P. (1995), 'European Banking and Insurance: Business Alliances and Corporate Strategies', in J. Greenwood (ed.), *European Casebook on Business Alliances*, Hemel Hempstead, 101–13

VRPEP (1993), *Verbatim Report on the Proceedings of the European Parliament*, Office of Publications of the European Community, Luxembourg.

WALLACE, H. (1995), 'Britain out on a Limb?', *Political Quarterly*, 66/1: 46–58.

WALLACE, W. (1986), 'What Price Independence? Sovereignty and Interdependence in British Politics', *International Affairs*, 62/3.

WALSH, A. (1990), *Statistics for the Social Sciences*, New York.

WARD, H. (1996), 'The Fetishisation of Falsification: The Debate on Rational Choice', *New Political Economy*, 1: 283–96.

WEDDERBURN, Lord (1995), *Labour Law and Freedom: Further Essays in Labour Law*, London.

WENDON, B. (1994), 'British Trade Union Responses to European Integration', *Journal of European Public Policy*, 1/2.

WESTLAKE, M. (1994), *Britain's Emerging Euro-Elite? The British and the European Parliament 1979–1992*, London.

WHITELEY, P., SEYD, P., and RICHARDSON, J. (1994), *True Blues: The Politics of Conservative Party Membership*, Oxford.

WHITNEY, R. (1996), *Time to Return to Euro-sanity*, London.

WIGG, Lord (1972), *George Wigg*, London.

WILKES, G. (forthcoming), 'British Attitudes to the European Community, 1956–63', Ph.D. thesis, Cambridge.

WILKS, S. (1996), 'Britain and Europe: Awkward Partner or Awkward State?', *Politics*, 16/3.

WILLIAMS, S. (1995), 'Britain and the European Union: A Way Forward', *Political Quarterly*, 66/1.

WOLFE, B. (1973), *Scotland Lives*, Edinburgh.

YOUNG, D. (1948), *The International Importance of Scottish Nationalism*, Scots Secretariat, Glasgow.

YOUNG, J. W. (1993), *Britain and European Unity, 1945–1992*, London.

—— and SLOWMAN A. (1981), *No Minister*, BBC, London.

INDEX